THE TIME
OF
MY DEATH

THE TIME OF MY DEATH

ALAN JEFFRY BRESLAU

E. P. DUTTON & CO., INC.

NEW YORK

Library of Congress Cataloging in Publication Data

Breslau, Alan Jeffry.   The time of my death.

1. Burns and scalds—Personal narratives.
2. Aeronautics—Accidents—1963—Personal narratives.
3. Breslau, Alan Jeffry.
RD96.4.B7   362.1'9'7110924 [B]   76–12583

ISBN: *0–525–21992–7*

Published simultaneously in Canada by Clarke, Irwin & Company Limited, Toronto and Vancouver
Designed by The Etheredges

10 9 8 7 6 5 4 3 2 1

First Edition

*"Whoever lives through a trial of the spirit
or who takes part in any event that weighs
on man's destiny or frees him, is duty-bound to transmit
what he has seen, felt and feared."*

—ELIE WIESEL

PREFACE

I have often been asked why I wanted to write this book. "Why rake up such a tragedy?" people ask. "Let well enough alone!"

I have wanted to write ever since I was editor of *le petite journal français* in Madame Bagar's sixth-grade French class. I have done a lot of writing since then, almost all of it technical and scientific: as editor of the College of Engineering's *Quadrangle* at New York University; and as editor-in-chief of both *The Alembic,* a monthly publication of the American Chemical Society (Trenton section), and *The Spectator,* put out by the Society of Plastics Engineers (Delaware Valley section). For a number of years now I have served on the editorial advisory board of the *Journal of Elastomers and Plastics* (Technomic Publishing Company). As a scientist, I have published technical papers in numerous professional journals and coauthored a major scientific book, *Epoxy Resins: Chemistry and Technology* (Marcel Dekker, Inc., New York, 1973). But all of this was not really writing.

In order to really "write," one must ideally be either a master of prose, or, lacking literary talent, to have gone through such a unique experience that just telling it as it was makes for fascinating reading. Until July 2, 1963, I hadn't the *chutzpa* to assume that anything I had experienced would be of interest to others. I knew what any scientifically trained person knows about plane flight: how a plane gets off the ground. I flew all over the world in all kinds of aircraft, and always enjoyed it. I knew little about burns except that they were painful and sometimes left severe scars. I had never considered the question before.

But on that date I became involved in a series of experiences so great, so overwhelming that it forever changed me, my life and the lives of my loved ones. Now I had had the unique experience, and it had given me a singular opportunity.

The idea for the book started slowly. The writing took almost ten years. There may be so many psychological reasons for my undertaking the task and staying at it for so long that I am not aware of them all. Perhaps, because I was made the center of attention by everything that had happened to me, I didn't want to stop writing. Perhaps writing about the trauma and horror was an emotional purgative. And who doesn't like to talk about his operations?

I kept brief notes during each of my nineteen hospitalizations. I also compulsively clip anything of possible interest from newspapers and magazines and carefully file it. My wife, Grace, finally bought me a sterling silver "Clip-It" from Tiffany's as a symbol of my prowess in that area. And I had access to my complete hospital records, plus thousands of pages of pretrial depositions, documents, manuals, correspondence, official reports, et al. accumulated by my attorneys. I myself interviewed a number of people: nurses and doctors; the medical examiner; my attorneys; personnel from Mohawk Airlines, the weather service and the control tower; my colleagues and several of my friends; and even a public-relations man for Mohawk Airline's insurance carrier, Insurance Company of North America, who was quite helpful and anxious to read the book.

Everything in this story is true, based on some evidentiary fact as best I could ferret it out. I took no liberties with dialogue or description.

This book is not meant to be a manual for the handicapped, but rather a manual for the healthy, because the so-called handicapped have no problems. It is those who have not yet faced the horror of tragedy who fear it most and need reassurance.

I am indebted to many people in this book's preparation. In particular, I am grateful to my attorney Lee S. Kriendler, Esq., who made available his extensive files; to my fellow victim Charles V. McAdam, Jr., for letting me read and quote from the unpublished manuscript he wrote of his experience; to Florence Greenhouse Jacoby, R.N., my special nurse at Strong Memorial Hospital, to whom I owe not only my life but much of the material on burns included in her own treatise *Nursing Care of the Patient With Burns* (C. V. Mosby Co., St. Louis, 1972) often referred to as "The Bible of Burn Nursing;" to Rebecca Reid Keene, who not only arranged my access to the hospital during my writing, but set up many interviews and managed, in the midst of her own busy schedule, to research many missing names; to my amanuensis Barbara McLaren, who worked so tirelessly and so well during a very difficult time in her life; to Kevin McAuliffe, for his editorial assistance in organizing this book; to my editor, Ann La Farge, who made the whole process so painless; and finally to my wife, Grace, who had to fight so hard for everything she edited out of the book and who suffered my continued presence so pleasantly.

Alan Jeffry Breslau

New York City
March 1976

ACKNOWLEDGMENTS

This is the story of the saving of a life—mine. Many people were involved in the drama. My rescuers, doctors, and nurses played major roles. The application of their professional skills spelled the difference between my physical survival and demise. My emotional survival was another story. It depended on a smile here, a friendly word there, a letter when needed, a friendship. It involved a multitude. I would like to dedicate this story equally to all of the people who helped me. There are many, I am sure, whom I have unintentionally omitted—either because of oversight or for lack of having met them in a conscious state. To those that I have so slighted (or whose names I have misspelled) I do humbly apologize, but I am, in my heart, equally grateful to them all.

Arthur Abramsohn · Marcia, Felissa, Roy and Jennifer Abramsohn · Mike and Emilie Addante · Mitzi, Philip, Jackson and Linda (Hart)

Adler · Dr. Roberto de Toro Alabado, Jr. · Dr. Russell Allenzo · Dr. Cecilla E. Allsup · Gale Ammon, RN · Pat, Russell, and Tommy Amore · Logan Anderson · Forough, Darius, and Professor William Kay Archer · Martha (d.)* and Louis L. Archer (d.) · Mildred, George and Douglas Ashendorf · Arlene Austin · Edith Avery · Guy Aydlett · Dr. Ivanhoe Baez · Dr. Harold W. Bales (d.) · Mike Barone · Janice Bartle, RN · Janet Bapst, RN · Dr. Robert Berkow · Adrienne, Alan, May, Diane and Dr. Morris Berenbaum · Bea and Jan Berlin · Dr. Roger P. Bernard · Collie Baines · Donna Barnett, RN · Anthony and Sue Biancosino · Ms. Bing, RN · Dr. G. C. Bird · Guy and Lo Bishop · Don and Adele Black · Hazel Blaker · Alfred (d.), Zelda, Billy, Lois and Marcia Bloom · Nancy Bloomer · Dr. Myron Blume · Oscar and Selma Bortner · Jeanne Bowers, RN · Dr. Lyman Boynton · Dr. Lawrence J. Bradley (d.) · Nancy and Ted Breen · Dr. Roger Breslau · Sandy Breslau · Barbara A. Bringhurst, RN · Melvina E. Brinson, RN · Ann and Dr. Bernard Broad · Col. Lyle A. Brookover · Ms. Brown, RN · Dr. Lawrence P. Brown · Dr. Alan Paul Brown · Rabbi Herbert Bronstein · Douglass Brummell · Jack and Pat Bucey · Dr. Carroll Burgoon · Ms. Burgos · Grace and John (d.) Burak · Noreen Burleigh (Mrs. Harvey) Wheeler · Dr. Richard Burton · Jane Bush, RN · Angelina "Gay" Butera · Leonard Butera · Henrietta and Stephen Calarco · Mary Callahan, RN · Elaine Campbell, RN · Sally Carol, RN · Charles Z. Case (d.) · Anne Kendall Castle · Dr. Don H. Catlin · Jeanne H. Champlin, RN · Lil, Saul, Beth, Jonathon, Jamie and Wendy Chavkin · Arthur Chester · Mrs. Michael Chomicki · Lani Stutsman Christie · Joanne Clarke, RN · Dr. H. Gerald Clermont · Dominic Colangelo · "Bootsie" and Samuel Colodny · Dr. James M. Colville · Karen Cornelius, RN · Annette and Dr. Lester M. Cramer · Dr. Norris K. Culf, Jr. · Bruce W. Curtis · Jo Daniels · Dr. Kenneth S. Danielson · Ms. Davino, RN · Goldia Davis · Dr. Albert Davne · Julia Salome Breslau Della Penna · Dr. Robert J. DeMuth · Dorothy, David, Joel, Philip, Bruce, Judy and Cara Dickstein · Dr. Dieler · Dr. Charles "Ed" Dixon · Edwin A. Downs, Jr. · Iola and Andean Drum · Mrs. Dolin · Winnie and Dr. Isaac Drogin · Jack and Gloris Dunnous · David Dworkin · Shirley Edwards · Loretta, Hal (d.), Peter and Roger Elkin · Theodore and Lois Ellenoff · Harvey Charles Ellner · Arlene, Ross, Jeff and Elizabeth Ellner · Marie "Isse" and Gerhard A. Elston · Ruth and David Elwell · Elsie, Jon, Adam, Jill and Dr. Irving Farber · Dolores and Walter Farley, Jr. · Dr. Mahmood Fassihi · Ms. Felberg, RN · Dr. Leonard D. Fenninger · Dr. Joshua Fierer · Saranne

Author's note: A "(d.)" notation means the individual is now deceased.

and Rabbi William Fierverker · Lo, Leslie and Dr. Douglas Fisher · Rev. Frank R. Fisher (d.) · Ms. L. Fitzpatrick, RN · Andy and Rene Flager · Pat, Susan, Debbie, Stephen and Dr. George Flamm · Mary Flannery · Dr. J. Raymond Fletcher · Catherine, Jim, Kevin and Mary Fredericks · Mr. and Mrs. John Fox · Karen Fugg, RN · Dr. Jim E. Fuller · Caroline Werner Gannett · Samuel A. Gano · Connie and Sanford Garland · Sally Gervais, RN · Dr. George Gifford, Jr. · Dr. Alastair J. Gillies · Joanne, Sophia, Nadia and Dr. Riad H. Gobran · Estelle Goldman · Grace B. Greene · Sandra Lynn Gregor, RN · Hildegard Gresens, RN · Dr. John M. Griffin · Caryl and Carol Bachman Griffith, RN · Dr. Lawrence S. C. Griffith · Eleanor, Cary, Eric, and Dr. Boris Gutbezahl · Dr. Eric Guttman · Delia and Shaw Hakim · Adele, Mike (d.), Greg, Brad and Richard Hamel · Jan Kirk and Annette Fox Hancoski (Mrs. Lawrence Kissick) · Bert and Jacquiline Harmon · Jack and Ramona LeBon Harris · Bea (d.) and Walter Hart, Jr. · Dot and Stell Hartman · Dr. James P. Hayes · Mrs. N. Heberling, PN · Cortlandt Herbst · Martha Heimhuber · Connie Henning · Ruth Hinkley · Dr. J. Raymond Hinshaw · Maria Hoebink, RN · Dr. Richard P. Hockman · Charles Hoffman · Peggy Hogencamp · Reverend William B. Holberton · William, Jeanette, Susan, Barbara and Pat Holleran · John, Dina, Barbara and Raymond Hoover · Marilyn Houseknecht, RN · Dr. Stuart J. Hulnick · Dr. David S. Hungerford · Dr. Muayad H. Hussaini · Aileen Huther (d.) · Ralph Ippiliti · Frank Indivino · Dr. Alexander R. Irvine · George, Terri, Stacy, Karen and Jeremy Ivers · Mrs. C. Ivison, RN · Karen Jacobssen, RN · Marvin, Richard, Stuart, Robert and Florence Greenfield Jacoby, RN · Dorothy (Mrs. Lane) Johnson · Phyllis and Joseph S. Jorczak · Antonia Jurado, RN · Carol and Lou Kamer · Joanne Kanty, RN · Rebecca Reid Keene · Margaret E. Keene · "Bobby" Keene · Dr. William Henry Kehrli · Joanne Kemper · Ms. Kennedy, RN · Dorothy Kilburn · Dr. John R. Kirkpatrick · Jane Klein, RN · Mabel and Spencer Knight · Melvin A. Kohudic · Beverly and Irving Koval · Lee S. Kreindler · Mimi, Jonathon, Jessica and Dr. Melvin J. Krant · Ruth, Sheila and Eugene A. Krause · Dr. Annemarie Karen Kreutner · Maureen Kruse, RN · Dr. Glen H. Kumasaka · Carol and Paul M. Kurland · Woodrow Lahr · Elizabeth O. Lang, RN · Ms. Larsen, RN · Joan Lash · Don Latzel · Helen Leadley, RN · Vera LeDuc · Dr. Fred Lee · Marcia Legru · Rose Lehr, RN · Dr. Gerold "Jerry" LeMole · Ms. LePore, RN · Betty LeVan, RN · Doris, Shep (d.), David and Janet Levine · Marvin, Shirley, Polly, Meg, and Jennifer Levitt · Sidney Levy · Stanley J. Levy · Gabriella Liddon · Jerry and Bea Liebson · Joseph Livertro · Dr. Alan W. Livingston · Adrienne and Dr. Marvin Loev · Jennie Luczyszyn, RN

· Maurice Lynch · Timmy and Eileen Lynch · "Tress" (Smith) Mac-Donald · Dr. Earl B. Mahoney · Edward W. Mahoney · Reuben Mallisham · Linda Mann · Jerome and Jean Marrow · Dolores Marzo · Gwendolyn M. Marshman, RN · Dr. Samuel J. Mazza · Sally and Charles V. McAdam, Jr. · Shiela McAndrews, RN · Johnnie McCants · Dr. Robert M. McCormack · Pat and Leo Jerry McCrone · Dr. Donald McGilligan · Barbara, Danny, Philip (d.) and Charles McLaren · Dr. Margo S. Mears · Betty and Dr. Howard Mele · Avia and Dr. Theodore H. Meltzer · Peggy Welch Merkley · Joyce Miles, RN · Linda J. Miller, RN · Lee and Mark Miller · Steve, Dolores, Eddie and David Miller · Marilyn E. Miller (Mrs. John F. Spears), RN · Dr. Stanley L. Minkin · Dr. Elmer Theodore Mitchell, Jr. · Georgia Mitchum · Rosemary Moeller, RN · Kevin and Noreen Moore · Dr. John Moreland · Dr. John H. Morton · Zack Mosley · Jasmine Muller, RN · Maxine Muller · Dr. Enrique Muyshondt · Helen, Milton, Larry, Bonnie, Don and Jane Myer · Dr. Robert R. Nesbit, Jr. · Harry and Thelma Neufeld · Lois Nichols, RN · Joyce, Lee, Bruce and Gary Neumann · Dr. Jan Nisonson · Ms. Nonsuch, RN · Selig O. Osband · June, Polly and Judy Owen · Henrietta "Anne" Parlow · Connie and Dr. Earl A. Parrish · Dr. Pearson · Reverend Russell Pendergast, CSB · Dr. Paul C. Pennock · Anthony Pentz · Dr. Stanley M. Perl · Margarete Peterson · Oscar, Bayla, Josh, Piera and Nicolai Piagentini · Patricia Pierce, RN · Dr. Dean L. Pierson · Barbara Ann Poet, RN · Sid and Bea Popkin · Georgia Porcelli, RN · Richard Press · Andrew Profeta · Carla, Dick, Adam, Seth and Jordan Rabin · Dr. R. V. Radcliffe · Catherine Ramsey, RN · Felice (d.) and Nathan Ratkin · Edith Ratkin · Toby, Irwin and Rachel Reich · Ms. Respicio, RN · Isobel "Rusty" Reed, RN · Ann Riedl · Wendy, Dominique, Simon and Professor Robin Riley · Dr. Murray H. Ringold · Reverend Frank Robinson · Gerald A. Robbie · Dr. Stanley M. Rogoff · Dr. George P. Rosemond · Jeannine Rosenborg, RN · Chany, Marvin (d.), Gene, Danny and Effie Rubinstein · Ms. Russell, RN · Charles, Hazel, Brian, Pat, Jimmy, Mary Ellen and "Chucky" Ryder · Violet, Haron, "Jackie" and Munir Saltoun · Astrid Sandburg, RN · John R. Santarsiero, Jr. · Toni, Ann, David, and Dr. Mike Samloff · Dr. Joseph Sataloff · Dorothy Sauers, RN · Dr. Edwin D. Savlov · Peggy Savlov · Charlotte and Joseph Schatz · Dr. Arthur Schmale · Darlene Schmink, RN · Marvin and June Schneider · Robert A. Schulman · Pearl and Sid (d.) Selwyn · Joan Burak Shaheen · Don, Joan, Andrew, Jeffry and Lauri Shifter · Katherine Shrove · Dr. Shugarts · Harvey, Marge, Michael and Sally Silk · Milton Sincoff · Ms. Small, RN · Dr. Albert C. Snell · David and Ethel Sokoloff · Pat, Arnold, Mark, Margo and Leslie Somers · Paul E. Starey · Adelaide Steedman, RN · Mary Sterling, RN · Betty, David, Amy, Linda, and Dr. Edward A. Stern · Dr. Harriet Carol Stern · Arthue Steve · Desmond and Lorraine Stone · Ann, Eric, Janet and Brian Strauss · Linton and Bonnie Studdiford · Irvin and Marie Stutsman · Kay D. Sullivan · Jean Sullivan, LPN · Helen Surline, LPN · Alice Suter, RN · Delores Torbit · Agnes M. Tarrant · Margaret and Irving Tauscher · Milton and Adele (d.) Tenenbaum · Dr. Frederick W. Tiley · Dr. Frank Marwood Tooze · Dr. Jonathon Baker Towne · Joseph and Marge Trachy · Lucille, Buddy, Randy, Johnny, Gina and Dr. William Trench · Shirley Tyler · Jessie Tyson · Stanley, Jane, Betsy and Jason Ungar · Franz Van Gennit · Katherine Ververs, RN · L. O. Vascerine · Beverly Volk, RPN · Alfred E. Vragel · Dr. Walker · Dr. Wallace H. Wallace · Robbie Warfield · Michael Welch · Jan Wheeler, RN · Dr. Donald R. Wieche · Linda and William M. Williams · Ms. Windsor, PN · LaRue, Holly, Jennifer and Dr. Stephen A. Wolfe · June Elain Wood, RN · Joan Woodward · Leah and Irvin (d.) Wurzel · Dr. Philip R. Yarnell · Bob Yates · Armen and Alda Yazujian · Richard and Carol Ziegler · Susan and Dr. Donald N. Zehl · Nancy Zwanco ·

and to my wife, Grace, who was my rock
and to my sons Leigh, Cory and Tod, who were my reason

PROLOGUE

I arrived in Rochester early that morning accompanied by my boss, Jerry Kurtz, the president of the company for which I was technical director. He was forty-two, tall, handsome and well built, but beginning to show the paunchiness of the good life that his wealth and position afforded him. And Jerry Kurtz knew how to live the good life, although he spent most of his time involved in his work. He was a tiger in following up an idea.

Jerry had his suits custom-made during his many visits each year to the two plastics molding factories he owned in Hong Kong. The company, Rico Internationale, Ltd., specialized in plastic flowers. Golf was his game, but he found so little time for it that his blonde, independently wealthy wife Connie had many more trophies to show for it than he did on display in their

Harrison, New York mansion. The first time I approached the house in Kurtz's Cadillac, he joked, "It isn't much, but we call it home." I had thought we were approaching the town hall.

The night before we flew into Rochester, I slept in the guest room so we could get an early start at 5:30 the next morning. I lived in Pennsylvania, and if I had left from home, getting together for the trip would have delayed us. We were to be joined in Rochester by Jerry Marrow, the company vice-president and partner in the firm, who planned to fly directly from LaGuardia Airport rather than drive up to Westchester County Airport in White Plains and depart with us.

Jerry Marrow, like Kurtz, was well over six feet tall. His attire was equally neat, but more conservative and always impeccable, the product of the same Chinese tailor. I was neither as tall as he nor as wealthy as either, but I too began having my suits made by that Chinese tailor after my first visit to the factories in Hong Kong.

I was thirty-seven years old in 1963 and married to my childhood sweetheart, Grace. With her blue eyes and light hair worn in bangs, she was very attractive on all counts and quite chic. She had always looked younger than she actually was, except when I first met her. Then she looked more mature and developed than her peers, something I regarded in her favor. Our three boys—Leigh, seven, Cory, three, and Tod, who would soon have his first birthday—were towheads too.

I met Grace when my family moved to her neighborhood soon after the death of my father, who had been an attorney in New York City. He was an accomplished artist and an outstanding classical pianist. He was thin and frail and very gentle. When I was just sixteen, he hanged himself from the back of his office door on Fifth Avenue in a spell of depression. He left my mother, my sister and me long suicide notes. I saved mine, but have never read it since.

I studied piano and oboe at the High School of Music and Art and was leader of the dance band. I also studied piano at the Juilliard School of Music, and had my own combo which played weekends and summers in the Borscht Belt in the Catskills. In January 1944, at seventeen, I enlisted in the army, but I never saw any action even though I was shipped overseas during the death throes of the Third Reich.

I was honorably discharged in June 1946 and was accepted at the engineering college of New York University, only a short bus ride from home. When I graduated in 1950, I took a job with a company in Trenton, New Jersey, but continued my education via scholarships to Columbia and Brooklyn Polytechnic Institue. On June 18 of that year, I married Grace. Leigh was born in the eighth year of our marriage. We needed more room —we were living in a small apartment in Greenwich Village— and when we could find nothing suitable we bought our present home in Levittown, Pennsylvania, only a few minutes drive from work instead of the hour-and-a-half commute by train.

A colleague offered me an exciting job as technical director with his company in Philadelphia at a considerable increase in salary which I accepted. Two years later, Jerry Kurtz came into our office to buy one of the plastics processing machines we manufactured. He bought everything I suggested; it was one of our easiest sales. Then at lunch he told me he wanted to buy me along with the machines and invited me to his New York office off Park Avenue to discuss the situation. I presented a list of difficult demands which he accepted at once. Then he threw in the clincher: besides almost doubling my present salary, I would spend several months in Hong Kong, where the factories were, followed by a tour of Japan to familiarize myself with the plastics industry there.

I worked on new projects at Rico Internationale, but in reality I was Kurtz's alter ego. Our company's plastic flowers were considered the best in the industry.

One day T. Spencer Knight, the president and board chairman of the Stuart Company, dropped into our office unannounced with a unique proposal, namely, setting up plastic-flower-arranging parties. His company was in the door-to-door selling business, using parties in the home as its sales gimmick, but in his conversations with Jerry Kurtz he let it be known that his company had several million dollars in the bank which it was hoping to put to work.

The existence of such a sum of money became a consuming passion of Kurtz's waking hours. We visited Stuart's headquarters, took the grand tour, returned home with, we hoped, a clear impression of their capabilities and narrowed down our ideas until we came up with a new invention: an aerosol-can spray gun that could blend two different liquid components with reasonable accuracy. At the same time we developed a multiple-aerosol can dispenser and designed a complete package around the concept. We had prepared models and renderings, and details of the whole program. It was the presentation of this program that was bringing us to Rochester to visit the Stuart Company in nearby Newark, New York on July 2, 1963.

Jerry Marrow's plane had landed in Rochester before ours did, so he rented a car at the airport. The rented car was not air-conditioned and although it was still early morning as we struck out on Highway 31 for Newark, the heat and humidity made us uncomfortable. We took off our jackets, loosened our ties and opened all the windows, to no avail. At least the countryside was beautiful and relaxing to look at in the clear sunlight.

Our meeting was held in Stuart's modern, orange-brick executive offices. We had lunch with several of the senior executives at a nearby country club and then returned to the company's facilities for a tour of the packaging operation.

Everything went better than we had expected. When our meetings were finished we retraced our way back to the airport under a sweltering sun, avidly discussing the success of our mission. Jerry Kurtz was driving, and as we sped along he began to sing. Kurtz wasn't the type to sing. He was usually tougher than that, and it was out of character for him. He would periodically reveal that side of himself, though, and this time it indicated his obvious pleasure at the way the meeting had been concluded.

In the distance we could see ominous dark clouds, but overhead it remained sunny and bright. Jerry Marrow, who feared flying even though he was a veteran traveler who flew around the world several times a year, expressed his hope that we would be long gone before the rain arrived.

When we reached the airport Kurtz and I checked in at the Mohawk ticket counter, while Marrow took care of his ticket on an American Airlines flight that was scheduled to depart a half hour after ours.

I was anxious to return home. We had no plans for the Fourth of July, but I'd already missed a day with my family, spending the night before at Kurtz's house, and I was due home that night. I planned to go to Kurtz's house in Harrison, where my car was, and drive home. I hadn't had a chance to call Grace all day.

We stopped at the airport café to get something to drink and I tried to convince Marrow to switch his ticket so we could all fly back together and continue the conversation on board. But he said no, that his car was parked at LaGuardia and that our flight would terminate at Newark, New Jersey, after White Plains. I persisted, and almost had him convinced. I even went out to the Mohawk counter to check on our flight status, where I learned that our flight was booked up and he could not have been accommodated in any case.

Kurtz and I rose to leave, passing the check on to Marrow. He stayed behind and had another beer. As we got up to go, Kurtz chucked Marrow under the chin and chided him, "Don't be afraid of the rain." I learned from Marrow several years later that this was pure bravado; Kurtz himself was deathly afraid of flying.

Clouds were gathering close to the field. To the northwest there was complete darkness. As we left the comfort of the café and lined up at the gate we again removed our jackets and slung them over our shoulders, hanging them by the loop from a single finger down our backs.

Marrow could see us lining up from his vantage point in the café. He could also see, at the same time, little swirls of dust devils tracing erratic paths on parts of the airfield.

Our twin-propeller Martin 404 was a small plane by today's standards; ten rows of four seats abreast, two on each side of the aisle. And it was a depressing aircraft—small, hot, crowded, dingy. The first man aboard it for "The Business Man's Flight," as Mohawk Flight 112 was known, was Henry Fetz, a sales supervisor for Cheeseborough-Ponds. He went straight for a seat in the rear of the plane, for safety's sake, and on the left side, for comfort. The stewardess, Mary Ann Miara, was blocking the very last row on the left, so Fetz squirmed his way into a window seat one row ahead. As he was boarding he noted that it was dark and threatening outside. Inside it was quite humid, almost stifling. He overheard a passenger comment on the bad weather to the stewardess, and her answer that there was a very bad storm back at her home town in New Jersey.

Charles McAdam, Jr. had just left his two youngest children with their maternal grandmother Caroline Werner Gannett, widow of the founder of the Gannett newspaper empire, in Rochester. An experienced traveler, he was concerned that the ominous black clouds overhead might ground his plane and keep him in Rochester an extra day and his uncertainty was reinforced when he heard over the public address system that two American flights would be postponed for thirty minutes to allow the storm to pass. And as he walked out to the boarding ramp, queuing up at the gate with the other passengers, he felt a stab of apprehension. The silver craft gave off no gleam; it looked like lead. The thought, "ghost ship," flashed through his mind. He chose the seat next to Fetz and introduced himself. Naturally, their discussion turned to the weather.

Two young plastics salesmen from Connecticut, Gary Higgins and James Kirkpatrick, chose seats close to the rear, too—Kirkpatrick at random, Higgins because he considered the tail section the safest part of the plane. They sat across from Fetz.

Three men from the New York State Commission on Human Rights—Edward Rutledge, John Sullivan, and Lloyd Trent Jr.—had been to a Rochester Chamber of Commerce meeting to explain a new state law against discrimination in housing. Their meeting broke up earlier than expected, so Trent, booked for a 6:35 P.M. return flight on American, tried to get on the Mohawk flight with the others and return that much sooner to his anxious bride of two months. He was placed on standby, and the three went into the café for an early dinner. While they were eating, Trent was paged and advised that a seat was available on the Mohawk flight and he had his ticket changed. When he boarded the plane he took his seat on the aisle in Row 8 next to Donald Carney, who was on a business trip for Sterling Precision Laboratories. John Sullivan sat down in the left window seat on Row 7 next to H. W. McCalley, a middle-aged man who was sitting there "so I can get off in a hurry," as he explained. Edward Rutledge took the last-row seat that Stewardess Miara finally exposed as she moved to the opposite side of the aisle. He sat next to the only woman passenger aboard, a housewife with a name made famous though not by her: Mrs. Richard Nixon. By now, frequent lightning bolts were striking all around and she tensely asked Rutledge, "What happens if lightning hits the plane?" He replied that the plane was a good conductor of lightning. Mrs. Nixon said she "didn't know whether this was good or bad." She didn't feel reassured, but did not pursue the matter.

Two vice-presidents of the Hickok Manufacturing Company, Charles Yelin and Walter Rappoport, both in town for a regular business meeting, slipped into the last row of seats on the right. Robert Christopher and Thomas Mayer, of the Crown-Zellerbach paper-manufacturing concern, took up Row 7 on the right. Richard Baldwin, a promotion representative for Remington Arms in Bridgeport, Connecticut, who was in Rochester to enter a skeet-shooting contest on behalf of the company, took the left aisle seat in Row 6, near the wing and next to Daniel Schwester, a New Jersey engineer who had been on a trip to the Xerox Corporation. Charles Martin, a sales representative for Kodak who lived in a town near mine outside Philadelphia, took a right window seat on Row 6. The last passenger to board, Nathan Shippee, making business calls for his packaging firm in Rochester that day, took the seat next to him.

There was a contingent of ten from International Business Machines Corporation on board. Two private consultants for the firm, George Bossi and Donald McCauley, took aisle seats in Row 4 opposite one another. Bossi was from Varese, Italy. He could barely speak a word of English. He sat next to the well-known architect John L. O'Brien, Jr. and McCauley next to an account executive with the J. Walter Thompson Advertising Agency, Laurence Johnson. Karl Schink and Louis Wirtz, who had been inspecting the Rochester Institute of Technology's graphic arts department for IBM, took Row 3 on the right. Another IBM employee, Thomas Callinan, who had accompanied them, sat on the left aisle in Row 2 next to Alan Crandall, at seventeen the youngest passenger, who had been visiting relatives. Across from them sat two representatives of the IBM research laboratories, Joseph Crimi and Morris Housel. Behind those two, across from Schink and Wirtz, sat Andre Nys and Charles "Chuck" Wright, a research chemist. Stephen Kissell, a buyer of chemicals and raw materials, took a seat in Row 8 next to the left-hand emergency exit. To him, the people on board "seemed to be apprehensive about the weather because it seemed that they were crowding to get on the plane." He put his hand through a little opening in a small metal plate covering the emergency exit partition, and tested the tension of the spring. Just in case.

At first, Thomas Forrest, a reservations clerk for Eastern Airlines flying on an airline pass, was seated next to him. But just as Forrest settled back after tightening his seat belt, he heard his name being paged over the cabin loudspeaker and knew he was being bumped for a paying customer. He returned to the terminal without seeing who took his place, phoned his sister, and once again stayed overnight at her home. His seat was taken by Robert Bernstein of Stamford, Connecticut, who said as he sat down next to Kissel, "I don't know if I want to get on this plane or not." Later, another passenger would blame Bernstein for the takeoff delay he had caused in bumping Forrest.

Gene K. Beare, the president of Sylvania Electric, sat next to the right-side forward emergency exit in Row 5, next to Dr. Lee Davenport, president of Sylvania's parent company, General Telephone and Electronics. Two Sylvania executives, David Elwell and Roy Drew, took seats across the aisle. On the left, the first-row seats were occupied by Morris Falk and Lee O'Dell, both New York management consultants.

Jerry Kurtz and I completed the first row. Jerry, because of his height, preferred the extra leg room of the first row. I was aware the rear was safer, and on long flights I became restless in the front row because the smooth bulkhead didn't allow me to put my feet up as the other seats did, but I voiced no objection. We kept our jackets off, stowed them, and fastened our seat belts. I turned to Kurtz and commented that it was a shame Jerry Marrow had not come with us. Kurtz looked at me, forcing a nervous smile. We said very little after that. In the cockpit, the two-man flight crew went through their preflight preparations.

Most veteran passengers of propeller-driven aircraft are familiar with the run-up check of the plane's engines just prior to takeoff. This check is usually performed adjacent to the runway. Knowledgeable passengers wait for the brakes to be locked as soon as the plane has drawn to a stop after taxiing up to the runway, and listen as each of the engines is run up to full power. They wait for this in much the same way that one waits for a second shoe to be dropped in the upstairs apartment. And so it was not unusual for some of the passengers to act like seasoned inspectors and direct their total attention to that sound after the plane had set its brakes. But the sound they waited for never came. This procedure was either somehow overlooked or deliberately eliminated by the crew in their haste to depart before the storm broke.

Passenger Charley McAdam heard himself say, "I hope the pilot won't try it." When he felt the brakes lock as the plane stopped adjacent to the runway, he murmured, "Good! He's going to wait for the storm to pass."

Before the words were out of his mouth, he felt the brakes release and the plane wheel to the right onto the runway to begin its takeoff roll. McAdam leaned toward his seatmate Henry Fetz and said, "Well, Henry, you'd better tighten your belt. This is going to be a rough ride." With that, he disregarded his own advice and loosened his seat belt, so he could bend his body into the aisle and observe the activity in the cockpit. This was still in the pre-hijack era, so the doors to the flight deck were left fully open.

Dr. Lee Davenport of GT&E was also surprised by the lack of engine run-up, and when the plane set its brakes next to the runway threshold he told his Sylvania colleague Dave Elwell, "It looks like we're going to spend ten or fifteen minutes on the ground until this blows over." Elwell nodded. As the plane made its turn, he too directed his glance toward the cockpit and noticed the windshield wipers grinding slowly away. He thought it unusual that the rain could be so heavy on the windshield and yet so light on the window where he was sitting. Peering into the cockpit from her vantage point at the rear of the cabin, Stewardess Miara also noted that the wipers were having little effect. She could see only vague shimmering shadows through the cockpit windshield.

Steve Kissel later remembered "the rain made horizontal streaks; not vertical streaks, *horizontal* streaks." He and Robert Bernstein began to discuss whether a plane of this size would even have windshield wipers, when they peered into the cockpit just in time to see Dennis reach up and manipulate a knob which started them sweeping across the windows. Then Kissel saw Dennis give Neff a go-ahead nod and the plane started its roll down the barely visible strip of concrete. Bernstein leaned over to say, "Doesn't this seem slow? Come on, let's go!" Nathan Shippee recalled the murmur of disbelief that ran through the cabin as the aircraft swung onto the runway, and Henry Fetz tensely told McAdam, "This is ridiculous! In fact, this is the most ridiculous thing I ever heard of—taking off in this kind of weather!"

I had flown in rainstorms and snowstorms prior to this, but never in one this severe in intensity.

I was slightly apprehensive, as I am on any takeoff or landing. Like most passengers, I relax only after I am airborne and the "Fasten Your Seat Belt" and "No Smoking" signs go off. I used to immediately light up a cigarette, which somehow would develop an improved taste on those occasions.

As we were rolling down the runway, I fastened my eyes on the backs of the heads of the crew and watched the action on the flight deck, the backs of their heads just visible above their high seat backs, their arms gyrating in all directions everywhere, even overhead.

Our motion smoothed out and I knew that the wheels had lifted, that we were now airborne. I was glad for that, because my main concern is usually that these giant machines will not lift off but will bounce along the ground to a fiery death at the edge of the field. No matter how often I fly, I never cease to be amazed at the ability of these monsters to remain aloft for a sustained period, even though I am totally familiar with the scientific principles involved. I noticed that the crew was beginning to react in an abnormal way: their movements were not the relaxed, casual motions that one usually observes in an airplane cockpit.

As soon as we ascended a short distance, the left wing of the plane tipped steeply toward the ground. I looked out the window to my right past Jerry Kurtz. Only dark gray sky was visible. It was then that I noticed Kurtz. His hands were clenching the armrests of his seat. His knuckles were white—drained of blood. His head was pressed firmly against the back of his seat, his mouth open and taut, exposing clenched teeth. On his face was a grimace of abject terror.

I suppose this was the difference between being an optimist and a pessimist, because, even after seeing his horrified look, I did not react similarly. I felt that he was foolishly over-reacting and in an effort to put him at ease I said to him in as light a manner as I could, "I hope we make it!" In reality, it was a prayer.

At that moment, the plane reversed itself. Now the right wing was pointing earthward and the left one to the sky. I stopped looking out the window and again had focused my attention on the activity in the cockpit. I can recall seeing the pilot (actually it was copilot Neff) straining with two hands on the wheel and I have a vague recollection of Dennis reaching over to do something in his direction.

It seemed we had ascended a considerable distance when the plane once again tilted suddenly to the left, its left wing pointing at the ground, and then I knew from the extreme angle and from the discomfort in my stomach—the feeling one experiences when a plane hits an air pocket or turbulence and suddenly changes altitude, or to a lesser extent on a high-speed elevator in a tall building—that this was not a normal takeoff, that we were in danger.

All the external noise was drowned out by the shivering, deafening, agonizing roar that suddenly engulfed the cabin. McAdam recognized it as a stallout; the plane did not have enough airspeed to get aloft. This realization froze the blood in his veins. He watched in horrified fascination as both crewmen struggled to pull back on their wheels. He prayed that they would try to land.

But the plane continued to rise, to about 125 feet above the ground, and rolled over on its left side. The pilots tried to right the craft but overcompensated, so that now it tipped over on its right side, then again back on its left—and then it happened. The left wingtip scraped the ground. A shudder of vibration, at a different frequency, began to rock the airplane. McAdam thought to himself, "Somebody's going to get hurt," as he quickly leaned back in his seat and cinched his belt as tightly as he could, bracing himself for what he knew had to come. The vibration crescendoed as the plane cartwheeled over the left wing, onto its nose, and over to the right wing. New vibrations in the rear signaled that the tail fin had struck the ground. This was only a momentary event as the plane righted itself and went bounding along on its belly, tearing itself apart as it slithered through the grass and the freshly formed mud. The shrieking, hideous, metallic screams could be felt as well as heard as they penetrated the cabin. Then silence.

In that one instant, the course of my life changed forever.

Part One
The Anatomy
of a
Plane Crash

1

It was Tuesday, July 2, 1963.

The sun was already up as Captain Richard Dennis swung his wife's Volkswagen onto the Garden State Parkway just minutes from his home in Elberon on the Jersey Shore. This was his first day back on the job after an eighteen-day vacation in the Virgin Islands with his wife and their three sons. He gunned the car toward Newark Airport, his home base.

The New Jersey Turnpike marks the eastern boundary of the airport. As the car came over a rise in the highway Dennis could see the runways, already busy with air traffic, and the terminal buildings sprawled in the distance. He checked his watch. It was 6:40 A.M., daylight saving time.

Captain Dennis strode into the Mohawk Airlines operations office. The rest of his crew had already arrived:

First Officer Neff and Flight Attendant Miara.

Mary Ann Miara lived close to the airport in Sayreville, New Jersey, directly in the path of the main runway. When she had joined Mohawk six months earlier she was put through a two-week training program intended to convert her into a glorified waitress-wife-mother-sweetheart-nurse. The training also included emergency procedures and required the satisfactory completion of a company medical examination. She graduated to become one of more than thirty-three thousand stewardesses and stewards employed by United States airlines. As she sat curled up in a plastic-covered chair in operations, First Officer John William Neff stood at the operations counter studying the current weather information.

Neff, who was thirty-one and good looking, had been hired by Mohawk on September 26, 1961, as a First Officer trainee assigned to the airline's Utica, New York, headquarters. He was given a forty-hour basic company indoctrination course and a sixty-four-hour initial ground-school course on the primary aircraft the line was flying at the time—the Convair 240 and the Convair 440. Following the ground training, he spent six hours and thirty minutes at the controls flying the newest addition to Mohawk's fleet, the Martin 404. He also rode on the Martin for seven hours as an observer. Later that month he was given a proficiency test flying the Martin on a one hour and fifty minute flight. When he passed this he was returned to the line as a dually qualified first officer in Convair and Martin aircraft. In October of the following year he received eight hours of recurrent ground training on Convair 240 and 440 aircraft and on January 10, 1963, he received eight hours on the Martin 404. This training included emergency evacuation drill. More than half of ground training simulates severe emergency conditions.

Neff passed his next regular annual proficiency check on March 16, 1963. On that test he qualified for the left seat, the seat reserved for the pilot. The Mohawk policy of on-the-job training permitted the first officer to fly the left seat if the captain had two hundred and fifty hours of command experience.

There is no FAA regulation that stipulates whether the pilot sit in the left- or right-hand seat, but the applicable Mohawk regulation stated that a first officer must log nine hundred hours in that type of aircraft and put in twenty-four months of active service with Mohawk before being permitted to fly in the left seat. Although the instruments and controls are essentially duplicated in both the pilot's and copilot's positions, it is only the left seat that controls the nose wheel for steering on the ground; the man in the right seat handles the ground communications equipment while the plane is taxiing. Scanning of the instruments is partially reversed in each seat. The single radar scope is located on the left side of the panel; each side also contains some important monitoring instruments that the other side lacks.

During the four-month period between March 16 and July 2, 1963, First Officer Neff logged an additional 154:51 hours in the Martin 404. He also flew 124:57 hours in the Convair 240 and 440 airplanes during this same period.

Entered in his personal flight log up to that July day in 1963 was recorded, in brief, Neff's entire flight history:

Total Flight Time	3,399:10 hours
Total Time in Convair Aircraft	627:40 hours
Total Time In Martin Aircraft	821:50 hours
Total Time as Pilot-in-Command	1,495:30 hours
Total Time as Co-Pilot	1,805:45 hours
Total Night Time	574:05 hours
Total Actual Weather Time	150:30 hours
Total Hood [Instrument] Time	31:20 hours
Total Link [Ground Trainer] Time	56:35 hours

Captain Dennis was an experienced pilot. He had logged fifteen thousand nine hundred seventy hours of flight time. Four hundred fourteen of those hours were logged in Martin aircraft. His record also testifies that he satisfactorily passed a qualification check on the DC-3 and proficiency checks on the Convair 240. In the middle of November 1962 Dennis spent five days in ground school taking a course on the Martin 404. For an additional two weeks he took transitional training in the Martin 404 and accumulated 8:04 hours of flight time and 7:16 hours as an observer.

Based upon this experience, Dennis was recommended for a type-rating in the Martin 404 on December 15, 1962. On

January 3, 1963, Dennis added 1:48 more hours of flight time and exactly the same amount of time riding the jump seat as an observer. He was again recommended for a type-rating.

At approximately 7:00 A.M. Stewardess Miara heaved herself up out of her chair in the Newark operations office and walked out to the Martin 404 parked at the Mohawk ramp. She was the first crew member to board the plane. She walked down the aisle, checking seats as she went to make sure that they were all upright and their safety belts properly placed. She also checked the emergency doors and the CO_2 fire extinguishers—two forward and one on the partition just in front of her swing-down seat in the rear of the cabin. She shuffled the leatherette-covered magazines in the rack on the forward bulkhead and rearranged some of the pillows and blankets in the overhead rack.

As she began to organize the coffee service in the galley, Captain Dennis and First Officer Neff boarded the plane and took their seats in the cockpit. It was now 7:10 A.M. Moments later the passengers began boarding. At exactly 7:25 A.M. this flight departed Newark Airport for Buffalo as Mohawk Flight 253. It made an intermediate stop at Westchester County Airport in White Plains, New York. No passengers deplaned. The stop was brief and one engine was kept running. The second engine was stopped so as not to present a hazard to the enplaning passengers. The active engine was needed to generate on-board power so that a ground-cable connection would be unnecessary. The flight continued on to Buffalo without incident, arriving at 9:43 A.M.

Aircraft departure and arrival times are precise and are carefully recorded by a number of people: the pilot, in his log; the local company agent; and the departure-control agent in the FAA tower. This information is also transmitted to company headquarters by the local company agent where, in Mohawk's case, it was fed into an IBM computer for evaluation of individual pilot performance. (Mohawk also rented time on Eastern Airlines' UNIVAC computer to keep their dispatchers current on passenger flight reservations.)

Mohawk had a policy that graded pilots in accordance with their on-time performance of arrival and departure. Crew members were queried on all delays. The pilot's current standing was printed on his paycheck voucher. From this information, a list was compiled each quarter, the purpose of which was to focus the attention of the flight managers on pilots who performed below par. An effort would then be made to discuss his performance with the errant pilot and retrain him if necessary. At least that was the plan.

Dennis was high up on the list for on-time performance, among the top ten. One day in late August 1962, Captain E. P. Rooney, a Mohawk air safety inspector and a Civil Aeronautics Board safety representative, overheard the assistant to the vice-president of operations needling Dennis, suggesting that Dennis should be number three on the on-time performance list rather than number ten. This conversation was dutifully reported by Rooney to Mohawk Captain Ralph F. Colliander, who also happened to be chairman of the Master Executive Committee of the Air Line Pilots' Association (ALPA), a title which can be freely translated into "shop steward of the pilots' union."

Colliander constantly had the ear of Mohawk's top management as he negotiated the various and sundry complaints and problems that arose between the pilots and the company. When he learned about the pressure being put on the pilots to improve their on-time arrival and departure records, he was perturbed because he felt that this represented a potential safety hazard. He conceded that the airline had the right to monitor delays caused by crew members, but he felt that the additional pressure on the pilots was unwarranted. Pilots could be tempted to overstep CAB regulations in order to improve their standings, he reasoned. They might, for example, not complete their checklists in order to cut their schedules to the shortest possible elapsed times. Time-saving procedures were being established without sufficient consideration given to safety factors.

The company had also established a policy of "Beat American." This was brought to Colliander's attention when Mohawk was granted a route from Syracuse to New York City in competition with American Airlines. Both airlines had flights departing Syracuse at the same time in the morning. Colliander had been asked by Mohawk management to "urge" pilots to get their aircraft out of the gate and into the air ahead of American. Colliander relayed this order to the pilot group. But he complained to the company management that these pressures might be responsible for some of the difficulties that pilots had become involved in. (In spite of all the efforts Mohawk made, in 1970 its on-time arrival rate was the lowest of all America's twenty-two scheduled airlines. Only 47.2 percent of its scheduled flights arrived on time compared with National Airlines, which had the highest rate at 82.7 percent.)

Captain Dennis, First Officer Neff, and Stewardess Miara had a two-hour-and-forty-five-minute layover in Buffalo on July 2, 1963. At 12:38 in the afternoon they flew Mohawk Flight 204, also a Martin 404 aircraft, from Buffalo to Ithaca, arriving at 1:08 P.M.

2

John M. Williams came on duty at the United States Weather Bureau at 8:00 A.M. on July 2, 1963. With twenty-seven years of experience behind him, he was chief meteorologist at the Rochester station which was housed in a single-story pale yellow brick building located directly behind the airport tower on the south side of the county airport.

The weather bureau's office is at ground level and consists of four rooms containing the usual assortment of institutional-gray metal desks and chairs. The building is surrounded by a chain-link fence to protect some of the weather-measuring instruments set in the small yard northwest of the building. The entrance hall is festooned with long, yellow teletype tapes held on clipboards. The tapes are periodically regurgitated by the weather teletype machines that line three walls of the room beyond. There are more than half a dozen such machines intermittently coming alive in seemingly random fashion and spewing out lengths of paper containing the codified symbols which convey to the trained eye the weather conditions in all parts of the country and beyond. There is also a facsimile machine that twenty-four hours a day slowly oozes out weather maps of the Western hemisphere, the United States, and local areas. It takes about fifteen minutes for a large map to emerge from the machine. These, too, are hung in the central entrance hall, each map covered with the amoebalike concentric lines that join areas of constant barometric pressure (isobars), and other symbols that indicate temperature, cloud, wind condition and direction, and other weather phenomena.

The weather observatory is in an office to the right of the center hall. It contains several desks and the recording instruments that constantly monitor the local weather conditions. The recorders are housed in a large gray console. The slanting panel on the left houses the aneroid barometer, which continually measures changes in atmospheric pressure. It is with this meter that aircraft make their very critical aviation observation surface altimeter setting, which tells them their distance aboveground. In the center are the wind instruments that indicate wind velocity and wind direction. These instruments share their sensing elements with the FAA control tower. A permanent record is made of these readings on the so-called triple register whose two needlelike pens scribble lines while a third pen taps out intermittent "hammer" markings of an arrow indicating wind direction. These are calibrated to print at precise time intervals. Once a day, when the charts are changed, a spring clock mechanism is wound and the time is synchronized with the observatory clock.

There were no instruments for measuring wind gusts or turbulence as such, although the wind speed indicator would indicate wind gusts, if you happened to be looking directly at it when such phenomena occurred.

An instrument for recording visibility directly on the field, called a transmissometer, had been installed in January. Located adjacent to the main east-west runway, runway 10–28, were two devices that comprised the sensing end of this instrument. They were spaced five hundred feet apart along the runway midpoint. The data acquired were fed by wire to a recording instrument on the weather-bureau panel where another pen scrawled its information on a chart. The instrument had not, as yet, been checked out for time accuracy. Because of this factor, the transmissometer had not been officially commissioned even though it had been in operation for almost six months. Thus, dissemination of its information to anyone outside the weather bureau was prohibited, although it was continually monitored by bureau personnel along with the other instruments. Official visibility readings were determined solely by eye; they were found to agree perfectly with the unofficial transmissometer readings. The purpose of monitoring the instrument was for it to be certified as accurate, allowing it to be commissioned into active duty. When it was time-checked each morning it was found to agree within sixty seconds of the observatory clock.

The observatory panel has readouts for other sensing instruments located in the outside fenced-off yard. "Extreme" thermometers give the high and low temperature readings for the day; a psychrometer indicates the relative humidity or moisture in the air. It consists of a wet and a dry bulb thermometer; the difference between the two varies according to the amount of water evaporated from the wet bulb which is directly effected by the amount of moisture in the air. There are also three types of rain gauges: a tipping bucket gauge which sends a remote signal to the triple register chart in the office each time it fills and tips to empty; a weighing gauge consisting of a metal structure with an opening on top through which rain falls into a bucket sitting on top of a pair of scales (the weight is indicated as hundredths of an inch of rain rather than as weight units); also mounted in the outside yard is an eight-inch rain gauge, really just a measuring cup, but it doesn't have a remote readout in the bureau office.

A hygrothermometer, which is another device for measuring humidity, had been installed on June 30, only three days before.

For determination of ceiling, i.e., height of the clouds above the ground, both a rotating-beam ceilometer and a fixed-beam ceilometer were used. Visibility was determined both day and night by eye from distances to natural and man-made local points, plotted on two charts. One chart covered a range of one-half mile; the other covered eight miles.

The Rochester bureau had weather-search radar, known as WSR-3, which had been in use for about three years. It was never used on the weather-dissemination network, but only as a tool by the local observer and forecaster primarily for local public-service messages. The only other weather radar in western New York was the much more powerful WSR-57 unit located in Buffalo. This instrument had more than ten times the Rochester unit's power, and was the primary radar instrument in the area. The information obtained in the WSR-57 was disseminated over the teletype network and a daily log was kept of the coverage of its echoes. Rochester did not maintain a log of its radar except to note at 7:00 A.M. EST that its radar was properly aligned and operating. It was so recorded on July 2, 1963.

The radar at Buffalo had a maximum range of two hundred fifty miles. It had a separate range height indicator (RHI) scope. Whenever unusual conditions appeared on either scope, a photograph was taken for the record.

Bobby C. Oehlerich, an eight-year employee of the weather bureau, manned the WSR-57 radar at the Greater Buffalo Airport on July 2.

Oehlerich came on duty in Buffalo at 8:00 A.M. for the eight-to-four shift. But because of the echoes that appeared on radar that day, he, in Buffalo, and Williams in Rochester would both put in some overtime.

Lake Ontario, which is deep and remains unfrozen during the long winters of the area, plays an important part in shaping the climate of the Rochester area. After "storing up cold" in the water during the winter, the lake "releases cold" in the spring, thus delaying the development of vegetation and reducing losses that would occur from spring frosts. (Actually cold cannot be transferred; only heat can. The lake surrenders its heat. By giving up more heat than its surroundings it becomes colder. The process reverses and it absorbs heat, but more slowly than the surroundings.) In the autumn the reverse actions take place: the stored summer heat is released to warm the air and so prolongs the growing and harvest seasons.

The temperature extremes in the Rochester area, both lower and upper, are moderated by the lake effect, so that the long-term range, as well as the daily one, is less than other continental cities at the same latitude. It very rarely reaches 100 degrees Fahrenheit in the summer in Rochester, and the winter minimum falls to zero or below on an average of only about five days a year.

A further effect of the lake is to promote cloudiness and frequent rain, especially during cold weather when atmospheric circulatory processes gather moisture and heat in the lower layers as air masses move over the water surface from northerly directions. Upon striking the colder land surface south of the lake, clouds form and snow develops. Such snowfalls are frequent but usually not heavy.

Rochester is also near the so-called St. Lawrence storm track. Cyclonic systems progressing from the interior of the Atlantic Ocean through the St. Lawrence Valley transport moisture from the Gulf of Mexico which is precipitated enroute. This is the source of a large portion of the rainfall in the Rochester area, and practically all of its major snow storms.

On July 2, 1963, Rochester had been in the throes of a six-week drought. For nine days the heat had been oppressive. The last measurable rainfall had been on June 14, when eight-hundredths of an inch had been recorded.

The temperature had been pressing forward all day to a summer's high of 95 degrees Fahrenheit. At noon, William G. Kerchbessner, a chemist at the Public Safety Laboratory, checked the temperature at the intersection in downtown Rochester known as Four Corners. He inserted oversized thermometers into holes he dug with his penknife in the sticky asphalt street. The thermometers registered almost 118 degrees Fahrenheit.

At forty-five minutes past noon a message was sent out on circuit 8022 of the Service A teletype system by the weather bureau's forecast center at Cleveland-Hopkins Airport Station in Cleveland, Ohio. This was the routine twelve-hour terminal forecast issued twice a day by that office. The Cleveland office is responsible for forecasting weather encompassing the northern third of Ohio, western Pennsylvania, and western New York, including the Rochester area.

The terminal forecast is a statement of expected weather for the forthcoming twelve-hour period and is specific for approximately sixteen commercial airports in the area. It is put out on the teletype twice a day in the code of the weatherman. The 12:45 P.M. forecast read in part:

FT I CLE 021645
17Z TUE-05Z WED

Then, near the bottom of the list of forecasts that followed for the sixteen airports, appeared this entry:

ROC 50① 120① 7→15 OCNL C15① 2 TRW→20+VCNTY. 1900
E COLD FRO PA 250-① ↘ 12 OCNL 40① TIL 21E.

In translation this becomes: "Twelve-hour terminal forecast issued from Cleveland on July 2, 1960 at 12:45 P.M. eastern daylight time effective from 1:00 P.M. on Tuesday to 1:00 A.M. on Wednesday."

Then: "For Rochester Airport and vicinity 5,000 feet scattered clouds, 12,000 feet scattered clouds, visibility 7 miles. Surface winds west at 15 knots. Conditions occasional. Ceiling 1,500 feet overcast. Visibility 2 miles. Thunderstorm and moderate rain showers. Surface winds west at 20 knots with gusts in the vicinity. This portion of the forecast is valid through 7:00 P.M. EDT. At 7:00 P.M. a cold frontal passage is forecast to pass through the station. Following that cold front, conditions are forecast to be 25,000 feet then scattered clouds, visibilities unrestricted. Surface winds from the northwest at 12 knots. Occasional cloudiness at 4,000 feet, scattered. Until 9:00 P.M. EDT."

If the forecasts for the other stations were studied, they would have shown that thunderstorm activity was predicted with a "chance at Cleveland, occasional at Pittsburgh, occasional at Canton-Akron and at Buffalo, a chance at Erie, occasional at Syracuse, Phillipsburg, Elmira, Allegheny County, Mansfield, Altoona, Bradford and Watertown." There could be no doubt that there were thunderstorms in the area.

* * *

At nearby Olmsted Falls, Ohio, Aviation-Forecaster Rodney C. Winslow was on duty at the Olmsted Falls center. The area under his official scrutiny was experiencing quite warm, moist, tropical air and had been for some time. But now a well-defined cold front was approaching from the northwest, promising some relief. By ten o'clock that morning it stretched from Quebec Province through Lake Huron into the extreme northwest portion of Ohio and was moving southward at about fifteen to twenty knots.

Winslow sent a weather forecast about the approaching front out over flight service station (FSS) by interfax machine, which relayed it via long-line teletype. Finally it was put out over the Service A teletypewriter, circuit number 8022. This service is used primarily for aviation weather reports. (There is also a Service C teletypewriter network used for domestic synoptic weather information and a Service O network used for international service.)

An unending stream of messages poured in day and night, on regular schedule, over the teletype networks. In addition to the twelve-hour terminal forecasts received on the Service A circuit 8022, there were also area forecasts; hourly sequences; pilots reports (PIREPS), which cover in-flight conditions observed by pilots, such as turbulence, reduced visibility, cloud cover, ice, tornadoes, thunderstorms, cold fronts, squall lines and other weather phenomena; significant meteorological phenomena (SIGMETS) such as tornadoes, thunderstorms, and so forth; notice to airmen (NOTAMS) of pertinent field conditions as far as navigation or obstructions to the field or air-navigation facilities that are shut down or being reactivated, or runway construction; severe weather warnings (SWW) when such weather is expected; winds aloft, giving velocity, direction, and temperature at various altitudes; radar advisories when storm centers such as thunderstorms or rain showers are picked up on the radar scope. Any amendments to the above if changes have occurred after the message have been put on the circuit. At half past each hour the scan of special and local reports is issued by the different terminals. In addition, there are emergency communications and messages relating to operations of the circuit. Obviously, the circuits are very busy.

Early that afternoon, at 2:15 P.M. EDT precisely, REWARC

Circuit 706, the radar severe weather circuit, came to life all around the country as an aviation severe weather warning went out over the line. It was issued by the (storm) cells officer at the Kansas City severe local storms forecast center. This circuit is used exclusively for that purpose. The message is then put on the circuit 8022 aviation-weather teletype and is also issued to all the communications media.

The forecast was marked "urgent" and stated in translation:

"Area One. Tornado forecast number 315:

"A. Along sixty miles either side of a line from fifty miles southeast of Buffalo, New York, to fifty miles northeast of Burlington, Vermont. Valid from 2:00 P.M. to 8:00 P.M. EDT. Public forecast issued.

"B. Scattered severe thunderstorms with extreme turbulence; hail to one and one-half inches in diameter; maximum surface gusts to 65 knots; possibility of isolated tornado or two. Few cumulus nimbus clouds with maximum tops of 60,000 feet.

"C. Squall line forming in Zone XI in Ontario, Canada, to the vicinity of Buffalo, New York, and Youngstown, Ohio; expected to intensify and move eastward at 40 knots."

This warning also went on to forecast severe thunderstorm activity in Area Two: Harrisburg, Pennsylvania, to Lynchburg, Virginia. And also for Area Three—Havre, Montana, to Sheridan, Wyoming.

Although a tornado never materialized, a report from Syracuse, New York, noted that a "Pilot reported a funnel cloud over Oneida; wake moving northeast toward West Lake Intersection."

As a result of receiving the SWW from Kansas City, Rodney Winslow at the Cleveland Falls Center issued a SIGMET at 2:30 P.M. EDT with essentially the same information, amending the regular terminal forecast within the area covered by the severe weather warning. His SIGMET mentioned extreme turbulence, hail from one-quarter to one and one-half inches, and at least he implied the presence of squall lines. The terminal forecast issued from Rochester at 2:45 P.M. EDT mentioned surface winds, gusts to sixty-five knots, possibilities of hail, and also a chance of a tornado.

This severe weather message alarmed John Williams in

Rochester and Bobby Oehlerich in Buffalo who kept their eyes glued to their radar screens as they watched the ever-growing amoebalike blob of light work its way across their respective pale green pulsating discs until it gobbled up the center dot, their very location.

The second of July storm began its buildup in Canada hours earlier. It moved south to the Detroit area. Then it began its move south and east toward Lake Ontario. By then it was clear that this was no simple summer storm and Kansas City issued the severe weather warning. Fifteen minutes later, the Cleveland weather bureau issued its SIGMET number one. Five minutes before this message was sent, the regular PIREP scan at twenty-five minutes past the hour went out, with the notation:

"Between Syracuse and Rochester, thunderstorms; tops to 30,000 feet, twenty miles west of Syracuse; small cell four miles north of Airway Victor Two; fifty miles south-southwest of Buffalo, thunderstorm, Jamestown, New York area, moving east-southeast. . . ."

One hour earlier, a Martin 404 took off from New York's John F. Kennedy Airport, then known as Idlewild. Painted in bold letters and numbers on top of the right wing, on the bottom of the left wing, and on the tail section was the identifying registry designation "N449A." Sitting at the controls of this aircraft was Mohawk Captain Herbert M. Silvera, an experienced pilot with ten thousand hours of flight time logged since he began flying eighteen years earlier. He was piloting Mohawk Flight 115 on a one-hour-and-fifteen-minute trip to Ithaca, New York.

During the last ten minutes of this flight he overheard a conversation on the plane's radio between a pilot of a private airplane ahead of him and the New York center ground control station. The pilot requested different routing to Buffalo "to circumnavigate thunderstorms." Silvera went on the alert. The weather was cloudy where he was flying, with visibility less than one hundred miles. But without a reference point, he could not estimate how much less. He could not see any thunderstorm activity in his region. His airborne radar, in use only a year, was on standby mode (which kept it warmed up but not operating). After overhearing the conversation of the aircraft ahead of him, he reached forward and switched the radar to its function position just as he was beginning his landing descent from seven thousand feet. The radar was set at its maximum range of one hundred fifty miles, which was indicated by the outer of the four concentric circles on the scope.

Although Silvera had seen hundreds of storms on the radar screen in the year it had been in use, the intensity of the echo return that glared out at him from the screen at 2:42 P.M. on July 2, 1963, was shocking.

"It was the worst thing I had ever seen as far as severity goes," he later reported. He had never flown through a squall; he had never even seen one while airborne, although he had witnessed them while on the ground and had a fair idea as to the unrelenting fury contained in the system as it passed through. On the radar screen the echo return showed as a hazy, green, cloudlike area which represented precipitation, nothing too ominous to the untrained observer. As he stared out of the cockpit window in the direction of the storm he could see no indications of severe weather activity; the storm was taking place beyond his visible limits.

He glanced back at the radar scope. The storm appeared like a finger, pointing from the eight on an imaginary clock, almost to the twelve; it ran off the scope to the southwest and so the left limit of the storm could not be determined. But the front appeared to be more than one hundred miles wide. At its northwest edge (near twelve o'clock) it broke up into isolated individual thunderstorm cells, and was about one hundred fifty miles away, which placed it over Marmora, Canada.

As he rolled out the plane for his landing in Ithaca at the 320 degree heading, the storm was directly in front of him on the radar. (Buffalo is approximately one hundred miles from that point at a heading of 310 degrees to 315 degrees; Rochester is about sixty-five miles on a heading of approximately 315 degrees to 320 degrees.)

Silvera's log shows that Flight 115 touched down at Ithaca airport at 2:52 P.M. and made a radar sweep of the storm. He arrived at the gate three minutes later, and secured the craft, locking the controls and switching off various plane functions after setting the brakes. He then packed his gear and deplaned with his crew (copilot and stewardess) and some of the passengers. This was only an intermediate stop for Flight 115, but a crew change was scheduled.

As he headed toward the Mohawk operations office he met Captain Dennis and First Officer Neff on their way out to the aircraft to take over command. After a brief greeting, Neff continued out to the plane while Silvera described to Dennis the storms he had observed toward Rochester on the plane's radar. Dennis asked if it were possible to get under them. Silvera explained that he had not made visual contact with the storms and from just the radar observations he could not determine how close to the ground they were. He passed on the details of their intensity and location. This conversation took place at about 3:00 P.M. At that moment the edge of the storm was about ten to fifteen nautical miles from Rochester, plus or minus five miles, or no more than twenty-three statute miles from that city. Dennis boarded the plane and we can presume that he and Neff went through the appropriate checklists: "before starting engines," "before leaving the ramp," and "before takeoff." (These are consequently followed by "after takeoff," "in range," "before landing," "after landing" and "securing" checklists.) Checklists are performed using the challenge-and-response method in which the copilot calls out each item on the left side of the list and the pilot observes or acts accordingly and responds with the appropriate information. The checklist itself is a scroll, like a small Jewish Torah, fixed in a metal container covered by a plastic window. The window permits observation of eight to ten lines of the list at a time. Lubber lines scribed across the face of the plastic window act as an index and let the copilot keep track of where he is in the list as he turns a metal wheel on the side of the case to advance the list, item by item. Mohawk operations procedures and the federal regulations do not permit either pilot or copilot to rely on their memories.

Once inside the aircraft, regulations also do not permit the crew to use the radar while parked at the ramp because of the danger of radar radiation exposure to persons in the area, and the possibility of fire damage from fuel operations in the area. But because it takes about three to four minutes for the radar tubes to warm up and the vertical gyroscope to erect, the radar is switched to the standby position, drawing its power from an on-the-ground auxiliary-procedure unit plugged into the aircraft, and an inverter, which is a type of alternating current generator, is switched on. Once out on the taxiway or runway, the radar can be switched to the function position. However, it doesn't start until after a built-in time delay which insures that the set is properly warmed up. Then the observer makes the necessary adjustments for sweep, intensity of returns, and range.

It wasn't until 3:08 P.M., when Dennis slowly pulled flight 115 away from the gate in Ithaca that he could switch the radar over to function and start observing the storm ahead of him, which we must presume he did. The plane left the ground at Ithaca at precisely 3:15 P.M.

The airplane that Dennis and Neff were flying was a Martin 404, registry number N449-A, manufactured on January 2, 1952, and sold originally to Eastern Airlines. Eastern used it for ten years in regular service before they sold it to an aircraft leasing company in Charlotte, North Carolina, in November 1962. Aircraft leasing is a common practice in the industry.

Ten years is the average age of this type of plane in commercial operation. This particular aircraft was one of two Martin 404's that Mohawk leased from Charlotte Aircraft Company on June 5, 1963, to handle its increasing passenger traffic. It was put into service two weeks later. There hadn't even been time to paint on the usual insignia used on Mohawk planes: the head of an Indian chief with bonnet feathers swept back the entire length of the fuselage. Instead, temporary decals reading "Fly Mohawk!" were used.

Over its ten-year history, the plane had logged 29,818 flying hours. Before adding it to its fleet of fourteen Martin 404's, Mohawk gave it a complete mechanical inspection. Planes receive routine inspections every eighteen hundred hours of flight time; servicing periods vary according to strict FAA safety regulations. A plane never becomes obsolete, but is rebuilt constantly and can be used year after year. New equipment including engine and parts are installed periodically. The costs of these replacement parts are figured in the original cost of the aircraft.

The Martin 404 was a small plane by today's standards. It had a wing span of ninety-three feet, three inches, its length was seventy-four feet, seven inches, and its height was twenty-eight feet, five inches. The two Double Wasp, eighteen-cylinder radial air-cooled engines could develop a total maximum of 4,800 horsepower for takeoff. The left- or number-one engine had been used for a total of 21,518 hours and had been overhauled 482 hours earlier. The right engine had last been overhauled 999 hours earlier and had logged 20,941 hours of use.

One of the characteristic features of the craft that made it easily identifiable was the self-contained so-called anal staircase that dropped down in the underside rear of the plane for loading passengers.

The plane's pressurized cabin enabled it to climb to 29,000 feet. It could do this at 1,905 feet per minute. Its maximum speed is 312 miles per hour at 14,500 feet and its normal cruising speed was 280 miles per hour, a snail's pace by today's standard of trisonic jet travel. If the plane's speed dropped to 79 miles per hour at sea level, it stalled. It required a takeoff distance of 1,980 feet to climb to a fifty-foot altitude at a maximum takeoff speed of 190 miles per hour.

The Martin 404 weighed 29,126 pounds when empty and could carry a payload of 13,874 pounds, giving it a maximum gross weight of 43,000 pounds. Compare this with a fully loaded Boeing 747B which weighs in at 775,000 pounds!

The Martin aircraft were really the end of an era. The jet age had already begun. The final generation of large propeller-driven aircraft could not even be given away as freighters because operating costs were prohibitive when compared with the costs of running new jets. It became axiomatic in the industry that if you operate a bigger and faster airplane, you make more money. And the giants were born! As soon as they were spawned, they were next issued in stretched-out versions making them even more cavernous and grotesque. A point of no return is ultimately reached where it makes sense to offer less unit capacity and more frequent service, rather than gambling on assembling a concentrated load at arbitrary departure times. The result was the development of the intermediate-sized airbus.

Some of these behemoths of the sky require crews of sixteen or more; the Martin required a crew of only three.

When Dennis picked up the plane in Ithaca he had to

cosign a facsimile of the flight release plan issued an hour earlier from Mohawk headquarters operations at Oneida County Airport in Utica. The second signature on the form was that of Robert C. Baker, the north-south dispatcher in Utica. It was written by the Ithaca local agent who initialed it; company regulations permitted this procedure. Both the pilot and the dispatcher retain joint responsibility and cognizance of a flight until it is terminated.

At 1:00 in the afternoon of July 2, 1963, Baker went on duty. He was scheduled to work until 9:50 P.M. He joined the other dispatcher on duty in the Utica dispatch office, Charles J. McIntyre, who, as manager of flight service at Mohawk, was in charge of the office, and in effect supervisor of the people in it. He had come on duty at 9:00 A.M. Both dispatchers were concerned with operational safety; the flight service manager was concerned with the economics of the operation—the cancelling of flights, setting up extra sections, taking care of passengers on diverted flights, and other related problems.

At 2:45 P.M. an amended terminal forecast (number one) came over the Service A teletype. It stated in translation "Now Rochester: ceiling 4,000 feet, broken; visibility 7 miles; winds west-southwest at 16 knots; scattered thunderstorms, possibly brief; ceiling 500 feet; one-half mile visibility; sky partially obscured; thunderstorms, heavy rain, hail; westerly winds 40 knots, gusts to 65 knots, chance of isolated tornado."

These conditions were forecast to exist until 7:00 P.M. EDT. The message continued: "A cold frontal passage; 25,000 feet, thin scattered clouds; surface winds northwest [a complete reversal in direction] at 10 knots; occasionally 4,000 feet scattered clouds; effective until 9:00 P.M. EDT."

As soon as McIntyre saw this message, he prepared a weather advisory which he issued on the company teletype network from Utica to "All Mohawk stations: post for pilots and pass to any pilots in areas mentioned. Weather bureau severe weather forecast indicates along and sixty-miles either side from fifty miles southeast of Buffalo, New York, to fifty miles northeast of Burlington, Vermont: expect scattered severe thunderstorms with severe turbulence, hail to one and one-half inches in diameter and maximum surface gusts 65 knots. Possibly an isolated tornado or two. Squall line forming in Ontario,

Canada, to vicinity of Buffalo and Youngstown, Ohio; expected to intensify and move south-southeastward at 40 knots. Company pilot reports indicate a line of thunderstorms through western Pennsylvania from north of Johnstown, Pennsylvania, extending southeastward and building rapidly. Expect these thunderstorms to move eastward." Signed "McIntyre, Flight Control, July 2, 1963, 2:53 P.M. EDT."

At least now the warning was disseminated to the company. McIntyre's message did not indicate the period for which these conditions were valid, however. The matter is academic since Dennis departed as captain-in-command of Flight 115 from Ithaca only moments before the message was issued, and was hence not aware of it through official channels. Dennis was required by Civil Air Regulations (Part 60, Section 60:11, Effective November 30, 1962) "to familiarize himself with all available information . . . including a careful study of available current weather reports and forecasts." Even if Dennis was unable to procure the McIntyre warning, the FAA *Air Traffic Control Manual* (Section 352.1) states that "Whenever storm areas such as apparent thunderstorms, rain showers or squall lines can be discerned on radar display, information concerning them shall be provided to a pilot when considered advisable by the controller."

Up to that moment, at least, Dennis's knowledge of the storm ahead was based only on a casual conference he had with Captain Silvera.

And as Captain Dennis, First Officer Neff, and Stewardess Miara were taking off from Ithaca on Flight 115 on July 2, 1963, some forty passengers destined for Mohawk Flight 112 had already begun to gather at the Rochester-Monroe County Airport. I was one of them.

3

The Mohawk operations office at the Rochester airport was a small, unattractive room directly behind the ticket counter wall. It had a temporary look about it, as though the occupants weren't planning to stay there long. A high counter, where the pilots examine their flight plans and weather information, divided it into two areas. A large three-paned window looked out to gate number four and the field beyond. You could see the tower from this vantage point. The crew's side of the counter had a lounge area consisting of vinyl-covered chrome-tube couches and chairs. A set of small metal lockers were off to one side.

The usual round clock was on the wall and there were a couple of gray-green institutional tables. The desks on the office side of the counter held the radio and telephone equipment.

The company teletype machine was located near the window; but there was no Service A weather teletype nor TELautograph equipment, either. This latter machine consists of a metal box covered with a glass window. A paper tape is mounted in it in a vertical position. When the weather-bureau operator writes a message with a metal pen on a metal pad, the TELautograph machines all over the field at the different agencies come to life simultaneously as exact facsimiles are transmitted electrically. The TELautograph has a mechanical-pen mechanism that duplicates the motion of the transmitting pen at the other end of the line. When the message is completed, the operator pushes a button that activates a buzzer at the receiving end so that the receiver knows that there is a message on the machine. The sender usually pushed the button several times in rapid succession. The buzzer was audible quite some distance from the machine. (These machines are also used at the parimutual windows at some race tracks to confirm the results of each race to the tellers.) The cost of installing such a device at Mohawk's Rochester office would have been twenty-five dollars for installation, twenty dollars a month to the TELautograph company, and five dollars a month to the telephone company, over whose lines the signals are transmitted. (Since 1963, an improved system called the Electrowriter has replaced the TELautograph system.)

The TELautograph was used to transmit changes in weather and other information that took place during the periods between regular teletype transmissions, keeping the information current.

Since Mohawk did not have this equipment in the Rochester operations office, they had to rely on an informal arrangement with United Airlines who did have such equipment. The United office was about two hundred feet away from Mohawk's operation at the other end of the terminal building. The agreement stemmed from an arrangement made four years earlier when Capital Airlines was still independent of United Airlines. The two companies, Capital and Mohawk, shared adjoining offices at that time. Mohawk had an agreement to use Capital's TELautograph machine which ran between Capital's offices, the American Airlines offices, the United States Weather Bureau, and the tower. Only the latter two had units that could both transmit and receive; the two airlines' units could only receive. Mohawk turned down an opportunity to install a unit of its own, but agreed to pay a prorated cost for the use of the TELautograph at United. They also agreed to split the cost of the rental of the machine and the rental of the line across the field.

This arrangement continued until 1959. Mohawk then requested cancellation of this agreement for economic reasons. Capital discontinued billing them for the service and took on the complete payment themselves. There was no agreement on the Service A teletype, but Capital allowed them to use it as well at no cost to Mohawk.

Capital's Service A teletype was an older unit that used purple cloth ribbon which produced only one copy, the original. Mohawk was not allowed to take this master copy, but Capital Airlines and subsequently United Airlines (after it absorbed Capital) permitted Mohawk to make a copy on their old-fashioned gelatin pad Gelofax copying machine. This copying machine could only make about four or five copies from one original and since United needed most for themselves, only one copy was available to Mohawk.

If amendments to the hourly weather came in on the teletype or on the TELautograph, United did not so advise Mohawk; it was left to Mohawk to maintain a constant surveillance, which they could not readily do under this arrangement.

The pilots often complained of the lack of weather-information facilities in Mohawk's Rochester office. They were too embarrassed to go, hat-in-hand so to speak, to United for the weather information. They sent the customer-service agents instead. American Airlines, the third carrier at the airport, also had weather teletype at its office in Rochester, but Mohawk never used this, perhaps because they were in competition with each other on several routes.

The company radio in the Mohawk operations office operated on 130.0 megacycles. There was no radio operator as such, but all of the customer service agents were qualified to use it. This equipment allowed them to communicate with aircraft on the ground and with company headquarters in Utica. (The Mohawk operations manual specifies that the customer-service manager or his representative must monitor the company radio frequency at all times.) They could also monitor conversations between the tower and aircraft taxing on the airport and flying in the vicinity of Rochester on the local control frequency of 118.3 megacycles. If Mohawk operations wanted to talk directly to a taxiing aircraft, the tower would first have to be called on the interphone and requested to tell the taxiing plane to switch their radio over to the company frequency.

A dozen Mohawk flights stopped at Rochester each day as an intermediate stop between two other terminals; two flights terminated in Rochester and two flights originated in Rochester. The latter two departed Rochester in the afternoon. One of these was Flight 206, scheduled to depart Rochester at 2:05 P.M. destined for Idlewild International Airport in New York City.

On through flights, no flight-plan release is prepared at the through station, only a weight and balance sheet. On such flights, the plane's crew rarely deplanes. If there is an unusual change in the weather, the customer-service agent will personally take a report out to the plane and hand it to the crew.

There were no other aircraft to be serviced between the departure of Mohawk Flight 206 and one and a half hours later, when Flight 112 was scheduled to depart at 4:45 P.M.

Richard Curtis came on duty at 1:15 P.M. and was assigned to loading and unloading baggage. The baggage room was adjacent to the operations office. Curtis was only twenty-two at the time and had been working for Mohawk just over three years.

The plane's crew sat around the lounge area on their side of the operations counter, reading magazines and talking to each other. Stewardess Miara and Captain Dennis went outside together for a drink of water, returning in less than five minutes.

While Dennis and Mary Ann were out of the Rochester operations office, Curtis told First Officer Neff that the flight plan was in and on the release blank, ready for him to complete. He told Neff that he would get the weather from United as soon as the hourly sequence was due. This conversation took place at about 3:50 P.M.

Dennis and Mary Ann returned to operations and the crew remained together until flight time. Curtis overheard Murray mention to Dennis that he had heard reports of tornadoes in the area on the news broadcast while driving to work at a little before 3:00 P.M. McIntyre's severe weather warning of 2:53 P.M. was already lying on the counter.

Mary Ann and Captain Dennis did not talk much together. She did not feel comfortable with him. But she and First Officer Neff had established a rapport. Neff talked about his wife, his children, and about painting his house. They didn't just talk about the weather, which is what they should have done under the circumstances.

While they were waiting, Dennis reached across the operations counter (sometimes referred to as the flight planning desk) and made two telephone calls. One call was to crew scheduling, to check on his flights for the following day. The second was a personal call to his wife. These were made just before 4:00 P.M.

He normally only called his wife when he expected to arrive home late. But Flight 112 was due in at Newark Airport on time, at 6:45 P.M. Dennis told his wife he expected to arrive at home for dinner at 8:00 P.M., and requested that she wait dinner for him. Mary Ann couldn't tell if Dennis had looked at the weather reports on the counter while he was telephoning. She asked him how the weather was and he absently replied that it was raining in the Red Bank area near both of their homes, information passed on to him by his wife.

At about 4:10 P.M. Curtis marched down to the United Airlines operations office to collect the weather information. He did this twice a day, just before the 2:05 P.M. and 4:45 P.M. originating flights.

Although a long list of weather information is put out on the Service A weather teletype and special information on the TELautograph machine, Curtis only looked at the 4:00 P.M. hourly sequence. He placed a sheet of paper over the gelatin pad and smoothed it out, picking up the reversed purple-ink impression. The whole procedure for obtaining the weather information lasted no more than five minutes.

The 4:00 P.M. sequence covered the area from Buffalo to Harrisburg and encompassed the entire route of Flight 112.

When he returned to Mohawk operations, Curtis remained on the crew's side of the counter and laid the 4:00 P.M. hourly weather sequence on top of the flight plan release on the counter. It was 4:20 P.M. Murray had already checked over the flight plan release while Dennis and Curtis were standing at the counter. Neff was standing nearby. The McIntyre severe weather warning lay alongside to the right. The flight plan had not yet been signed by Dennis. To do so (which he did at 4:25 P.M.), he would have had to move the 4:00 P.M. hourly weather sequence or raise a corner of it. Curtis had already signed on his designated line.

Curtis did not brief the crew on the weather. He did not see any of them touch, read, or handle the severe weather warning. He did not call it to their attention or attach it to the flight plan. Usually the first officer attached the weather report to the flight plan after filling it out, otherwise it gets in the way. But since the plan had been completed prior to his return from United's office, Curtis could have clipped both the hourly sequence and the severe weather warning to the flight plan. Curtis did offer to take both Dennis and Neff down to United's office to obtain weather information. Neff said that they had current terminal forecasts on board the airplane from the release in Ithaca and he didn't think it would be necessary to go down to United and look at them. (The terminal forecast that he referred to was the 2:00 P.M. forecast and he did not have any amendments that were issued after that time.) Dennis also turned him down, saying that the hourly sequence would be sufficient and with that they would have all the weather information they wanted.

Curtis could not know if Dennis or Neff had a copy of the 2:45 P.M. amended terminal forecast for Rochester; he himself was not aware of its existence at the time.

(Mohawk operations manual, page 03:01:03, paragraph 3A, states that the customer-service agent "shall be alert and take the initiative in supplying captains and dispatchers with all pertinent information including obvious changes in local weather.")

Curtis made no calls to the weather bureau, the FAA tower, or to the Dispatch office in Utica during this preflight period. No weather documents were physically attached to the flight release plan as per regulations. No duplicates were retained in the Rochester station files of all the documents supplied, as per regulations. All of the weather information—the 2:15 severe weather warning, the 2:30 SIGMET, or the 2:45 amended

Rochester terminal forecast—was not supplied, as per regulations. This latter message read in part for the Rochester area: "Scattered thunderstorms, possibly brief, ceiling 500 feet one-half mile visibility, heavy thunderstorm, hail, heavy rainshower, west winds at 40 knots gusts to 65 knots. Chance of isolated tornadoes."

The amended forecasts for Elmira and Syracuse terminals were identical in all respects to the Rochester forecast.

The 3:00 P.M. hourly weather sequence on the Service A circuit referred to thunderstorm activity at DuBois, Pennsylvania, which was also in the 2:00 P.M. sequence. It continued, "towering cumulus clouds to the west of Wilkes-Barre-Scranton . . . Allegheny County, at Pittsburgh, reports thunder."

Neither pilot was aware of these messages. Neither Murray nor Curtis thought to call the weather bureau for a complete weather briefing. They had almost never called the weather bureau in the past.

They were not aware of the 3:25 P.M. PIREP which stated: "Elmira, aircraft radar, line of buildups 20 miles north of Rockdale, 100 miles south; tops of clouds 25,000 feet plus. Buffalo to EWC [Elmwood City] line of thunderstorms penetrated north of EWC." Elmwood City, Pennsylvania, is southeast of Youngstown, Ohio, and north of Pittsburgh. DuBois was again mentioned as having thunderstorms.

The only weather information the two pilots were known to have received was the 2:00 P.M. hourly sequence which they picked up in Ithaca, McIntyre's 2:53 severe weather warning and the 4:00 P.M. hourly sequence just obtained by Curtis from United's office. For the area encompassing the flight of 112, the 4:00 P.M. hourly sequence read as follows: "Rochester: ceiling estimated 5,000 feet, broken clouds; higher broken clouds, 12,000; visibility, eight miles; pressure 1,007.6 millibars; temperature 94 degrees Fahrenheit; dew point 66 degrees Fahrenheit; wind, west-southwest at 16 knots; altimeter 21.79 inches of mercury."

As they walked toward the plane, off to the side the sky was turning gray and it was quite windy. Mary Ann found it difficult to get on the steps entering the plane's belly because of the wind. Her jacket, which was unbuttoned, was blown open as she grabbed for her hat in a strong gust. The light in the sky was changing around her rapidly. It was turning quite dark. It was then that she considered the flight might be a little bumpy.

It is one of the dispatcher's duties to cancel a flight if reports of widespread turbulence would indicate extreme passenger discomfort. McIntyre's message of 2:53 P.M. read: "Extreme turbulence and maximum surface gusts to 65 knots." Baker, who was aware of this message, did not cancel Flight 112 because the weather report was for a *general* area rather than for a *specific* station, even though he acknowledges that 65 knots was extreme weather.

But Mohawk operations manual (page 05:15:01) lists for the Martin 404 takeoff "Maximum Cross-Wind and Cross-Wind Components":

Maximum Cross-Wind Component, Martin 404	26 knots
Maximum Down-Wind Component, Martin 404	8.5 knots
Maximum Wind in Gusts, Martin 404	60 knots

Since the forecast winds were above sixty knots, Baker should have cancelled Flight 112. He had cancelled the two landings scheduled for 4:30 P.M. at Utica that day, because that station was below limits due to a thunderstorm. The manual also states that "turbulence, sufficient to cause real passenger discomfort over a small portion of the route to be flown would *not* [italics mine] constitute a reason for cancellation, i.e., if most of the flight could be conducted in relative comfort."

Flight 112 was to fly from Rochester in almost a straight line that would take it over Geneva, Ithaca, Binghamton, south of Liberty and Newburgh, northeast of Wilkes-Barre and Scranton, and on to White Plains.

The dispatchers were required to notify the station agents of weather conditions that could cause passenger discomfort over part of the route, so that each passenger could decide for himself whether to fly or not to fly. It was for this reason that McIntyre and Baker sent out the joint weather advisory at 3:45 P.M. which advised of air-traffic-control delays, possible thunderstorm activity, and turbulence aloft.

Mary Ann Miara did not know of this warning, nor were any of the passengers so advised, as far as is known. Although the crew could have been advised by many sources as to the exact and immediate weather situation and were not, it was still their duty to maintain a continuing watch on the local weather as they walked out to the plane, and from the cockpit itself.

Dennis and Neff followed Mary Ann on board and squeezed past her. They entered the cockpit, stowed their gear, and strapped themselves into their seats.

Mary Ann, after stowing her pocketbook, and giving the cabin one last glance, stationed herself at the top of the staircase on the right side and awaited the arrival of the first passengers.

4

When Richard Curtis finished loading the last of the baggage in the aft (rear) belly bins of N449A, he walked around to the left side of the aircraft to ask the captain if it would be all right to remove the ground power unit after starting the right engine in order for him to have it ready for Flight 186, which was just approaching the gate. But it was First Officer Neff who was seated in the left-hand, or pilot's seat, against regulations. Captain Dennis was sitting in the copilot's seat.

With permission granted, Curtis took his position under the right wing as fire guard; a fifty-pound CO_2 fire-extinguisher cylinder on wheels, with its black conical nozzle, seemed to stand at attention beside him. Making a circular motion with his right hand while his left hand with its index finger pointed skyward, he signaled the crew to start the number two or right engine. The last passengers were just boarding. The plane was facing to the east with gate five of the terminal off to its left. Starting up of the number-one, or left, engine first would have presented a hazard to the enplaning passengers.

Pat Murray had been working up the weight and balance for the load plan on the flight manifest. The gross weight of Flight 112 was calculated as 41,946 pounds. Passenger weight is calculated at 165 pounds average from May 1 to October 31 and at 170 pounds average in the winter months to allow for heavier clothing. An additional 990 pounds had to be added, making the total weight 42,936 pounds, thirteen hundred pounds less than the maximum certified gross weight of 44,271 pounds.

It wasn't until Murray walked out to the plane and boarded it to deliver the manifest that he learned from Stewardess Miara that there were forty passengers on board, a full load. He corrected the manifest sheet, crossing out the "34" he had written earlier and entered "40" above it. He could hear thunder as he handed Mary Ann the manifest. She hunched her shoulders and shuddered as she covered her ears with her hands to indicate her concern about the weather. Murray turned and rapidly descended the staircase. Then Curtis gave the signal to start up the number-one engine. The number-two engine had been running for about two minutes. The noise of the engines, much louder on the outside of the plane, prevented Curtis from hearing the thunder which was then rumbling onto the field.

As soon as Murray was out of the plane, Mary Ann actuated the handle that raised the anal staircase into the belly of the plane, sealing them all into their hot, humid capsule. The air-conditioning system had not yet become effective.

Murray quickly walked to a position about thirty feet forward of the six-foot-long engine, snapped to attention, and smartly saluted the aircraft—the usual signal for sending an aircraft on its way. It was exactly 4:45 P.M., right on schedule. It had just started raining, a light sprinkle. The sky was black. There was a rumbling of thunder and a light wind of ten to fifteen knots began whipping about him.

Mohawk Flight 186, minutes behind schedule, had already landed and was parked at gate five. The time was 4:41 P.M. as

Captain Shimel locked the brakes. A fuel truck pulled up in front of it. Looking out of the cockpit window Shimel could see black billowy clouds directly ahead of him. Visibility was rapidly decreasing. He had left his number-one engine still operating as this was scheduled to be only a short stop to take on and discharge passengers. Five passengers disembarked from his plane in Rochester. Curtis started unloading the baggage from Shimel's Convair on to one of the little baggage trains that are used to service smaller aircraft.

When he finished, Curtis quickly mounted the tractor seat and sped to the baggage area on the southwest corner of the operations office. It was still raining as he backed around. He unloaded what little baggage there was and entered the operations office from the baggage room. The telephone was ringing. Curtis picked it up. McIntyre was on the line from Utica. He informed Curtis that Flight 186 was going to require additional fuel to give the plane more holding time because of the weather. The entire conversation lasted less than half a minute.

Seconds later, Murray came into the office and Curtis informed him of the change. Murray went over to the desk to correct their copy of the manifest for Flight 112, for the additional passengers on the airplane. Curtis went out to the gate and signaled Captain Shimel to cut his other engine so that the plane could start taking on fuel. This was going to delay their schedule even longer. Normally, the enroute stop at Rochester lasts only six minutes.

Refueling of Shimel's plane began almost simultaneously with the first drops of rain, the rain so anxiously awaited by the parched community. First, there was a light sprinkle which was almost immediately followed by a deluge of single large heavy drops that splattered one at a time on the dusty gray superstructure of the plane, printing the ink-blot ectoplasmic splotches over the skin of the craft until the entire plane was finally wetted down. It glistened dully. The sky suddenly turned black and there was a sharp increase in the winds. In less than a minute the rain had become intense and lightning flashed all around, contrasting sharply with the darkness of the sky. Shimel knew that the squall line had hit the field. It began to hail.

Shimel became concerned and ordered the fueling to stop and the fuel truck to withdraw until the passage of the storm.

He was worried mainly about a lightning strike starting a fire. Only his left wing had been fueled, and then only partially. The right wing would also have to be fueled with an equal amount to balance the weight load. Each wing had a capacity of five hundred gallons of fuel. The tank man complied and pulled his truck away from the aircraft. Shimel and his copilot, Philler, slammed their cockpit windows closed as the wind whipped the rain onto their laps.

As soon as Stewardess Miara had closed and locked the staircase of N449A, she walked to the front of the plane, smiling left and right to the passengers. She made a mental note of a briefcase in the overhead rack. She entered the small cockpit and laid the manifest on the throttle quadrant pedestal that separates the two pilots. But she didn't notice, or if she did, it didn't register at the time, that the copilot was seated in the pilot's seat and vice-versa. Only the backs of their heads were visible. One of them was speaking into his microphone.

On her return trip to the rear of the cabin, she left the cockpit and galley doors open. Seat belts and smoking were checked as she worked her way along. She removed the offending briefcase from the overhead rack and slid it under the passenger's seat with appropriate comments. All belts were secure and no passengers were smoking. This took only a few seconds. When she reached the rear of the passenger cabin she lifted her microphone from the wall bracket and went into her usual singsong spiel:

"Welcome aboard Mohawk Flight 112 for White Plains and Newark. Your captain is Richard Dennis and your first officer is John Neff. I am your stewardess, Mary Ann Miara. Our estimated time of arrival in White Plains is 5:45. Please see that your seat belts are fastened and observe the no-smoking sign. Coffee will be served as soon as we are aloft. We hope that you will enjoy your trip."

She sat down in her fold-down seat at the very rear of the plane on the left and fastened her own belt. She was distracted by the sound of the rain.

"I sort of looked up toward the ceiling," she remembered, "because I couldn't believe it was raining so hard. I never heard it rain this hard before. It sounded like stones were being thrown at the plane. To make sure it was raining, I turned to look toward the cockpit, noticing the windshield wipers were going back and forth, so I just thought it was raining very hard."

The rain was so heavy that the wipers had almost no effect in clearing the visual field. Mary Ann busied herself with recording the passengers' names.

In the weather-bureau observatory on the opposite side of the field, Chief Meterologist Williams watched the storm echoes approach the field on the radarscope. The line of about twenty cells varied in depth from three miles to twenty miles and were approaching at about thirty-five miles an hour. Some of the echoes had sharp edges characteristic of a tornado, but not other typical tornado features.

Because of the approaching thunderstorm, he continued working past his regular quitting time in order to assist Claude W. Chapman, the meteorological technician who had come on duty at 4:00 P.M. He had measured the rate at which the storm was moving toward them and advised Chapman of it at 4:30 P.M. They both watched the scope as if hypnotized—the way one stares into a crackling fire, or perhaps at a cobra poised to strike.

At 4:45 P.M. the storm was within two and one half miles of the weather bureau, which placed it about two miles from the airport terminal building. While Williams had his eyes pinned to the radarscope, the sudden pounding of hail on the windows distracted him. He quickly stepped outside and grabbed some of the larger hailstones. He measured his specimens using a ruler. Some were as large as one inch. One inch is large for a hailstone, but not uncommon. Hailstones as large as 5.4 inches in diameter and seventeen and half inches in circumference—as large as a good-sized canteloupe—have been authenticated. Williams entered his measurements of the hailstones onto his weather bureau form WBAN–10–B.

When Chapman came on duty he discussed the severe weather warning with the men he was about to replace. He knew that the warning was in effect because he had been listening to a commercial AM radio program while eating lunch and heard the warning on the weather report. He conducted a self-briefing of existing conditions by first reading the Kansas City severe weather teletype message which was attached to the map on which the area in the forecast was outlined. At-tached to it was the call list which tabulated those that were to be telephoned and advised when such a warning goes into effect: the police department, fire department, civil defense, and so on. Then he worked on the television weather summary that was to be issued at 5:30 P.M., as it was each day. When that was finished, he gathered together the list-synoptic map, prognostic charts, five hundred millibar chart, analyses of the Chicago and Washington forecasts, and put them all on his desk to go through them as time permitted. He also had to check the observations on the instruments and enter them on punched computer cards, and also review the work of the previous shift.

He heard the first thunder at 4:40 P.M. and he recorded that as the time the storm officially arrived at the Rochester station. A thunderstorm is considered to start "at a station if thunder is heard during a fifteen-minute period or, if during a fifteen-minute period, noises are such that thunder could not be heard, but hail or overhead lightning are observed." As soon as a thunderstorm is within ten miles of a station as indicated by radar, the observer goes outside to listen for the first thunder. Chapman made and recorded his first observation between 4:40 and 4:42 P.M.; the next observation began at 4:49 and ended three minutes later. He noted on the form clipped to two clipboards on the observatory console that the thunderstorm was heavy or severe and thunder and lightning was frequent. The thunder was continuous, sharp, and pronounced.

Using the data from the ceilometer, he estimated the ceiling at 4:42 P.M. to be five thousand feet. He was outside at that time; it hadn't yet started to rain. Black clouds loomed to the northwest running from north to west on the other side of the field. Visibility was about eight miles. It wasn't until after he returned to the office that the first drops started to fall. When it came it was heavy, since it was falling at a rate in excess of three-hundredths of an inch per six minutes. Chapman estimates that it was actually falling at a rate somewhere in the vicinity of ten- or eleven-hundredths of an inch per six-minute period. And when the hail came, the ground was covered with white. It was the largest hail that Chapman had ever seen during his eleven years at the airport. The hail lasted for only five minutes and fell in a narrow band at the weather bureau and along Scottsville Road, which runs along the south side of the airport behind the bureau.

Just as he noted the rain beginning to fall, the telephone mounted on the console rang. This was the field interphone that links the weather bureau, all the airlines offices, the county operations office, and the FAA tower. Chapman picked up the phone. The call was from American Airlines requesting a visibility check. Chapman said he would take one and put it on the TELautograph. But the caller said never mind; he would get it from the tower.

Chapman immediately went to the observatory and took a transmissometer reading. It indicated a visibility of eight miles. He wrote the current observations on the TELautograph and pressed the buzzer twice to alert the tower that a message had been sent. He didn't wait for the return buzzer, which would acknowledge receipt of the message. Instead, he hurried to the teletype room intending to transmit his station report over the teletype. But the 4:45 P.M. scan had already begun, preventing him from doing so. So instead, he busied himself clearing the teletype and facsimile machines, tearing off the pale yellow paper sheets that emerged from them with each transmission. He entered the pilot briefing room. Calls came in from pilots and the public. The pilots received briefings of weather over their planned routes. These calls came in between 4:00 and 4:30 P.M. No calls came in from Mohawk.

Some pilots actually came into the briefing room for information during this period. At about 4:40 P.M. Chapman received a telephone call from a newspaper reporter who wanted information about weather in the past to compare it with the current dry spell they were experiencing. Chapman begged off helping him at that time because he wanted to keep an eye on the impending storm. He suggested that the reporter call him back later. From that point on, he kept a close watch on the storm.

Two county airport employees came in to get a weather rundown because they had some planes parked in the open and the air, they noted, was getting "a little flush with wind." They laughed when Chapman gave them the forecast; they didn't think it could hail in the summer (the average of fifteen to twenty hailstorms in the United States occur mainly during the months of May through July). Chapman advised them to get all aircraft inside and under cover. And even though they were skeptical about hail in the summer, they nevertheless hurriedly returned to the field to move their planes under cover.

Moments later a navy pilot stopped into the office. He, too, had a plane in the open. He was aware of the severe weather warning and wanted advice on whether or not to take precautions against damage to his aircraft. They stood talking in front of the observatory console and noted that the wind was blowing out of the west to the west-northwest at a velocity of from twenty to twenty-five knots. Chapman warned him that gusts to sixty knots had been forecast. As they watched, the wind gusted suddenly to forty knots (about forty-six miles per hour) and the pilot needed no further advice as he rushed out to secure his plane. But as he rushed out, the deluge began and the navy pilot retreated back into the office.

The wind was blowing straight down east-west runway 10–28, which was the one in use at the moment. Occasional gusts came from twelve degrees off to the right. Thus, a plane taking off (from east to west) would be hit by the wind from the right front which would tend to cause it to drift off to the left.

The last temperature reading taken before the thunderstorm hit the field was 94 degrees Fahrenheit at 3:59 P.M. It had been one degree higher a little earlier, the high for the year.

It was the weather observer's duty to notify the tower if he had information of significance that the tower didn't. Neither Chapman nor Williams reported any of their information to the tower. They, in turn, had no knowledge of any planes planning to take off at this time.

The FAA tower is across a blacktop roadway toward the field just northwest of the weather bureau. It is a four-story-square building sheathed in corrugated metal walls painted institutional beige. This tower is kept under tight security as are all FAA towers.

The IFR room hummed with activity and the constant crackling of radio communications over several loudspeakers. The room was small and dimly lit. Along one wall, side by side, were three ASR–4 radar scopes, the ASR standing for air surveillance radar. Only two were operating; the third scope was used for training or kept on standby in case of failure of one of the other units, or when routine maintenance caused one of the other units to be shut down.

John R. McSweeney was the watch supervisor operating in the IFR room that day. He was working the arrival and departure flight data position. Working radar departure control on one side of him was Charles Leon Sufrin, a seven-year veteran with the FAA. When he came on duty he was advised of the severe weather warning in force. He took his position in front of the radarscope and started to identify the faint green marks and points smeared across it. The range switch was set at thirty nautical miles with each concentrically scribed circle representing ten miles. The center dot corresponded with the antenna out on the field, which was about one hundred yards south of runway 10–28 and about seventy-five yards east of taxiway 6 (now called taxiway fox or F) which runs south toward the tower.

The tower ASR–4 radar was different from both the weather-bureau radar and airborne radar. The weather-bureau radar at the time was a directional-type unit. The antenna could be tilted upward and downward to determine the heights of echoes. The tower radar antenna was fixed, so that it could not do this. It could not even indicate air traffic above twenty-three thousand feet. It could not paint weather cells, either, the way airborne radar could, because it lacked the contour feature. In fact, the tower radar was purposely designed to eliminate, to the greatest extent possible, all interference in order that its prime function, the provision of data concerning moving aircraft, not be compromised. The radar is usually kept switched to this mode unless the controller wishes to examine precipitation areas or other such phenomena.

Unfortunately, although this circular polarization can remove ground clutter on the scope, it also will eliminate the pilot who is flying a circular path around the station.

Sufrin's radar screen had superimposed upon it the holding patterns, runways, the shoreline of Lake Ontario across the top, and a restricted area along the lake reserved for military use during the daylight hours up to twenty-three thousand feet. Radar reflectors positioned near each of the runways painted sharp marks on the scope which were used for aligning the runways, so that all of these other scope markings were then in their relatively exact juxtaposition. The checking and alignment were done each morning.

Even though Sufrin's radar was set on circular polarization to minimize weather and ground features, his scope still clearly showed an ominous fingertip moving toward the center from the northwest or ten o'clock position. Over a half-hour period it moved closer and closer to the radar antenna site on the field, becoming ever larger, and like an amoeba under the microscope, took on a gelatinous shape, with buds developing off the main mass. It so impressed itself on Sufrin's brain that he later reproduced it on paper in precise detail.

The actual total storm area may, in fact, have been much larger than it appeared on the scope, but it was rendered partially invisible because of the circular polarization mode. During this same half-hour period since he had come on duty, Sufrin had handled three IFR flights, but not Mohawk Flight 186, which was handled by approach control.

Only minutes ahead of schedule to avoid the impending storm, Robert L. Fairweather (a man who obviously took his name seriously), First Pilot Captain with American Airlines and Captain of American Flight 453, hurriedly took off from Runway 28 at exactly 4:45 P.M. The flight had originated at LaGuardia Airport in New York City and had stopped at Syracuse and Rochester; it was now enroute to Buffalo. The plane was a Lockheed Electra.

Three veteran FAA controllers were working in the glassed-in square room two floors above the IFR room in the Rochester tower: Robert B. Thorp, working the local control position; Carl A. DiStasio, working the ground control and flight data position; and Robert "Dixie" Howell. The latter was the flight-service specialist handling the enroute traffic. His position was at the left side of the tower cab, next to the TELautograph machine.

The tower-control console ran the entire fourteen-foot width of the tower cab facing the field to the north. It was covered with a dazzling array of switches, instruments, and controls. The three controllers usually worked standing, rather than sitting, because of the tension and for a better view of the action. Thorp had the position on the right; DiStasio was in the middle.

Parallel to the console along the opposite wall of the tower cab, a narrow flight of concrete steps worked its way up from the floor below, making a left turn directly behind Thorp's position. The remainder of the space adjoining the stairwell was filled with a file cabinet and water cooler. Two teletype machines, one for Service A weather information and one for Service B for sending flight plans and messages, lined the stair rail. A spare teletype printer, tape perforator, and other related teletype equipment were positioned next to them.

Much of the gadgetry is concerned with field lighting and communications. A loudspeaker hangs above the head of each controller, each emitting a different message. The controllers could use earphones if they wanted to but seem to prefer the blaring confusion of the speakers as this creates a more exciting and tense atmosphere. Microphones dangle on coiled wires nearby. Each operator can tune his radio to a different frequency. They have three-position switches enabling them to talk to aircraft (push to the right), the IFR room (push to the left) or to both simultaneously (mid-position). Telephones connect with all field installations including one out to the approach light system so that the field maintenance man can call the tower when he wants to take over control of the lighting on the field for servicing.

A large red button on the left side of the cab next to the enroute position sets off the field emergency siren mounted on top of the weather-bureau hangar. Should the siren fail, there is also a red emergency telephone. And the siren did fail that day, at exactly 4:44 P.M. A bolt of lightning struck the airport crash-unit alarm, short-circuiting it and setting it off. The emergency crews and their four ponderous trucks rushed into the raging storm from the comfort of hangar number four.

The crews raced around the field looking for the trouble, but could find nothing to indicate an emergency and returned to the garage and began to remove their raincoats, hard hats, and boots. But this turned out to be an amazing coincidence that saved many lives that day.

Each day at noon, the siren is tested from the tower. A separate button is used for this; the real emergency button sets the siren howling for six very long minutes. The emergency crew also checks the communications equipment at each shift change.

The instrument landing system (ILS) monitors the localizer and glide slope. The system continually transmits ROC, the three-letter Morse code key for the station: .—., — — —, —.—.. There is a second localizer station at Rochester, but it continually transmits the code MCU, so that there cannot possibly be a mistake in navigation. Each code is transmitted on a different frequency as well. Should the system malfunction, a buzzer sounds and a red light goes on, so that local traffic can be warned.

When Chapman in the weather bureau heard the first clap of thunder, he started to take a special observation and indicated this on his WBAN–10B form with the letter "s" under the column headed "type." He next entered the time: 1542 Z (4:42 P.M.). Under the "sky and ceiling" column he listed the letters, numbers, and symbols indicating that the height of the clouds was estimated to be five thousand feet and the sky was overcast, that is, completely covered with clouds.

He entered visibility as "eight miles" in all directions along the ground. The entry "TRW+" in the next column meant thunderstorm (T), rainshower (RW) and the plus indicated that it was heavy.

The entry in the "wind" column noted that the wind was blowing from the west northwest at eighteen knots. His "remarks" stated that the thunderstorm began at forty minutes after the preceding hour (TB 40); that it was at the northwest moving east (TNW-MVG E); and that there was frequent lightning from cloud to ground (FQT LTG CG).

It was this information that Chapman sent to Howell in the tower cab on the TELautograph machine. Howell did not buzz back to acknowledge receipt of the message. In any case, Chapman did not wait for the acknowledgment.

This was the kind of information that Howell would broadcast to all aircraft flying in his sector as part of his regular duties. He time-stamped the transmission 2044 GMT (4:44 P.M. EDT) and gathered the rest of the information he needed for his 4:45 scheduled broadcast. He made the broadcast on time. The special weather observation was given at the beginning and repeated at the end as required by current procedures. But aircraft on the ground were tuned to a different radio frequency and would not receive this broadcast. The procedure was for Howell to then pass the message over to Thorp at local control, so that he could alert any aircraft he was handling on the ground. He would then insert the message in the clipboard lying on the console in front of him. Neither Thorp, Sufrin, nor DiStasio were aware of the message when it came into the tower; none of them had heard the buzzer. But when Howell finally did pass the slip over to Thorp at the other side of the tower cab, it was too late to be of any use to Mohawk Flight 112.

All of the controllers were so engrossed with their duties that none was aware of an FAA maintenance man—an electronics repair technician—who was working in the tower cab all the while and who was a witness to all that followed in the cab and down on the field.

The panorama from the tower cab is breathtaking when viewed for the first time. It is unimpeded for miles to the north, west, and east. Only to the south is the view partly blocked by hangar number two, and by the trees of Gennesee Park, which spread out like a green-velvet apron. Almost none of the airport activity took place in this southerly direction.

Down on the field in front of the tower, that is, to the north, is a blacktop area with a large circle and some lines radiating from it, and the letters "VO" painted in white on the macadam surface. The tower controller, Chester Brundage, explained several years later that this was a spot onto which small aircraft taxied, aiming directly at the VOR and aligned their receivers, checking them against their radio compasses for true north and magnetic north. The diagram had been painted on the ground by a man who had worked at the airport for twenty-five years, often working sixteen hours a day, and credited by his colleagues as having done "some wonderful things" there. He originally worked at the old airport tower, and when the present tower was built, he was transferred to the maintenance department. His name was Carl Reiner, but he was affectionately known at the airport as "Truth Ball" for a reason or reasons no longer remembered. While he was painting the VOR alignment marker, he suffered a heart attack and succumbed before he could finish it. Out of respect for him, no one has gone out there with a paint brush to add the conspicuously missing "R."

Crisscrossing beyond the VOR alignment area were several small runways: 7–25 (4,399 feet long running from northeast to southwest), 12–3 (3,241 feet, running from northwest to southeast), and the southern end of 1–19 which was the main north-south runway of the airport (5,030 feet). The smaller runways had begun to deteriorate and had been phased out; painted white X's covered their surfaces signaling that they were no longer in use.

The runways were intersected by a number of taxiways which led to aprons associated with private aircraft, whose activities were restricted to the south side of the airport close to the tower.

The bulk of the commercial-aircraft activity took place on runway 10–28, which stretched on the horizon to the front of the tower. This was the east-west runway (the prevailing winds were from the west) and was little more than a mile long (5,500 feet) from end to end. All the runways were 150 feet wide.

Four taxiways cut into runway 10–28: one at each end, one perpendicular running directly north to the terminal building, and one close to the western end of the runway. This last taxiway approximated the location of the new jet runway that was at that moment under construction. This new seven-thousand-foot-long runway (later extended to eight thousand feet to accommodate the jumbos) was at that time only a strip of multiple tracks scraped and compressed into the dry, parched soil. It was the scraping away of this soil that may have made the difference between life and death for many people that afternoon.

At 4:44 P.M. Captain Dennis squeezed the button on his radio microphone and spoke to DiStasio in the tower cab, requesting permission to depart. Conversations between aircraft and ground control were not recorded, and so the actual conversation between Dennis and DiStasio can only be surmised from prior experience and the hazy recollection of witnesses.

DiStasio was aware that Flight 112 was departing under IFR because their flight plan had been filed earlier. He called downstairs to Local Controller Thorp in the radar room to advise him that Flight 112 had requested permission to depart at a certain altitude structure. Would it be safe to do so with respect to the air traffic in the area? DiStasio asked. Clearance was granted.

It should be remembered that clearance is an authorization to proceed insofar as traffic conditions exist, with the purpose of preventing collision between known aircraft. Any airport conditions which might be hazardous to the flight must also be considered. However, the decision to go or not to go rests solely with the pilot and the company dispatcher. The pilot must decide to go, delay, or stay.

The clearance passed down the chain of command until DiStasio cleared Mohawk 112 to runway 28 on taxiway number one. At the same time he gave the plane the wind direction and velocity—three hundred degrees at fifteen to twenty knots. He also gave the all-important altimeter setting and a time check.

The distance from the gate to the run-up position next to the runway is about three thousand feet. DiStasio watched as the plane crawled along the taxiway most distant from the tower. The regulation for taxiing speed is to taxi at a "reasonable rate with the aircraft under control." This would be about ten to fifteen miles an hour, and would make the taxiing time to the run-up area between two and three minutes.

While he was watching Mohawk 112 holding short of the runway, he relayed the Cleveland control clearance to the plane. The Cleveland air route traffic control center has jurisdiction for aircraft flying above five thousand feet, which was the flight plan for Mohawk 112. At the same time, DiStasio added the standard departure instruction for a plane departing Rochester, which was for Mohawk 112 to maintain departure heading for radar vectors to victor thirty-four.

When the Cleveland clearance was granted, McSweeney, the Rochester tower watch supervisor, working the arrival and departure flight-data position in the IFR room, copied the information onto a flight-departure slip and handed it to Sufrin working radar-departure control next to him. At 4:48 P.M. DiStasio called Cleveland center and gave them the departure time for American Airlines Flight 453, which had just departed on time at 4:45 P.M. Then he asked Cleveland to please stand by on the line for the departure time of Mohawk Flight 112.

Passenger Jim Kirkpatrick was not concerned as the plane

started its roll. "It was difficult to see the terminal as we were going down the runway," he later reported.

When Murray returned to the operations office, the lightning, thunder, and rain were all heavy. The winds were strong. He was going to call the Utica dispatch office to inform them of the conditions at the station, but stopped a moment to look out of the office window. The rain was now a constant downpour. Although he could see Mohawk Flight 186 parked outside at the gate, he could not see Flight 112 on the runway. Then conditions got even worse and he could no longer make out Flight 186 at the gate.

While he was standing there, Murray heard the last communication Flight 112 ever made. He heard it over the local control frequency speaker that monitors tower communications with the departing aircraft.

This conversation was recorded on tape in the recording room of hangar number two. It was between Captain Dennis flying as copilot, with Local Controller Thorp and Radar Departure Controller Sufrin in the control tower. Their three voices could be readily distinguished. The entire transmission lasted for only fifty seconds.

FLIGHT 112 (Dennis): "And tower, Mohawk, ah, 112 ready to go on twenty-eight." (This was a request for clearance for takeoff on runway twenty-eight.)

THORP: "Release Mohawk off twenty-eight." (The local controller is asking the departure controller for a release for an aircraft.)

FLIGHT 112: "Rochester Tower."

THORP: "Roger 112. Mohawk 112 cleared for takeoff on runway twenty-eight."

The transmission continued:

FLIGHT 112: "Yeah 'kay. We'd like to make a left turn out as soon as practicable to avoid those thunderstorms coming in from the west." (This was a request for change in the original clearance. It showed that the crew was aware of the storm approaching the field. But it also indicated that they were not aware of how close the storm was to them.)

THORP: "He wants—"

SUFRIN: "Ah, give him—"

THORP: "Okay, you can make a left turn, ah, on course Mohawk 112."

THORP: "Mohawk 112, delete your runway heading. Make left turn on course. The wind at the moment is three four zero; velocity one five." (This is the authorization for a revised clearance and also notifies the flight that the wind is blowing at fifteen knots from the north northwest or 340 degrees.)

FLIGHT 112: "Okay. We'll make a left turn out, ah, right away."

THORP: "All right."

After that, only silence.

5

I was neither a waking victim nor a witness to what happened next; God or nature, in infinite wisdom and mercy, caused me to black out. As it turned out, the majority of passengers mercifully passed out as well, some later than others and for varying periods. Most regained consciousness quickly enough to enable them to take action to save their lives. I myself cannot remember regaining consciousness hours, days, or even weeks later, although I am told that after a short time I was not only awake, but doing some pretty amazing things.

In those last few seconds between the initial fear and the blackout, no panorama of my life flashed before my eyes, nor did any of the other survivors report such an experience. Based on my own experience, I believe that up until the final moment one is solely preoccupied with survival.

There was no sound. It was as though they were in a vacuum. Nobody moved or spoke. Only silence. And there was no panic. Perhaps they were all too dazed.

McAdam thought to himself, "Don't they know? Are they all asleep?"

Then he realized that his seat had been torn from its moorings and catapulted into the forward section of the cabin. A sickening pain wracked his chest, stomach, back and shoulder. He lay in silence and utter blackness, then he suddenly became aware of being ringed by crimson flames emanating from the blazing wings. For a moment he thought, "I'm dead and in hell!"

Suddenly the cabin burst into a ball of fire and McAdam instinctively covered his face with his left arm; his right arm was completely useless. The ball of flame, however, alerted him to the fact that he was still alive, and he thought, "I have to get the hell out of here!" His body was humming with pain all over and was barely responsive to his will. He could not walk, but he managed to crawl toward a gaping hole he could see in the fuselage, about fifteen feet away.

Henry Fetz was looking out the window during the takeoff and only then did he realize the plane was on its side because all he could see was the ground.

"We'll never make it; we're out of control," he shouted in panic. His next memory is of hitting his head on the back of the seat in front of him and saying, "Oh, no!" A crawling, clammy sensation enveloped him with the realization that they were going to crash. He fell back into his seat, unconscious.

Coming out of his dazed condition moments later, he attempted to stand up, but found himself engulfed in a maze of electrical wires and had the sensation that he himself had caused a short circuit. He turned his attention to the redheaded McAdam who was slumped in the seat alongside of him.

"Come on, Red! Get up! Let's get out of here!" he shouted.

Fetz can't remember opening his seat belt. He stood up and looked to the rear for an exit because that was where he had entered. There were two men sitting behind him, and he shouted at the one closest to the window, Walter Rappoport, "How do you get out of this thing?" Rappoport replied, "Up front, through that opening."

Fetz walked up front, down what he assumed was the aisle, to where the plane had ripped open, pushing McAdam, who was crawling along ahead of him. He watched McAdam jump and crumple into the mud below and realized he had to jump far out in order to clear McAdam, who lay prostrate just below him, his head mashed in the mud.

Fetz leaped with all his energy, landed in the gushy morass, and saw that it was still raining heavily. He reached back and tried to rouse McAdam, but McAdam did not move. Someone yelled, "Run!" and Fetz ran—straight ahead. To his right was a fire; it looked like the grass was burning. Some distance away to his left was a crumpled propeller, looking like a large discarded daisy. He continued sloshing through the mud as it sucked at his feet with each agonizing step he took and it suddenly struck him that "I better not get too far away; otherwise they will never find me." He saw other huddled figures running in all directions and, just then, noted the arrival of a yellow fire truck, its gleaming nozzle spewing out foam as it came roaring up to the fire. A station wagon pulled up next to him and the driver shouted, "Get in!" Fetz gratefully obliged. Several people were already lying on the floor in the back. They stopped a few more times to pick up additional victims, then slithered through the mud onto the blacktop and to the hospital.

When Charley McAdam reached the opening in the fuselage, the jagged edges of the tortured metal seemed like daggers directed toward him and he drew back.

A voice from somewhere outside the plane shouted, "Get out! Get out!"

He muttered to himself, "Relax, you idiot! I'm coming!" He slid out of the plane head first, dropping seven feet face down into the mud. The jolt revived him enough to enable him to rise to his feet and, supporting his limp, painful right arm with his left, he waddled gorilla-like away from the wreckage.

A pilot from Page Airways found him staggering around in a daze, and led him away from the plane toward a muddy rise in the ground. McAdam gave the pilot his telephone number and asked him to call his wife, who as it turned out had already heard the news on the radio back in Connecticut and called Mohawk in Rochester to get confirmation that he had indeed been aboard the plane. When he reached a slight incline, Mc-

Adam didn't have the strength to mount the slope, so he slowly sank to the ground and rolled over to face the plane. He thought to himself, "I've got a grandstand seat to watch the plane burn."

Mary Ann Miara felt the bumpy sensation in her jump seat at the left rear of the cabin as the plane tipped left and right. She stared across the aisle at Rappoport and Charles Yelin, at the masks of terror stretched on their faces. Seeing their expressions, the young stewardess closed her eyes and proceeded to black out. She did not remember impact.

After the crash, she revived, unbuckled her seat belt, and got up from her seat. She was able to walk by supporting herself on the aisle seats. Her right side was in pain. She saw people lying down. Some were bleeding; some were moaning. The fire seemed to be close to them. She got out of the plane through the crack at the front of the tail section.

She could see two passengers who had made their escape and trying to locate someone still inside the plane. They called out his name. Then they went around to the other side and she couldn't see them anymore. Gary Higgins and James Kirkpatrick, the two salesmen from Connecticut, carried her up the hill and set her down on the ground. Over and over again, in pain and in shock she murmured, "Oh, God! Oh, God!"

McAdam heard her and mumbled with a thick tongue, sounding almost drunk, "Lady, if I had an ounce of strength in me, I'd try to help you. But I can't."

By now, his shoulder, which he knew was broken, had become a torment. He looked at his hands, which were clenched involuntarily. As the raindrops hit them, the skin made small popping noises, but he was grateful for the coolness.

Other passengers were being helped from the wreckage or from the area surrounding it. A man was lying next to McAdam, moaning. McAdam asked him where it hurt the most. The man replied, "The leg." McAdam in turn asked the man to look at his face and tell him if it was burnt. The man, distracted, slowly looked up and reassured him that it was only blackened and muddy.

Richard Baldwin, the rifleman, watched through his window as the left wing hit the ground and broke off. Impact tore his seat loose, but he did not lose consciousness. There seemed to be yellow-orange flames everywhere inside the cabin, and he didn't expect to get out of the inferno alive. Finally he flipped the buckle of his seat belt and freed himself after fumbling with it for what seemed an eternity, and crawled out a hole over the left wing. He ran, thinking the fuel tanks had not yet blown. Then, after he waited and nothing happened, he realized they already had and returned to the wreckage to help others. As he looked back at the remains of what had until moments before been an aircraft, he promised himself, "I'll never fly again." It was a promise he would keep for almost a full year, until the 1964 annual skeet shoot brought him back to Rochester to compete once again.

Stephen Kissel of IBM became frightened as soon as the plane tipped to the left for the first time, but still he thought, "Well, at least we're high enough so the wing span didn't touch." Then, as he could see Dennis grabbing the wheel with both hands and feel the plane tilt back to the right, he did as he had once read to do on the back of a card describing ditching procedures—he pulled his head and legs into his chest, braced his feet against the seat in front of him, and covered his ears. He covered his eyes as well when the plane made its final tilt leftward again, and even then still saw orange and brown as the plane crashed. Then he felt that he was wet, and being thrown in many directions. Realizing he was alive, he took his feet from their braced position and brought them to the floor, only to discover that there was no floor and that he was stuck deep in mud. Unbuckling his seat belt quickly for fear of the explosion, he ran fifty yards, felt he'd better go back to the plane, and then became frightened again. When he walked behind the tail, he saw he was not the only survivor.

Engineer Daniel Schwester walked about thirty feet from the plane, his arm and chest in agony. He noticed his wallet was missing and started back for it when he saw the plane in flames, turned and ran the other way. Yelin woke up suspended in a pile of rubble. He started to holler for help, but there was no one. He saw flames and hoped he'd get out in time. Trying to remain calm, he unbuckled his seat belt, managed to climb over the rubble, and crawled away with a broken leg. Advertising executive Laurence Johnson suffered a double fracture of the right leg from the impact of either the crash or his jump from the plane.

Donald Carney like McAdam, noticed the silence. Then he saw someone leaving through a small hole to his right. He was still sitting in his seat. A tall man outside wearing a cap told him to unlock his seat belt and get out, which he did. Carney could see the flames as he made his exit. He saw Mary Ann Miara lying on the ground holding her leg and crying out in pain but she wouldn't move when he tried to help her, so he left her, took the station wagon to the hospital, and ten minutes later, fainted in the emergency ward from shock.

Dr. Davenport of GT&E could see First Officer Neff in the left seat leaning far to his right as he tried to correct the plane's position. Even after the left wing tip hit, he still hoped the plane might make it. As it finally slithered and jostled to a halt, flames shot back into his section, but his face was covered with debris. He quickly pushed it away, but his seat had shifted left and forward, jamming up against the one in front. That made it hard to reach his belt buckle, and it took him half a minute—an eternity—to finally get it undone. Then he freed his stunned colleague Gene Beare, and the two of them wormed their way through the maze of controls, pipes, and wires that bridged the cracked fuselage. From there they dropped to the ground.

Outside Davenport could see other passengers running from the plane, and the wing on fire. He helped Beare as far away from any explosion as possible and went back for Jane Nixon, whom he saw crawling down through the tail. He helped her down to the ground.

She was in good shape and left under her own power. Nathan Shippee got out to safety with only slight head injuries when the plane cracked open right at his seat. Bernstein was also able to walk away from the crash. He sat down on the grass, next to architect John O'Brien, and waited for help to arrive. O'Brien had regained consciousness still strapped in his seat some distance from the aircraft, discovered he could not stand, and slithered 100 feet in the mud. The plane broke open immediately in front of Thomas Mayer and Robert Christopher, but Christopher walked away with no injuries at all and Mayer made it to safety with only a cut hand, sending word to his wife, waiting for him at Westchester County Airport, that he was safe. Gary Higgins was not scared by the takeoff, but the next thing he remembered was crawling through twisted and broken metal. Though in shock, he and his partner Kirkpatrick managed to carry the stewardess to safety. Then they walked to one of the many vehicles that had converged on the scene and went to the hospital. Lloyd Trent, the newlywed member of the New York State Human Rights Commission, remembered both Carney throwing an arm around him to catch himself during the terrorizing gyrations and the mud sucking the shoes off his feet almost 100 yards from the wreckage, but he remembered nothing in between.

But not everyone was able to walk away from the burning hulk.

As the plane slid along the ground it literally tore itself apart. The center section, to which the wings were attached, broke open behind the fifth row of seats on the left side, the crack continuing on behind the sixth row of seats on the right side. The forward section cracked and separated completely across the cabin behind the second row of seats. The cockpit area resembled a grotesque mechanical dump.

The forward section became known as the "death section." It was in this incredible jumble of bits and pieces of charred and twisted wreckage that seven men met their deaths: Captain Dennis and First Officer Neff; the two New York management consultants, Lee O'Dell and Morris Falk; Roy Drew, the comptroller for the Sylvania Electric Company; Thomas Callinan, manager of paper and ink research at IBM; and the president of my company, Jerry Kurtz.

One at a time, they were unstrapped from their seats as rescuers reached them, and removed from the still-smoldering wreckage, burned beyond recognition. Their limp, wet bodies were laid side by side like pieces of cord wood. One corpse lay face down, the head cradled by the arms as though asleep. What remained of their clothing was in shreds. Two large tarpaulins were spread over them to hide the grisly sight from the proliferating horde of rescuers and onlookers. A local priest, the Reverend Edward Tolster of Our Lady of Good Counsel Church, arrived to administer last rites. As he moved in front of each corpse, two firemen raised the edge of the tarpaulin covering each victim, and the shaken cleric made the sign of the cross, not touching their blackened remains but absolving them of their sins, Christian and Jew alike, with the prayer that began *"Si vivus ego te absolvo . . ."*

The fireball that exploded in the forward section as the fuel tanks ignited apparently lasted only about five seconds. But that was long enough to seal my doom. Since I was unconscious, I could not protect myself in any way. The ball of searing flame enveloped me, eating away at my unfeeling flesh, welding it the way a blowtorch melts steel.

6

Because the accident occurred at the airport in the heart of the third largest city in the state of New York, many eyes on the ground were witness to the actual events as they transpired.

Mary Foster, a forty-three-year-old woman who works for a catering firm, was on her way to pick up her husband who was just getting off from work. She was driving along Beahan Road just north of the field where the road was under construction, when she was suddenly engulfed by the violent thunderstorm. Lightning was all around her.

"I just happened to turn my head," she recalls, "and saw the plane. It was at eye level. Suddenly, from the center outward it burst into flame and went wholly to the ground just as if the Lord had put two huge hands on top of the plane and put it down.

"I remember saying to myself, 'My God, dear Lord, help those people!'"

She didn't stop the car, but continued on to Millstead Way where her husband was waiting outside his factory. She excitedly told him and some of his coworkers nearby, what she had seen, but no one would believe her story. She shakily asked her husband to hurry and drive her home. As they were again passing the airport, they could both see the smoke and the activity on the field and now he knew that what she had just related to him was in fact the truth.

Mrs. Beatrice L. Irich who works at the state school in the town of Industry, New York, was on her way home after leaving work at 4:30 P.M. Her normal route is Scottsville Road to Beahan Road. It was raining before she turned onto Beahan Road but as soon as she made the turn, the rain eased up for a moment. As she approached Weidner Road (which cuts into the field where the new jet runway was being built), the rain suddenly came down very hard—so hard that her windshield wipers could not clear the windshield. The storm lasted like this for only moments as it whipped its way past her. Suddenly it slowed down to a few large drops. As she reached the construction detour on Beahan Road (she could not have been far from Mrs. Foster's car), she saw a lightning bolt strike the ground at the airport just over her right shoulder and simultaneously heard a loud POOF sound. Immediately flames shot up into the sky.

"It was a very large blaze," she remembers, "and in this blaze I could see a tipped wing of an airplane at an angle like this." And she drew a line to indicate what she had seen.

She remembers that the man driving a car in front of her did not appear to see or notice what had happened at all and did not even slow down. But Mrs. Lynch slowed down to a crawl and inched her way through the detour until she had crossed the Baltimore and Ohio Railroad tracks and the flames were out of sight.

"I just couldn't believe my eyes!" she ruminated.

A twelve-year-old boy, Michael DeWind, whose home borders the airport on Beahan Road, was looking out of his kitchen window which faces the east-west runway 10–28 about a half mile away. The tracks of the Baltimore and Ohio Railroad block the view of all but the tops of aircraft on the strip.

He and his brother went out on the porch to watch the lightning.

"I heard a plane start up, and I could hear it about ready to take off," the boy said.

"Seemed as though it was about at the end of the runway. Then there was a great big noise like thunder, and a big flash of reddish-orange light. There were pieces of things flying through the air."

Michael yelled that a plane had crashed and the whole family gathered at the kitchen window. Smoke from the wreckage belched from the field, but his mother did not believe that he had seen a crash until she turned on the radio and a news flash verified his story.

On the airfield itself J. Sheldon Lewis, an employee of Page Airways, was in the Page Airways passenger lounge which is adjacent to and overlooking the eastern end of runway 10–28. With him were two pilots from Dresser Industries, who had just moved their DC-3 into the Page hangar. There wasn't enough time to fit the DC-3 fully into the hangar because the Page linemen were too busy securing small aircraft out on the ramp.

They all noticed N449A as it taxied out to the runway and were shocked to see it start its takeoff roll.

The plane disappeared behind the T-shaped hangars off to their left—a point about two thousand feet from the east end of runway 28—and they did not see it lift off the ground.

But just as the plane disappeared behind the hangars, they were struck by the full fury of the storm. The wind shifted abruptly to the northeast with a velocity sufficient to swing DC-3 belonging to Page Airways around ninety degrees. It had been parked on the grass just off the runway facing west with its parking brakes set.

Lewis commented, "The hailstones and heavy rains accompanying this wind were as severe as I have ever seen short of a typhoon."

The hail actually pierced the fabric control surfaces of both the Page and the Dresser DC-3's.

The storm was so fierce by this time that their attention was diverted to their own equipment being battered before their eyes. As a result, they were not aware of the crash itself until they learned of it when the tower called on the field telephone a few minutes after the accident, apprising them of the catastrophe.

Two telephone poles adjacent to the Page Hangar on Scottsville Road were snapped like toothpicks.

Neil C. Anderson of Camden, New York, was working with the line cargo division of American Airlines fleet service and was sitting in the ready room near the ramp at American Airlines gate three. The door, which was open, faced south across the field. It was his job to load the baggage on American Airlines Flight 265, which was parked on the ramp in front of him.

About two or three minutes after Mohawk Flight 112 taxied past Anderson on its way out to the runway, it started to sprinkle and Anderson decided to load the plane right away even though he still had a half hour to do so.

By the time he and the other agents were finished, it was pouring. He decided to make a run for the building.

Just as he made it to the door he heard the Martin go by. At that time he didn't know it was a Martin, but he could tell it was a plane under full power.

Anderson cracked to his coworkers, "Good Lord! Look fellows, somebody's trying to fly in this weather."

Then, he recalls, "As I reached the door, the wind was in the west. It had been blowing quite hard. And as I reached the door one of the fellows had unhooked it. We have a hook to hook it open on the side. This door swings into the west. And as I reached it, he had unhooked it and I grabbed it. And at this moment hail began to fall. I went to go through the door . . . the wind was pushing on it, so I didn't grab for it. But we turned to look because this was the moment that the plane went by. And as it did, I grabbed the rail on the door. At this moment, the wind switched to the opposite direction and tore the door out of my hand.

"There wasn't a lot of hail; about the size of marbles: three-eights to one-half inch; it did not accumulate."

They neither heard nor saw anymore of the aircraft. The weather was such that they could not see much beyond their own DC-6 parked at the ramp—a distance of about one hundred fifty feet.

Within one to two minutes, the heavy rain and hail passed over and visibility increased and they went into operations. As they entered the door, they heard the siren and they turned in time to see the crash crews speeding up runway 28.

Anderson did not venture out to the crash scene.

Anthony Nuccie was a motor equipment operator for the department of public works, working the four o'clock to midnight shift on July second. He usually arrives at work fifteen minutes early, as he did on that day. After checking in at his department, he walked over to the weather bureau to obtain the latest conditions. He was told to expect rain, hail, and damaging winds.

He returned to hangar number one on the south side of the field where the county operations office was located and conveyed this information to LaVerne J. DePaul, Sr. (known as Buster to his friends), who was a foreman at the airport. At the same time he suggested that they had better hangar the aircraft parked outside.

They grouped together in the doorway and watched the storm approaching. They were joined by Frank Rossney and Gordon G. Stoppelbein.

Nuccie said, "I've never seen it hail in July!"

Just then it started to rain—large drops, but not heavy—and a hailstone rolled into the office.

They could hear the engine of an aircraft about to take off. Then the weather broke. It was so strong and violent they were forced to close the door and their heads crowded together, watched the unfolding of events through the glass panes of the door, clouded with their collective breaths.

Stoppelbein describes the action in his own words:

> I heard this aircraft. I thought it was the sound—like it was going to be an approach. It seemed to have full power on. I didn't think anybody would be landing in such severe weather. . . . It kept getting louder and I realized it might be a takeoff. . . . There was about three-quarters of the field . . . covered with very hard precipitation. . . . There was severe turbulence, air moving across the field, high winds, rain, and there was some hail. I viewed the hail in front of the hangar on the ground. There wasn't much of it but what there was . . . was about a quarter of an inch or three-eights of an inch in diameter. . . .
>
> I looked over the northwest where I viewed the aircraft come

76

out of the storm area. . . . The wall of rain had already gone by and the plane passed through it. . . . You could see for about, I would say, a mile and a half or so. I don't know what the (visibility) condition was on the runway. . . .

When I first observed the aircraft, it was when it broke out of the severe weather. It was a very peculiar attitude for an aircraft that close to the ground. It was probably forty-five or fifty-five feet, nose up. . . . But it was not climbing or only slightly. It was certainly in a stalled condition. It could never recover from that close to the ground. It was still about seventy-five feet from the ground. It may have been one hundred feet—that is what I estimated. . . . You could see daylight between it and the horizon. . . . It was almost impossible to recover any way at all, a size airplane of that type that close to the ground. . . .

As they continued, they dropped out . . . I was approximately three hundred feet east of the north-south runway. And at that time . . . the weather was overcast . . . I could see it; it was in a nose-high altitude and . . . was progressing down the runway in a situation which was impossible to fly.

I knew something was going to happen. The nose turned to the right—I would say about twenty-five degrees—and then it came back to the left. It wasn't very high; pretty low. And at that particular time the nose was about forty-five or fifty-five degrees (indicating with his hand) on the left side of the runway . . . I believe . . . the left wing hit first and the tip dropped off. And then there was a large flame going up. It disappeared below the level of the ground where I was standing in the building.

Frank Rossney told a similar story:

I heard the plane taking off. We had just been commenting [on] how the wind had built up to a terrific point—and the rain and hail were coming down hard.

I couldn't believe that someone was taking off in that weather.

I couldn't actually see him until he was just about over the intersection of runways one and twenty-eight . . . the plane was taking off on twenty-eight to the west.

I noticed that the plane was tilted at an odd angle of about forty-five or fifty degrees—kind of nose up—which is unusual for planes taking off.

Pilots are usually quick to notice anything unusual about a plane's flight.

He looked like he was going into a stall . . . which at that altitude is almost always fatal; he was less than one hundred feet off the ground.

It hit on the left wing first and cartwheeled onto its nose and then the right wing. The wings were torn off on impact. . . . There was a big puff of flame and black smoke—it appeared no one could live through it.

Stricker, who had been sitting in the office, walked over to the door and stepped outside to join the others already out there.

A clap of thunder drowned out the engine noise, but he was just in time to see the wing hit the ground. He saw a flash of light, then a fireball followed by a mushroom cloud.

Just before impact, Stoppelbein yelled, He's not going to make it—it's going down. Let's go!

They all raced to the county station wagon. It was raining only lightly at that moment. DePaul sat in the driver's seat, Nuccie next to him. Stoppelbein, Rossney, and Stricker jumped into the back.

The plane was about 2,500 to 3,000 feet away from them, so that they could not see it, except for the flames and smoke that billowed up beyond the rise in the ground.

Jack Lynch, a private plane pilot, was driving his station wagon in front of hangar three when he saw the fireball and mushroom cloud of smoke on the field out past the OMNI station. The county station wagon, with its dome light on the roof flashing, was just starting up and Lynch stepped on the accelerator and drew up alongside of them.

On the radio in the county wagon a message crackled out from the tower closing the field to all air traffic. Nuccie took the car-radio handphone and called the tower requesting permission to enter the field, which was instantly granted. They had pulled the wagon around and had just gone through a gateway when the rain, which had eased up, suddenly turned into a relentless downpour. The wind whipped up again. Stoppelbein recalled, "I remember how the wind was blowing. There was [sic] several ashcans that were going down the ramp." According to Lynch, "The wind had sucked a couple of ashcans out of hangar number three and they were blown across the field in front of our cars."

Stoppelbein continued, "I believe it must have been blowing forty knots or so . . . it seemed everything was coming from the west . . . small papers and things. And like I say, there was a couple of ashcans. I remember we had to stop for them. They blew in [to] the side of the station wagon."

They could see almost nothing now through the windshield and they sat still for almost two minutes waiting for the pounding weather to subside. Nuccie opened the door a little, hoping to be able to see a little better, but only succeeded in getting drenched. It was then that he spotted the flashing lights of the fire vehicles behind them. He shouted to DePaul, "Keep to the left so the fire trucks can pass us."

They reached the wreckage site in less than five minutes after the impact. As they approached the area, the three engines from the field's rescue hangar had already gone into action. The firemen were pouring foam and dry chemicals onto the blazing inferno. Other engines from all over the city arrived moments later.

About forty feet to the north of the plane's nose, Nuccie spotted four men and the stewardess lying on a rise in the ground. When Nuccie reached the girl she said she couldn't breathe and was holding her right side. Not knowing the extent of her injuries, he was afraid to touch her, but he helped her sit up and this seemed to relieve her breathing. He then asked her to move her legs for him which she did. He got a blanket from one of the firemen and covered Miss Miara with it and instructed another fellow to hold her in the sitting position until an ambulance arrived.

Nuccie turned his attention next to a man lying on the ground, who was complaining that his arm hurt him, "so I knew that he was alive and conscious," he recalled. He checked the other three men; they were all alive.

Seeing that there was nothing further he could do there, he ran to the wreckage itself and carried and helped anyone in sight who was limping, crawling, or walking around in the area. Mud quickly encased everyone, so that it was difficult to differentiate between victim and rescuer.

Just in front of the fuselage where it had broken away from the cab, Nuccie spotted a man who was dazed and didn't know where he was going. Pulling the man's arm around his neck and grabbing him around the waist, they slithered away from the wreckage.

The man was covered with blood, but Nuccie could not spot the source of the bleeding because the man was also covered with the firefighter's foam. The man was very weak and faint and was getting very heavy.

Just then, he spotted DePaul and yelled to him for help. Together, they took the man to the station wagon. Four other victims were already in the wagon.

Stricker was at the wheel; Nuccie shouted, "Rush these people to the hospital immediately!"

Stricker had put two of the people in the wagon himself and told them he would get them to the hospital. He ran back to the plane and stopped to talk to some people on the ground. Then he returned to the wagon.

Before he had a chance to pull away, a sixth victim was placed in the car.

Lynch recalls that when he arrived at the crash scene, there were people spread all around on the ground like bowling pins.

Many of the survivors were dazed and staggering around muttering, "Where am I?"

"A lot of them didn't know what they were saying because of the pain," Rossney said. Stoppelbein got blankets for some of them. Some people were standing more than three hundred feet west of the wreckage; they may have been FAA personnel who had been working in the OMNI shed. Stricker saw a crash truck moving in on a small fire, spewing out foam from its chromed nozzle as it went.

"I picked up the first seven dazed and hurt passengers that I came to and loaded them in my station wagon," he recalls. "The county wagon was also picking up passengers."

One of those he found was Stephen Kissell. He told Kissell to "get in!" and Kissell replied, "Well, there's people worse than I am here and you ought to take them."

Again Lynch insisted, "Get in!" and Kissell didn't argue any longer but obeyed.

Both vehicles started across the field at almost the same time.

At the airport's driveway, they picked up a sheriff escort, and with siren screaming they were led through the deluge of traffic that had converged on the airport as a result of the alert that had gone out. Sightseers, thrill-seekers, and would-be rescuers jammed the roads in all directions.

As the Brooks and Beahan Road sectors around the airport became jammed with automobiles, neighbors and pedestrians flooded the field on foot, crossing the muddy, debris-strewn expanse in the airport's southwest area. Some curiosity seekers were looking for parts of the airplane as souvenirs. Police and deputies banned all nonemergency vehicular traffic into the airport.

It is less than three miles from the airport to Strong Memorial Hospital, part of the University of Rochester Medical Center; the Genesee River and Genesee Valley Park are all that separate the two. But all traffic between them is funneled down at the Elmwood Avenue bridge. The trip seemed interminable.

The accident coincidentally took place right at rush hour on a weekday in the third largest city in the state of New York. The homecoming traffic was so heavy that some ambulance drivers were forced to mount the curb and drive down the center island that separates the traffic lanes on Elmwood Avenue near the hospital.

After the wagons had departed from the crash scene, Nuccie returned to the wreckage. He found a man standing in a daze with his hands held up in front of him. He was covered with mud and blood was oozing through it on his face and hands. The man could speak no English—only Italian. (It could only have been George Bossi, the IBM consultant from Varese, Italy.) He kept repeating over and over again, *"Che e'successo? Dove mi trovo?"* ("What happened? Where am I?")

Nuccie, who fortunately was of Italian extraction, was able to comfort him in his native tongue.

"Don't worry," he said in Italian, "you will be taken care of."

Nuccie carefully placed Bossi in the front seat of a pickup truck and drove him to the hospital. When they arrived at the emergency entrance courtyard, a Pinkerton guard, in a crisp gray uniform, was waiting. Nuccie told the guard he had an injured man and a stretcher was brought out and Bossi was gently placed on it and quickly rolled into the red brick building. Nuccie told the guard to keep the emergency drive open because more ambulances were on their way bringing in the injured.

Nuccie headed back toward the airport. Traffic was very heavy in both directions and the emergency vehicles were having a difficult time getting through. When he reached the Elmwood Avenue bridge, Nuccie pulled the truck over to the curb and started directing traffic in an effort to get a lane open for emergency vehicles. He did this for a half hour. By then the congestion had eased and he returned to the crash scene. All the injured had been removed by that time.

During Nuccie's absence, Rossney was busy extinguishing small fires and helping the injured. He can never forget one last man being pulled from the wreckage. The man was burning very badly. Buster DePaul was spraying foam directly on him. (I may have been that man. I may also have been one of the first to arrive at the hospital in a station wagon. At least that is the recollection of one of the hospital's Pinkerton guards, Leonard Butera, who remembers off-loading me from a station wagon and described me as looking like a burned, toasted marshmallow. He took an interest in me and frequently visited me in my hospital room to see how I was coming along. I was quite touched by this interest. Eventually, he was transferred to undercover work on the university's main campus and I lost contact with him.

Jane Nixon could not remember how she got out of the plane; her first recollections were of being taken by car to Strong Memorial Hospital. She was sitting in the front seat. Her hands were busy searching her face for damage and they quickly located a bump next to her right eye. She bent forward to examine it in the rear-view mirror to assess the damage. Her face was swollen and bruised. She didn't notice that her right ankle sported a bad cut and that she was without shoes. They had been sucked off her feet by the mud. She also didn't realize that she had lost her earrings and her purse. She was just glad to be alive.

After Davenport had helped Mrs. Nixon from the wreckage he turned his attention back to the plane just in time to see the first rescue engines arrive. He remembers vividly the first piece to arrive was a large yellow fire truck which pulled up a respectful distance from the right wing and began pouring its fire-quenching foam on the inferno. Davenport spotted a passenger near the right side of the wreckage at the front of the center section of broken fuselage. He was pleading to him for help, but Davenport could not get close enough; a raging wall of fire blazed between them.

A second yellow fire truck pulled up seconds later. It was smaller than the first. It went to work at once on the fire in the crushed pile of debris that had once been the forward section of the airplane. The fire fighters did not initially get involved with rescuing passengers, but concentrated on extinguishing the blaze.

McAdam, from his vantage point at the rise in the ground, watched in awe as the glistening yellow trucks arrived and started pouring massive quantities of Foamite on the flames, dousing them rapidly as they went. It was then that Higgins and Kirkpatrick arrived carrying the stewardess in their arms and laid her gently down beside him. Almost at once, four men arrived with a stretcher. They gently placed McAdam on it and carried him to a waiting ambulance. Once inside, he heard the attendant radio Strong Memorial Hospital that he was on his way with four "seriously injured."

It was not until he heard these words that McAdam considered that he might be fatally hurt.

When Stricker returned to the airport from the hospital, he assumed the task of trying to keep the thousands of onlookers away from the crash area. Some had reputedly arrived with picnic baskets. They made the rescue efforts more difficult, and might have obliterated the telltale markings inscribed on the ground that investigators use to fathom the cause of these accidents. A later critique and evaluation of the event led to the construction of a fence around the entire airport at a cost in excess of one hundred thousand dollars. FAA Facilities Chief Wagner recalled that there had been another incident in which an airliner made an emergency landing despite a faulty landing gear. He, himself, had to take two cars and block an access road to keep spectators and police from crossing the runway, since there were still ten planes circling the airport that had to land. Long after the Mohawk crash, all of the involved agencies worked out plans for sealing off all streets bordering the airport in future emergencies and improving communications by means of a "hot line."

The activity at the crash scene crescendoed to a dizzying pitch. During all the excitement, DePaul, much to his chagrin, lost the thirty-dollar Stetson hat he had been wearing; it was ground underfoot in the muddy morass.

The airport emergency trucks had arrived at the crash scene unusually fast because of the lightning strike that had set off the airport crash alarm. The crews scurried out into the storm and, finding nothing amiss, were told by the tower to return to their hangar where their vehicles were berthed. The excursion had taken less than three minutes. When they arrived back in the hangar, one of the crewmen, Richard Ziegler, a twenty-six-year-old automotive mechanic, telephoned Howell in the tower on the local airport telephone and told him that their siren was out of commission and that any alert be given them over the crash phone if they were needed. This call was logged at 4:45 P.M. Ziegler also called the telephone company to apprise them of the damage to the alarm system, so that they could make repairs. But this false alarm had gathered all of the firemen, most of them volunteers, from their various locations on the field, and many were still in fire-fighting gear when the real alarm came in four minutes later.

Howell describes what happened next in the tower:

"I turned to the receiver rack with my back to the runways and was in the process of writing a note to be posted for our information. Mohawk 112 was just departing. As I turned around I saw a large ball of fire in the vicinity of the VOR building on the west side of the airport. I then picked up the crash phone and notified the Airport Fire Department that Mohawk Flight 112 was down."

Howell was almost continuously on the phone after that, answering queries concerning the accident.

Local Controller Thorp watched from the tower as Mohawk 112 started its takeoff roll. He could actually see the storm front lined up with the center taxiway that leads from the terminal building to the runway. The terminal building looked fuzzy through the edge of the storm front while the Martin 404 was sharply defined, as it was still out in the clear. The plane rolled down the runway and though it was coming closer it suddenly disappeared completely from view in the wall of precipitation which was moving from west (on his left) to east. Only ten or fifteen seconds had lapsed since his last communication on the field telephone.

When the plane again came into view as it emerged from the precipitation front, it was already airborne and just about over the north-south runway (1–19).

DiStasio's eyes were also glued to the plane. There was no other air traffic on or near the field at the time. The Martin's wings were almost parallel to the ground as it penetrated the storm front and emerged on the other side in a slightly nose-up attitude. Then as the left wing tipped toward the ground, DiStasio shouted to Thorp in panic, "Hit the siren!"

Thorp reached over and slammed the big red button setting off the siren on top of the weather-bureau hangar, taking his eyes momentarily off the field as he did so.

When he looked back, the plane appeared to be about one hundred feet up. He continued to watch as the plane fell off on its left wing and hit the ground. He witnessed the ball of flame which exploded and then seemed to go right out. Thorp had been in the process of notifying departure control that Mohawk 112's departure time was 49—4:49 P.M. Instead, this became the exact time of the crash, the number indelibly inscribed on the wings and tail of the plane itself, its identifying number, N *449*A.

The alarm went off this second time even before the plane had actually impacted. The emergency crews, still fortunately gathered in their hangar getting out of their uniforms after the first false alarm, rapidly reversed the process, like a film running backward, and smoothly rolled out on the field once again.

The sight that greeted them was overwhelming. Besides the blaze itself, torn metal, seats and unidentifiable debris was scattered everywhere about the Martin's ravaged hulk. Both pilots' caps were clearly visible in the mud. One of the engines was twenty yards off to the side. But they had arrived at the scene quickly enough to douse several flareups before they could get out of hand.

Rescue workers—regular firemen and volunteers—appeared, sloshing through the mud with stretchers, bearing the dead, dying and injured.

Charles Holcomb, education reporter for *The Rochester Times-Union,* was one of the first to arrive of more than forty reporters that eventually showed up to cover the story. When he arrived, the dead had already been lined up in a row in the mud; dazed survivors were being helped from the wreckage into ambulances. He watched, as a fireman, with desperate strength, chopped a hole through the taut aluminum skin of the broken-off tail section to see if there might be yet another survivor. Finding none, fire-smothering foam was injected through the opening.

The broken tail section lay on its left side; the right tail fin loomed up like a tombstone at a grotesque angle. Five windows, the last five in the cabin, were on the top side of a piece of fuselage. Rescuers used ladders to get to one of the last of these windows and smashed it to gain entry.

Silhouetted atop the tail section in the downpour and confusion, another fireman shouted, "Can you count the bodies? Are there forty-three?"

The roster had shown forty-three persons on board. Forty-one were accounted for including the seven dead; two were still missing.

At 4:47 P.M., FAA Inspector Capp, riding the jump seat on Mohawk Flight 186, was told of the crash while his plane was parked at the gate waiting for the storm to pass. Capp had watched as Flight 112 taxied from the adjacent gate as large raindrops splattered their parched craft. Lightning illuminated the darkening scene around them which forced them to call a halt to the fueling operation for fear of explosion. As soon as he received the word, Capp scurried from the safety and comfort of the plane, called his office and then went out to the crash site, taking charge of the wreckage. He stayed in charge until almost midnight when the CAB investigating team arrived to assume command.

When concern developed that two passengers might still be trapped in the wreckage, Public Safety Commissioner Donald Corbett, clad in a red fireman's coat, asked Capp for permission to lift the wreckage to look for the missing victims. Even though such movement might conceivably destroy evidence as to the cause of the crash, Capp acquiesced. A cable was attached to the still-intact nose wheel and the mangled front section of the wreckage was winched ajar with the efforts of more than a score of rescuers, revealing the horrifying jumble of the plane's innards. It resembled a large sausage stuffed with junk! Where had all the pieces come from? It didn't seem possible that they had been part of the plane itself.

Not only was there concern for the two unaccounted-for passengers, but there was a desperate fear that the gasoline flowing from the punctured tanks would reignite despite the voluminous mass of foam being poured on by the ever-growing horde of firefighters gathering at the scene. The air reeked of gasoline and smelled of wet, burned grass.

The entire wreckage had been covered with a thick layer of foam three times. The first two times the rain had washed the foam away, allowing the highly volatile fuel to evaporate into the air, creating an explosion hazard. The third time the rain had let up enough so that the suffocating foam remained in place. The white foam covered everything and looked like the ethereal formations found in limestone caves. Later on, even more gallons of foam were poured on—as an extra precaution against further outbreak of fire, almost completely hiding the grim, grayish mass of almost utter destruction. This was done at the instigation of City Fire Chief Joseph Donovan. The airport rescue crew resented having to take orders from him. Donovan later explained to Monroe County Manager Gordon A. Howe that Airport Rescue Chief Francis Flagg was too busy at the crash with his own equipment to be able to effectively direct the efforts of a larger force of city firemen and it was therefore incumbent upon him to take command.

As late as 6:00 P.M. it was still feared that another body remained buried deep inside the shattered remains of the plane. But this proved to be unfounded.

FAA Watch Supervisor McSweeney was notified of the crash over the tower phone as soon as it occurred. It was he who then proceeded to call the ambulances and the Rochester Fire Department for additional equipment. This set in motion a complex plan throughout the region known as the "Mutual Aid System." Fire-protection coverage was given to those areas whose fire companies went to the airport. By the time

McSweeney completed his calls and had gone up to the tower cab to view the scene for himself, the emergency vehicles had already started arriving. He immediately told the enroute specialist to issue a NOTAM closing "the airport until further notice on account of disabled aircraft" and to start the accident notification procedures. The airport remained closed for two hours.

No sooner had Ziegler called the tower to notify them that their siren was out of order due to the lightning strike than a call came in on the field phone from Dixie Howell to tell them that Flight 112 was down near the VOR shack just south of runway ten. It was Fireman James Locus who received the call on one of the three phones that lined the wall. The phones looked impressive because they were each a different color: red for the fire phone to the field, white for the "hot line" to the manager's office, and black for the crash phone to the tower, over which the call had come. While running out of the office, Locus yelled, "Crash on the field."

The external electrical heaters that are used to keep the motors of the trucks warm, and the quick-disconnect cables that keep the batteries fully charged so that the trucks are in the pink of condition at all times, had not yet been reconnected after the false alarm. The men were back in uniform in less than thirty seconds. Four of them wore aluminized protection over their fire outfits including asbestos hoods with fireproof glass masks. They sparkled like chrome-plated robots.

The three trucks started to roll out of the hangar almost simultaneously, their red dome lights flashing and sirens blasting a fanfare to herald their coming. Locus was driving CH-9, the dry chemical truck; Robert Clark was at the wheel of the Walters CH-12 engine with Ralph Cochrane and Ziegler on board; CH-10 was the third vehicle in the convoy that sped down the taxiway. Although the crews never had had to fight a major crash at the airport before, they averaged an emergency call about every three or four days for an engine or cabin fire, gasoline spill, or the like.

When they reached taxiway one, Ziegler heard Locus call the tower and tell them to close the field and to call the city fire department. Then, when the radio was clear, Ziegler picked up his handset and broadcast: "CH-12 to city fire dispatcher. Send all available equipment to the airport! We have a crash." He repeated the message again on the alternate frequency, but no one reported back that they would send equipment.

They still hadn't located the crash site. It was blowing rain so hard they could barely see the front of their own engine. When they turned down runway 28 and passed the intersection with runway 1–19, the flames became visible. The wind had abated somewhat as they pulled abreast of the inferno and turned off the blacktop onto the grass and mud. It looked like the whole plane was enveloped in flames.

The large pumper started spraying copious amounts of foam from its hydraulically operated turret gun even before it stopped moving. The gun is operated from inside the cab. It could automatically be wobbled up and down or from side to side in order to gain greater coverage of the fire. Foam shot out like large snow flakes, deluging the hulk. The truck had been purchased earlier that year by the county for $79,000 and was responsible for saving many lives.

Ziegler jumped off the pumper, unreeling a hand hose as he went, and started fighting a fire in the wheel and engine section of the wing. A piece of broken fuselage to which the wings were attached contained only two windows, above which were painted the two letters "AW" from the word "MO-HAWK." Ziegler suddenly realized that help was needed in rescuing passengers. He called Cochrane, who had already started helping victims out of the wreckage and into the arriving ambulances. Ziegler had Cochrane help him put on a Scott Air Pack so that he could enter the still-smouldering cabin. Cochrane then relieved John Huntoon on the hand line from the Walters truck.

In minutes, dozens of fire trucks, ambulances, and police cars lined the scooped-out mud and grass that the plane had bulldozed as it skid to a halt. City Police Chief William M. Lombard, in a brilliant orange raincoat, barked orders to the rescuers. Other city police wore yellow slickers that glistened in the downpour. Inspector Anthony DiCroce wore an ambulance driver's red jacket. Not all of the outfits were so colorful. Detective Lieutenant Andrew Sparacino worked stripped to the waist; and of course everyone was covered with mud.

City Fire Chief Earl J. Weber got out of a sick bed when

he got word of the crash, and came to assist Acting Chief Donovan despite his ailing condition. He took on overall command of the fire operations. Supervisor Kenneth Weindenborner, of the state police in Batavia, was on hand shouting instructions and slithering around in the mud like everyone else. State and city police, sheriffs' deputies, a town constable, police from the town of Brighton were all at the scene. Sheriff Albert Skinner wore a coat belonging to the Gates-Chili Fire Department. Civil Defense personnel, disaster units, and a raft of volunteers were all there as a result of the mutual-aid agreement. FBI agents appeared. They always investigate a plane crash to determine if sabotage is involved, which is a federal offense.

Two resident physicians and an intern from Genesee Hospital were brought to the scene by police car. By the time they arrived, all of the injured had long since been removed to the hospital. They returned to their hospital with a desperate feeling of frustration.

When Mohawk's lead customer service agent, Pat Murray, learned that one of his planes was down, he went out to the crash area. It was about five minutes after five. It was still raining. The fire was already out. Ambulances were everywhere and people were milling about. There was little for him to do but watch, and to search his mind to fathom whether he was in any way responsible for this tragedy.

Charred seats were strewn in every direction. He saw the propeller that had come to rest more than one hundred yards from its position on the engine wing, its tips bent at right angles.

An air force reserve ambulance, capable of negotiating in the mud, was utilized in hauling away some of the bodies.

From time to time, firemen and other rescuers would walk over to a large canvas tarpaulin and drop personal items that they had uncovered in the oozing slime. The tarp held seven briefcases, several wallets, a pile of muddy shoes, a crated tape recorder, and a pocket notebook undoubtedly belonging to one of the IBM contingent on board. Embossed in gold on the black cover was imprinted one word: "THINK!"

Airport Fire Chief Francis Flagg arrived at the scene in a pickup truck a few seconds behind the fire and crash equipment. About a dozen or so passengers were staggering or crawling outside the plane in dazed shock. The stewardess had been placed on the grass next to the giant yellow fire truck. Flagg ran stumbling to the wreckage as best he could through the mud and looked inside the plane and around the outside of the aircraft. He retraced his steps to the CH-12 truck and called the county fire radio requesting all available ambulances and tank trucks (known as nursers). Since there are no fire hydrants out on the field, the fire crews must bring all their water with them. A full supply lasts only four minutes. There is enough foam chemical on board to feed four tanks full of water.

Flagg turned his attention back to the rescue efforts. He found a body lying face down in the foam and mud and gasoline. "I put him into a sitting position," he reported later, "and he started to talk to me." At that point the chief noticed another lifeless form about fifteen feet away. He dragged this second body over and held the two of them in a sitting position until someone came over to help carry the two victims over to the grassy area. Flagg estimated that the fire was extinguished in about a minute; dry chemical had been used to smother the fire in the engine well.

Ziegler, a quiet, steady-going man, had entered the bowels of the wreckage wearing one of the silver suits and the air pack while Foamite was poured over him. He looked very much like an astronaut. He began handing out victims to Rossney, Stoppelbein, Nuccie, Stricker, and Flagg massed outside.

Locus, in the meantime, worked his way to the far side of the plane and found more victims scattered all over. Just then more help arrived in the form of the Gates-Chili and city fire departments. The new arrivals started to chop holes in the plane's scarred skin. Locus suggested that they not disturb the wreckage too much since he believed everyone alive was already out.

The city firemen from engine seven proceeded to pull apart the front of the plane and extract the dead passengers and crew members. They found the plane's records and turned them over to Flagg who placed them in the cab of CH-12. It was then that permission was received to pry open the tail section and Flagg told Lucas to man the winch on CH-12. Locus passed the hose he was holding to Fireman R. Byrd and assisted in opening up the tail section. Then Locus was instructed to place a victim (Bossi) in his pickup truck which was then driven to the hospital by Nuccie. Locus was ordered by Flagg to return the CH-9 truck to the firehouse and put it back into service. On the way he picked up two other firemen to help him—E. Czerkas and D. Zaraglia.

Cochrane climbed on top of the Walters truck where the spare drums of the chemical used for creating the fire-smothering foam were stored and reloaded the tank, obtaining water from the auxiliary tankers that had just arrived. Then Cochrane, too, was ordered back to the firehouse with the CH-10 truck and instructed to reload it and have it ready to go when the field was reopened by the tower to air traffic.

When they returned to the hangar they couldn't believe their eyes. A pool table that was kept in the firehouse between the trucks to help the men while away the time was wrapped around a flight of stairs inside the building by the wind. Billiard balls had blown as far away as the next building. An old-fashioned washing machine used for towels and rags for cleaning the vehicles had blown out of the building only to be stopped by a fence outside. Other objects were blown out of the building and across the adjoining ramp. Considerable damage had been done to the doors of the firehouse itself.

The men set about the task of getting everything back into order. The trucks were reloaded, and they and the hoses were scrubbed down to get rid of the defacing mud. CH-12 remained out at the crash with its two hand lines connected because of the continuous leakage of gasoline from the right wing tank. Flagg was able to release some of the off-field equipment, allowing them to return to their respective quarters, thus reversing the complex shifting of fire departments throughout the region. The Walters truck stayed on duty all night accompanied by four volunteer fire-department klieg-light trucks that illuminated the eerie scene like a surrealistic stage show. The grizzly work was thus able to continue without a letup.

There were heroes aplenty within moments of the crash. Foremost among them was perhaps Joseph Pearson, a construction worker from Tonawanda, New York, employed by Schwab Brothers of Kenmore, the subcontractors on the new runway construction. He was partly responsible for the torn-up field in the crash area and the life-saving mud that resulted. He had just climbed into a truck some four hundred yards from the impact site to find refuge from the sudden rainstorm when, as he described it, "I saw fire and what sounded like some kind of explosion. It was an inferno. I started running to the scene; it was slow going through all the mud.

"As I got to the plane wreckage, it was a sickening sight. There were moans inside and some faint cries for help . . . people inside were screaming, 'Oh, Jesus! I'm in here under the fire. Help us! We're alive in here.'

"I saw a man's leg sticking out. His leg was burning . . . flames were shooting up his back . . . I managed to get hold of him and pulled him out. [I] had to unbuckle his seat belt.

"Then I dragged out some more. By now, a fellow who works with me—I only know him as Greg—got there. Between the two of us we must have dragged out at least five people. All were alive. We just got them clear and left them in the mud while trying to get more out. I was sure that all the ones buried under the plane's front section were dead. There was no sound from there.

"But a lot of the injured kept saying things like, 'Jesus help me! I'm on fire.' and 'Help me! Help me!'

"One man had a leg off." [Only one passenger, however, lost a leg and that through surgery in the hospital.] "One was walking around with his ear torn and bleeding. He asked for help, but I said 'There's no time; we gotta get those people who are still in there.' "

Pearson was concerned about the fire raging on the side of the plane close to the runway and was both relieved and impressed by the speed with which the airport rescue engines had arrived and gone into action. He took it upon himself to administer last rites to some of the badly injured, just in case.

It was not until nearly an hour later that he began shaking from the shock and horror of what he had just witnessed. Then he discovered that both his forearms had been singed by the fire and one wrist was either sprained or fractured. Over his strenuous objections, an ambulance aide taped a splint to his arm and took him to the hospital for x-rays.

Two electronic maintenance technicians employed by the FAA found themselves by chance in the tower cab at the time of the crash. John F. Mahoney had been assigned to systems maintenance section number seventy at Rochester airport ever since he joined the agency in 1956. He began his career as an electronics technician in the navy and served three years as a member of an air-sea rescue team—training that would stand him in good stead this day. He was bright and full of energy. His duty tour began at 4:00 P.M. and he reported directly to the SMS office in hangar three. He had to run a routine maintenance service on the three radar sets in the tower and arrived at the IFR room at 4:25. The sets were switched to circular polarization which cancels out the effects of round raindrops. This it does well. But in high wind, the raindrops are not perfectly round, but are teardrop shaped and would thus not be cancelled out on the scope, which accounts for the visibility of the storm on the air-traffic-control radar. These storm echoes, which the radar is designed to minimize, interfere with the visibility of the air-traffic blips.

Mahoney was another who watched the gigantic storm cell edge across the field of view on all three scopes. It was a little less black than it would have been under linear polarization. The setting indicated that the edge of the storm was about twelve miles away from the radar antenna site. It took him only ten minutes to check out the instruments. Then he mounted the two flights of stairs to the tower cab to check out the equipment there. Once in the cab, he glanced at the log to see if there were any indication of technical malfunction recorded. Then he just listened to a few conversations coming in over the loudspeakers from the planes in the area to determine if the communications equipment was up to snuff. His presence went unnoticed by the tower personnel.

He looked out the window toward the field and could see the approaching storm about five miles or so to the west. The storm looked "dark and nasty" to him, corroborating what he had seen on the radar moments before. He couldn't estimate the height of the storm, but it was dark right down to the ground. There were no breaks in it anywhere and he didn't observe any internal motion of the clouds. About 4:40 P.M. he saw the first lightning, but could not hear the thunder associated with it. Because the storm could possibly cause damage to the radar equipment, he decided to wait and watch its progress. All equipment was operating normally at the time.

While monitoring the communications equipment, he heard the conversation between DiStasio and Thorp in the tower, with Mohawk 112, and watched as Thorp leaned over to switch on the runway lights. He hadn't noticed the aircraft until it started its takeoff roll. Almost at the same time he diverted his eyes toward the terminal building which at the moment was only a dim specter barely shining through the wall of precipitation moving across the field. His gaze snapped back to the rolling aircraft which slowly lifted and then disappeared into the same wall of precipitation after using up about one hundred feet of runway. The next time he saw the craft, it had penetrated the storm front and was just past the center taxiway about fifty feet above the ground. The right wing was tipped downward. The plane appeared fuzzy through the weather, but the bottoms of both wings could be seen clearly from the tower. He watched, fascinated, as the plane recovered; it appeared as if the plane was off to the right of the runway at this time. As the plane crossed the intersection with runway 1–19, it was in a normal climbing attitude, level, and approximately seventy-five to one hundred feet above the ground.

The plane immediately tipped into a left-wing-down attitude and never recovered. The wing tip hit the ground, dragging along in that position for about 150 to 200 feet. Then it went over onto its nose, hitting in that attitude. Mahoney saw a tremendous burst of flame on the impact, that rolled forty or fifty feet into the air and then extinguished itself quickly.

DaVia was also in the tower cab checking out the ILS and VOR equipment. He, too, watched the takeoff and crash. He remembers how his view was obscured by the raindrops coming from the northwest impinging on the green tinted-glass windows. He could barely see the plane's outline from his vantage point and missed out on some of the more intricate details of the accident.

Before the plane had shuddered to a halt, the two maintenance men raced down the three flights of concrete steps of the tower, out the door, and over to the SMS office in hangar three. Three other maintenance technicians were working there at the time: Robert H. Mauerman, acting chief of the section, James J. Gesel, an electrician, and Gerald P. Mack, also involved with electronic maintenance. Mauerman was working in the southwest corner of the hangar, sealing envelopes, when he heard Flight 112 gunning for its takeoff roll. Mack, who had been working on time sheets, moved to the window where Mauerman had already positioned himself, when he heard the sound of a plane taking off in that black, foreboding weather. They watched in disbelief as the Martin, barely visible, dipped its wingtip, hit the ground, cartwheeled onto its nose, and exploded in a blinding flash. Mauerman was sure that it was the left wing tank that had exploded. He could see no other flames after that initial burst.

Just before the accident, the three men had been discussing the weather. Gesel, at first, did not realize what was happening. Then, the panic reached him, and he ran to the window in time to witness, as he recalled, "the huge ball of orange flame—then nothing. I was stunned."

Within a minute, while they were excitedly deciding what they should do, Mahoney and DaVia raced in from the tower, breathless and wet. They quickly decided to go out to the crash site and check the VOR shack, since it was close to the burning wreck. Several grabbed raincoats as they headed for the door; Mahoney's coat was in the agency's Ford station wagon parked on the west side of hangar two, toward which he and Gesel were racing. DaVia and Mack followed along several minutes later in their own cars which were also government vehicles.

Mahoney pulled off runway twelve onto the narrow road that leads out to the localizer shack. They continued past the shack about one hundred fifty yards until they came upon a quarter-ton panel truck blocking their way. An injured man was lying beside it. They were in direct line with the tail section; some injured were crawling and walking around the remains of what once had been an aircraft. The rescue vehicles were just arriving.

Mahoney and Gesel jumped out of the wagon. A construction worker, about three-hundred feet away, hailed them and asked them to pick up two survivors. Mahoney returned almost at once with one of the injured men in tow. The man was very tall. His ear was torn and the bottom half was hanging loose. A severe scalp laceration behind the right ear and a smaller gash at the base of his skull had painted his face a grotesque red mask. The man indicated that there was nothing wrong with his legs so Mahoney helped the bleeding victim into the front seat of the wagon. Not to be out done, Gesel appeared almost immediately with a smaller and younger man who appeared to be suffering a pelvic injury and had difficulty in bending. The two maintenance men supported him as he was gently laid down in the back of the wagon.

They backed the car up to the VOR shack. DaVia, who was just driving into the area in his own car, heard Mauerman calling the tower on the ground control radio requesting that ambulances be sent to the VOR shack. When he entered the shack, he found Mauerman and Mahoney struggling to open a bale of rags. DaVia ran to his car to get a pair of wire clippers from his tool box and returned to cut the wires that secured the bale. They spread the rags all over the floor in the shack. They were clean rags used for wiping machinery and equipment. Mack had arrived by then, and the four maintenance men carried the two victims from the wagon and laid them on the rags in the shack trying to make them as comfortable as possible.

DaVia remained behind to tend the injured and await the ambulances while the others returned to the field. A telephone repairman came into the shack and asked DaVia to make a voice check on the VOR monophone with the tower, which he did. The phone was in working order. While he was about it, and perhaps to relieve some nervous tension that had built up within him, he diverted himself by checking out the VOR equipment as well. When he finished, he walked out the door and began searching the tall grass in the area of the shack for other victims. The rain was heavy. Mauerman was coming around from the back and Mack pulled up in his vehicle almost simultaneously. They could see a green and white National ambulance stopped at the tower. National was one of the two ambulance services that operated in the city. They went back into the shack and called the tower to tell them that the ambulance needed directions. Mauerman suggested that DaVia drive over to it and lead it back to the shack. DaVia intercepted the ambulance and motioned the driver to follow him. When they arrived at the shack, the ambulance kept on going, thinking that its services were needed closer to the wreckage. Mauerman ran out and flagged the ambulance to a halt and backed him up to the shack. They all entered the building, placed the smaller man on a stretcher, and carried him out to the ambulance. The other attendant started putting a rough bandage around the head injuries of the taller man, who was lying on his stomach on the rags in order to protect the wound on the back of his head. Mack entered just in time to help roll the tall man over onto a flat board. Then they all lifted board and victim onto a stretcher and carried him to the ambulance which left immediately for the hospital, retracing its route cautiously at first until it reached the hard-surfaced runway area.

While DaVia returned to the shack, the other three sloshed back toward the still smouldering aircraft. The fire engines had already quenched all visible flame. The firemen were now at work frantically on the near section of the plane searching for passengers that might be trapped.

Mahoney recalls that, "It was raining very heavy and going down in a northwesterly direction. The rain and wind were hitting me in the right front."

Several people were crawling away from the aircraft. Some were screaming for help.

"The first I assisted was a young girl [Stewardess Miara] who was lying in the grass just beyond the muddy area." (When all testimony is pieced together, one cannot but conclude that a pretty girl draws men like bees to honey; it seems that just about every rescuer had a hand in assisting the stewardess.)

"Her color was good," Mahoney continued, "but she had some difficulty breathing. I assumed she had a possible rib injury. Someone came and held her head and shoulders up [Nuccie]. I grabbed a cover from someone nearby and covered her with it. I believe it was canvas of some type.

"I then turned to a man that (sic) was lying a few feet from the girl in the muddy area [Yelin]. I do not recall the approximate age of this man. He was a slim man. He had no open cuts, but he did have a badly fractured right leg. I pulled him, head and shoulders first, so that his head and shoulders were on the grassy area. I removed my raincoat and covered him with it."

Mahoney saw another man lying face down in the mud with his arms stretched out under him toward his groin, about twenty-five feet west of the aircraft nose. He ran to the prostrate form. Using his knee, he partially rolled the limp figure over and felt for a pulse by pressing his fingertips to the carotid artery on the left side of the man's neck. His training was paying off.

"There was no pulse and I assumed he was dead," he related.

Seeing two other men lying about three hundred feet further west, he raced toward them, grabbing a blanket from someone as he went. A rather large man did not seem too badly hurt, but he was having trouble with his back and legs. Mahoney stretched the blanket over him but the driving wind and rain kept blowing it off. Mahoney was kept busy replacing it until someone arrived with a stretcher. The large man was placed on it and Mahoney assisted five other men who staggered under the load as they carried it to an ambulance on the grassy knoll. He noticed rescuers removing a man through the crack in the right side of the plane, the same opening that several people had escaped through moments before. The rescuers were calling for help. After depositing his precious load in the ambulance, Mahoney ran to their assistance. He implanted himself partially within the jagged opening in the fuselage, and with the help of another man took a limp body from the arms of two other rescuers further inside the plane.

"I believe he was the last man to be taken alive from the plane," he reported.

By now many ambulances were at the scene. All of the injured had been removed. Mahoney was drenched and covered with mud. He sloshed over to his government station wagon and took out a pair of coveralls that he keeps in it and went to the VOR shack where he changed his clothing. Then he returned to the wreckage, taking a quick survey of the plane and the area surrounding it. He made a mental note of a blade from one of the propellers stuck in a bank of sod like some pagan cross on an ancient grave.

Seeing that he was of little further use, Mahoney returned to the VOR shack and picked up Mauerman and drove back to the SMS office where they advised their district office of the crash. Later, Mahoney was awarded a citation for heroism for his sterling efforts.

After assisting with the removal of the injured, Gesel also returned to the VOR shack after the professionals had arrived in force and, by his own words, "became an interested specta-tor." Then he and DaVia also drove back to the south ramp. From then on they ran a shuttle service for police and govern-ment officials between the tower and the crash scene.

Mack had gone out to the localizer with DaVia to check its operation before returning to the VOR shack. He remained in the area directing traffic and keeping nonessential vehicles from parking near the site, so that emergency vehicles could be routed there.

Several of the rescuers suffered injuries. Besides Pearson's sprained wrist and burned arms, Richard Ziegler suffered from smoke inhalation. An ambulance attendant, Arthur Swan, suf-fered acid burns to his feet.

Both of Rochester's ambulance services took part in the rescue operations. Among the first to reach the scene of the dead and the more fortunate glassy-eyed survivors were Billy L. Booth and George Heisel, Jr. of National Ambulance Service. "We broke out stretchers faster than we ever had before," they reported. Booth was no novice when it came to this type of operation. He had served in a similar capacity at two other plane crashes in other cities.

James W. White, an ambulance driver for the competing Central Ambulance Service, was anxious to report that he had "firsthand information" that the plane "didn't have its landing gear up" on attempted takeoff and that "one wing tip hit the runway, tipping the plane."

When the tarpaulins were finally lifted from the torn, black, lifeless forms that lay in a row in the mud, so that the ambulances from the Monroe County medical examiner's office could take the bodies to the morgue, several onlookers turned away. Those with stronger stomachs hoisted the limp forms onto stretchers like so many sacks of potatoes and loaded them into the waiting ambulances.

Dr. Robert Greendyke, the chief Monroe County medical examiner, a giant of a man with a warm manner, a broad smile, and a deep, resonant voice, who grows orchids as a hobby, was at the scene in his medical-department sedan, its red light flash-ing. He had gotten there the wrong way on one-way streets because the traffic was backed up for miles. There were fifteen to twenty-five vehicles and hundreds of rescuers and would-be rescuers milling about. He saw to the handling of the bodies and then returned to the Monroe County Hospital on Mt. Hope Avenue just outside the city line in Brighton.

The morgue is located in a one-story, orange-bricked, tiled-roof, pseudo-Spanish building in front of the county hospital. The hospital itself is of the identical orange brick but five stories high, topped by the same red, Spanish-tile roof. It is picturesquely set in a clear expanse of green lawns.

The medical examiner's building contains a row of large unloading bays each with overhead garage doors so that the ambulances can enter and unload their grizzly cargoes in privacy.

The morgue is lined with rows of stainless-steel refrigerators used for storage of bodies until disposition can be arranged.

Dr. Greendyke had already performed four autopsies in the morning on bodies unrelated to the crash. The seven new additions kept him working until four A.M. the following morning. He, himself, performed five of the autopsies on these recent arrivals. An assistant had taken care of the other two.

The autopsies included toxicological examinations for alcohol, drugs, and carbon monoxide. All results were negative except for two passengers who had small amounts of alcohol in their blood.

All fatalities resulted from injuries sustained at impact. None were badly burned, that is, charred, although three of the seven fatalities showed evidence of second- and third-degree postmortem burns. The pilot's and copilot's bodies were badly damaged, but careful examination uncovered no evidence of any significant contributory preexisting disease in either of the crew members.

Investigators from the CAB team arrived very late that night to tell him what they wanted done. Dr. Greendyke, in his thoroughness, had already seen to all the details and the CAB men left, quite pleased, and headed for their motel for a short night's rest before picking up their duties again early in the morning.

Dr. Greendyke's secretary stayed on duty all night as well, manning the three telephones continuously. Calls continued to come in from the three local TV stations, the two newspapers, a radio station and both the United Press and Associated Press wire services, for detailed information concerning the deceased and for any clues to foul play. The names of the dead were not released immediately pending the usual notification of next of kin. But the body of one had been identified earlier as that of the pilot, Captain Dennis.

The evening was not complete without the usual roster of crank calls, which tragedy always seems to draw out of the woodwork. Several such calls came in. One call came into the morgue stating that there were three more bodies over at Strong. Ambulances and crews were dispatched. Dr. Greendyke, himself, made the trip even though he was exhausted, only to find to his disgust that a hoax had been perpetrated.

When the autopsies had been completed, and positive identifications were made by relatives and friends, the remains were turned over to local authorities for final disposition.

7

Numbers written on a sheet of paper do not tell the whole story of the weather that swept the area. The storm left a swath of devastation across western and central New York State. It knocked down power lines and trees; it blacked out several communities and caused extensive property damage. The storm continued through midnight in the Hudson Valley-Catskill Mountain area and western Long Island.

In Stillwater, Saratoga County, a boy was struck and killed by lightning. He was one of two killed by lightning in the state that day. Wellesville in Allegheny County and Camden in Oneida County were among several communities that were blacked out by power failures. Lightning started many fires throughout the region.

It hadn't rained in Rochester for the eighteen preceding

days. The last measurable rainfall had been on June 14 when 0.08 inches were recorded. But on July 2 between 4:48 P.M. and 6:22 P.M.—a little over an hour and a half—almost a half an inch of rain fell (0.48 inches). Chapman classified this rainfall as "heavy" but not "excessive." This was more than double the amount of rainfall that was recorded for the entire preceding month (0.22 inches). A lawn-sprinkling ban had been in effect in the county. The storm still only permitted alternate-day sprinkling of lawns, since the long-range forecast did not predict rain again in the near future.

The mercury rose to its summer high of 95 degrees Fahrenheit when the storm struck. (This was only four degrees lower than the all-time high for that day when, in 1931, the thermometer recorded a blistering 99 degrees. Even the lower temperature on July 2, 1931 set a record; it was the highest low ever recorded—76 degrees.) Ninety-four minutes after the high temperature had been reached the temperature plummeted twenty-six degrees to a comfortable 69 as the cold front passed through Rochester. The low for the day ended up only four degrees lower. This was the fourth day in a row that the temperature topped ninety degrees. Home air conditioners were quickly sold out in the Rochester stores.

But wind was the biggest culprit. Fifteen hundred telephones were knocked out of service in the area and were not restored until the following day. Fallen trees and seepage caused severe problems according to Justin Smith, customer-relations manager for the Rochester Telephone Company. St. Mary's Hospital reported all outside dial lines not operating. They were not out of order, according to Smith, but they could not handle the deluge of calls on three exchanges brought on by the crash itself.

More than six hundred homes lost electric power and were blacked out. A barn was flattened in the Henrietta suburb of Rochester. On Sweden Road in Sweden, another Rochester suburb, an empty silo on the John Markham farm was struck by lightning. Firemen from Brockport and Bergen were able to save the adjoining hay-filled barn. The fire radio was jammed with fire reports. Fire companies from the west side of the county were dispatched to three alarms on the east side of the county. They all turned out to be false reports.

About five or six miles southeast of the airport, Floyd Goodberlet, a sixty-three-year-old farmer, watched in horror as the wind blew his silo down. Four barn doors blew off their tracks bending some of the steel rails beyond repair. The wind took a large section of shingles off the west side of his barn roof and blew the barnyard fence down.

Goodberlet commented somewhat in awe, "The hailstones were as large as hickory nuts and turned the ground white . . . the wind seemed to be blowing at about one hundred miles per hour."

Fifty-seven-year-old Roy Hylan, proprietor of Hylans Flying Service located at the Rochester airport, was sitting in his office when the storm struck. He was concerned about the wind which was coming in from the west at better, he estimated, than seventy miles an hour. He observed it shift to the north through to the east and back again through the cycle to the west without any letup in velocity.

"Usually with a wind shift," he said, "the velocity will let up, but it didn't with this wind shift—one of the most peculiar storms I have ever seen and I have been in this vicinity for over forty years.

"Three years ago," he continued, "we had 102-knot winds. . . . Wind sock on top of the hangar did not blow off at that time. But it *was* torn off by this wind. I have never seen such huge hailstones. I have seen many storms, but never one that acted like this. I would estimate the peak winds to be about seventy-five knots."

Two sisters, Kathleen and Jeanne Amman, aged twenty-one and fifteen respectively, were playing cards in the living room at their home in the suburb of Henrietta, when their father, Willard Amman, called from a friend's house to inquire about the weather at home. Both girls raced to be the first to answer the telephone just as the storm struck outside. It shattered the large plate-glass picture window in the living room. Large glass splinters, transparent daggers, were catapulted over the chairs that the girls had just vacated and over the rest of the room. The girls, fortunately, were unhurt.

Radio stations were knocked off the air for short periods of time: station WHAM was out of service from 5:52 to 5:59 P.M.; WROC-AM was out from 5:00 to 5:15 P.M. Television station

WOKR was off the air from 4:59 to 5:06 P.M. and again from 5:36 to 5:40 P.M.

The relief from the rain was apparently as scattered as the damage. The police in the suburb of Irondequoit reported that it rained only "enough to wet your finger." Rain was very light in the towns of Greece and Webster, but Brighton was drenched by a twenty-minute deluge and the Henrietta state police barracks reported a forty-minute storm accompanied by hail.

Lightning is believed to be the culprit that downed an overhead line along the Pennsylvania Railroad tracks south of Chili Avenue, causing an underground circuit failure. It also blew a fuse on a 4,150-volt power line in the area of Marlborough and Roxborough Roads in the nineteenth ward, according to Schuyler Baldwin, an assistant vice-president of the Rochester Gas and Electric Company.

Southeast of the airport the terrain is quite open and flat. It encompasses Genesee Park. The land gradually slopes upward, reaching its highest point about one and a half miles away. Along this line from the Hylan hangar to the apex of the slope, the top of a large tree was blown off; another silo was blown down on top of this knoll, and the west door of the barn to which it was attached, was torn off. About one-half mile to the southeast of the silo, from which the very open ground sloped downward, two very large and stately willow trees had been blown down on the northeast side of a house. A hundred yards beyond, the top of another tree had been blown off and an even larger tree had been completely uprooted as though a giant had plucked a daisy. Yet, nearby houses were unharmed.

In a cemetery two hundred yards further on this southeast trail, several more large trees were downed. Further on, a large barn was blown down and a house two hundred yards to its west lost shingles from its roof. Limbs from the top of a nearby tree were torn off, but a small, spindly barn of rather flimsy construction was unharmed. The owner and his wife were isolated in their car about three-quarters of a mile away, unable to move because the torrential downpour obstructed their vision. Bits and pieces of the house and barn were dropping down around them like some nightmarish rain. They watched unbelievingly as their horsedrawn-type hay rake was picked up by the flailing storm and carried approximately one hundred yards and then deposited with ungentle force in the middle of the road. The wheels were smashed by the impact. Their children at home panicked at the violence of the storm and hid in a storm cellar until their parents returned.

The storm departed as quickly and as suddenly as it had arrived. The rain stopped; the hail stopped even earlier. The rumble of thunder faded into the distance and the lightning became weaker and less frequent and then ceased. The welcome storm was over and it was a pleasantly cool July evening. The weather forecast for the following day was for "cooler, mostly sunny and less humid; high 75 degrees; winds westerly 15 to 25 miles per hour." A large high pressure system had moved into the area which would portend fair weather for several days.

Loren Wagner, the facility chief of the airport tower, was told of the crash over the interphone while the siren was going off. He jolted out of his office and took the steps three at a time to the tower cab. After the excited flurry of emergency activity settled down, Wagner picked up a telephone and called Charles Anthony Salato, who was relaxing on his day off as watch supervisor at home. Salato, forty-nine, had held that job for three years. He had been with the agency since 1939. He was sitting looking out of the window of his home in the direction of the airport when he noticed a cloud of smoke rise in that general direction.

"I thought something might have happened," he reported, "and I called the tower to ascertain and to verify exactly what did happen. I then offered my services."

Salato was told to stand by at home until he was needed. It was then that Wagner called him back to accept his offer of assistance.

Without giving him too much detail, Wagner told Salato he could use him and to come to the airport right away.

Salato's home was only seven-tenths of a mile from the airport and he made the trip in six minutes. Wagner was waiting for him at the base of the tower. It was 4:57 P.M. Wagner instructed Salato to get the tape of the conversation between the tower and Flight 112 from the recording room in the hangar and bring it to him in the tower. Wagner watched Salato unlock the door to the equipment room and then returned to the tower alone.

Salato entered the stillness of the room. Everything seemed to be operating normally; he had seen it frequently before. One set of reels was in motion; the standby set was in place. Salato moved to the recorder and pushed a button which started up the standby reels so that both sets were operating. He waited almost a minute before he stopped the first set of reels. Then he wound up the remainder of the first tape onto the take-up reel and removed it from the machine. He picked up a red grease pencil and carefully printed on the reel the number of the recording unit from which it had been removed and his initials—"CS," followed by the Greenwich meridian time, "2130 Zulu" which would make it 5:50 P.M. EDT. He placed a fresh six-hour reel on the first machine before leaving the recording room; he was careful to see that the door was locked behind him.

Wagner was looking a little haggard under the strain of events when Salato reported to him in the tower. Wagner was becoming defensive as he started to assume, undeservedly, some of the guilt for the accident. When the newspapers called to obtain the name of the controller who released the flight for takeoff (implying, perhaps, an error in judgment), Wagner refused to release that bit of information. Wagner instructed Salato to make a duplicate recording of the all-important tape and to then turn the original over to him for safekeeping. Then Salato was to make a transcript of all of the recorded conversations on the tape starting at five minutes before the crash until an equivalent time following it.

Salato set the tape up on a recording machine and proceeded with his assignment. He recognized three separate voices during the fifty-second fateful transmission involving Flight 112. He recognized the voices of Thorp and Sufrin.

When he completed the recording, Salato turned the original tape over to Wagner, who locked it in a cabinet to which there were only two keys and Wagner had them both—one he kept at home, the other in his pocket. Whenever he went on vacation, he turned one key over to his relief with the admonition to "never leave it out of your sight."

The day following the crash, Wagner removed the original tape from the cabinet and gave it to Salato so that he could play it for the CAB investigators. It wasn't removed again until November of the following year when Salato replayed it to refresh his memory before his deposition was taken by lawyers involved in the legal suits that ensued.

Just one hour after the crash, William L. Lamb, a thirty-eight-year-old veteran navy fighter pilot received an alert notice at his home in northwest Washington, D.C. from the Civil Aeronautics Board Bureau of Safety duty officer. Ten minutes later, Joseph Fluet, chief of the investigation division called Lamb, told him about the Mohawk crash, and gave him the assignment of investigator-in-charge. This was the first time that Lamb had been placed in charge of an investigation since joining the CAB in 1959, although he had participated in numerous investigations in the intervening years. (A few years later, Lamb was made chief investigator for the CAB. By then, the agency was known as the National Transportation Board under the aegis of the Department of Transportation.)

The handsome pipe-smoking ex-navy pilot, who hailed from North Little Rock, Arkansas, was no novice to the aviation business; he had been involved with it for twenty-one years.

When Lamb was advised of his command of the crash investigation, he set to work at once. He called George Van Epps of the CAB's New York office and asked him to arrange to procure and initiate a study of the maintenance records pertinent to N449A. Van Epps immediately dispatched Francis Mosher to Mohawk's headquarters in Utica to accomplish this task.

Calls went out to eleven other men of the investigation team who were on-call at their homes in the Washington, D.C. area. They were instructed to assemble in hangar six at Washington National Airport at 8:30 P.M. This team was one of four such groups at the CAB. One team is always on call. Each of the twelve crash-team members was a specialist in a particular area of crash investigation. The team concept at the CAB had only been in effect six weeks; prior to that, representatives from the regional office (in this case it would have been New York City) went to the crash scene and then summoned experts from Washington as needed. Now the team was sent as a group.

Investigation by the CAB is made according to Title VII of the Civil Aviation Act of 1958 as amended, which directs the board "to investigate accidents involving civil aircraft in order to determine the facts, the conditions and circumstances relating to each accident and the probable cause thereof, and to ascertain measures which will best tend to prevent the recurrence of similar accidents in the future." Up to that time, during the twenty-seven years of commercial aviation history, 95 percent of all government investigations of aircraft disasters had been solved. This accident would be no exception. Where strikeouts did occur, it was generally the result of missing planes whose wreckage could not be examined.

Each man of Lamb's team arrived at hangar six on time, carrying his luggage which was kept packed and ready to go on a moment's notice. In addition to Lamb, the team was comprised of Alan I. Brunstein, weather specialist, whose group would gather all the weather information; Claude Schonberger, hearing officer, who would preside at the public hearing on the crash; Harry H. Black, structures specialist, who checks on the general condition of the aircraft structure; James H. Lewis, in charge of power plants which include engines and propellers; Billy M. Hopper was responsible for hydraulics and electricity; John J. Carroll and Dr. Richard Chubb were responsible for human factors; their investigation would be concerned with autopsies, the nature of injuries, effects of seat belts and so on. (Dr. Chubb was on loan to the CAB from the Armed Forces Institute of Pathology.) Bruce Hoch was in charge of operations and would trace the history of the flight, the fueling, weight parameters, the time in the air before crashing. Robert D. Rudich would investigate air traffic control, working with the control tower checking the tape recordings of the communications between the tower and the aircraft. Corwin C. Grimes was responsible for investigating witnesses, interviewing all those available and recording their statements. And, finally, there was Edward C. Slattery, Jr., who was the public-relations officer for the CAB. He predicted for the press upon the team's arrival in Rochester that the investigation would take from ten days to two weeks.

The team caught a 9:10 flight out of Washington, arriving in Rochester at 11:15 P.M. They quickly were lead out to the bizarre scene, stage-lit by the fire department klieg lights. Each team member conducted a quick check of the wreckage and, with the assistance of the state police and the county sheriff's department, established complete security.

Also on the scene, but not part of the team, was Ivan Strachner, a tall man with graying hair and thick features, who was a CAB air safety investigator, and Dr. Lawrence Marinelli, an FAA regional flight surgeon whose deepset eyes peered out from his forward-thrust head as he poked through the wreckage. The team was also augmented and assisted by the airline, the Airline Pilots Association, the Flight Dispatchers Association, and other groups. Each of these groups was obviously present to protect its own interests primarily, and to learn what they could from the investigation to prevent recurrence of the events. ALPA was present to fight any verdict of "pilot error" if one was arrived at. The other groups also had reason to be on the defensive.

The official, formal investigation would not begin until seven-thirty on the following morning with an organizational meeting in the conference room of the airport terminal building. At that time Lamb organized working teams, each under the chairmanship of a CAB investigator and staffed by interested parties. Then began the painstaking task of going over the wreckage inch by inch to determine the positions of the hundreds of switches and dials in the cockpit, to juxtapose each scrap of metal, glass, plastic and rubber to its original position like some giant jigsaw puzzle.

During the night, the checklist scroll was found in the rubble. Although investigators claimed that it was not significant, the scroll was set at the "before takeoff" position. It was a strong indication that the crew failed to complete their checklist procedure prior to the crash (something Dennis was known to have done on at least one prior occasion).

The investigation at the crash site by the various teams lasted just about a week. The thoroughness, technical knowledge, and painstaking patience is both fascinating and awe-inspiring.

The Structures Investigation Group, chaired by Harry Black, was staffed with representatives from the FAA and Mohawk. Later on, they were joined by representatives from the

CAB, ALPA, and the International Association of Machinists. The team spent the first day searching isolated areas, locating and photographing the major components of the wreckage. The following four days were spent mapping the distribution of the wreckage, documenting each part and taking additional photographs. Teams of surveyors headed by County Public Works Director Alexander Z. Grey, helped in spotting all pieces of wreckage. Once this was completed and the distribution diagram made, the pieces could be picked up for examination. They were then taken back to a hangar and placed again in their relative positions according to the diagram. This was done to ensure that all major components had been recovered and to help determine the angle of impact and other factors. One hundred and twenty-three parts were so located and identified. The wreckage was ultimately placed inside the hangar adjacent to the airport rescue squad and on the sixth day of the investigation, it was loaded on 6 trucks and transported to a Mohawk hangar in Ithaca where it was again laid out. The structures group reconvened there for two more days for further detailed examination, photographing, and documentation.

John Carrol drew a diagram, labeled "Crash Kinematics" to a scale of one inch equal to fifty feet, which showed all of the scoops and gouges in the ground caused by different parts of the plane as they made contact with the ground. It clearly shows the initial contact point made by the left wing and the three-foot-wide by one-hundred and twenty-five-foot-long trench it dug until the left propeller clawed its staccato imprint into the mud. There followed a four-foot-wide trench and then some wider gouges beginning a few feet further on. The right propeller left its imprint easily read by one skilled in the art, the way an Indian hunter of yore could read the forest floor for the telltale tracks of his prey. A small cut in the mud was made by the right wing tip; fragments of the right wing navigation light were found embedded in it.

The Structures Group summarized their conclusions in their report:

"Wreckage Pattern and Destruction: The plane hit the ground on the left wing tip and lower surface and began to disintegrate in an intermitting, long left curving direction, cartwheeling, and coming to rest on a magnetic heading of 280 degrees in a drainage excavation approximately six feet deep adjacent to runway twenty-eight.

"The aft section of the fuselage fractured around the circumference at approximately fuselage station number 510, pivoting approximately ninety degrees and came to rest in an almost upright position against the remaining portion of the left wing and engine nacelle [housing].

"The airport fire equipment extinguished all fires at 4:55 P.M. EDT, approximately four minutes after arrival at the site.

"Evidence of cartwheeling was substantiated by the location of glass fragments from both the red and green [left and right] wing-tip lights, the slices in the ground made by the left and right engine propellers, and the grass that remained impacted to the top of the cockpit windshield and the bottom of the forward fuselage.

"The forward fuselage section from station number 87 aft to approximately station number 372 on the left side and approximately station number 411 on the right side was demolished during ground impact and the succeeding ground slide into an indescribable mass of torn, twisted and compressed metal. This section was further destroyed when cabling was attached to the nose landing gear and the section pulled apart to assist in the rescue operation.

"Center Section: This section of the fuselage remained intact and attached to the center wing panel, sustaining only interior furnishing damage."

The report continued with a description of damage to the aft section:

"The aft section of the fuselage consisted of one intact section. . . . This section . . . and the attached empennage [the tail assembly of the aircraft] separated after fracture occurred around the circumference . . . during the ground slide and came to rest approximately ninety degrees to the left of the center fuselage section, resting on the outboard portions of the stabilizer and elevator. The forward section rested on the remaining portion of the wing and engine nacelle.

"The outer skin covering and the interior overhead furnishings on the left side of the fuselage . . . were burnt away when the fuselage came to rest against the burning left nacelle during the ground fire that followed after impact."

The report went on to tell how the tail cone remained intact, but was found to have sustained severe internal damage. It described how the left wing was separated from the engine nacelle during the ground slide causing partial disintegration of the nacelle skin and approximately half the fire wall. The spar ends suffered severe fire damage. The largest piece of outer wing panel measured twelve by thirteen feet and was found attached to the crumbled wing tip. The report described the condition of the aileron, trim tab, flaps, slats and shutter doors —all wing components—in minute detail.

The investigation determined that the right engine and mounts separated from the nacelle during the ground slide. The nacelle itself was fractured around the circumference at the leading edge of the wing and was further destroyed by fire.

The report continued, "The outboard portion of the leading edge, the upper and lower skin [of the right wing] . . . including the tip, was found buckled, torn, and compressed under the forward fuselage near the cockpit area."

A subparagraph made an interesting disclosure concerning the right aileron:

"a. Aileron: Upon opening the upper skin of the aileron to examine the trim tab mechanism, a large straw bird nest was found covering the bottom skin in the vicinity of the tab control rod." From what was known of the accident and the behavior of the craft prior to that time, the nest is a curiosity but of no particular significance.

The center wing panel was found intact and attached to the fuselage, sustaining only minor impact damage. The tail empennage section was attached to the aft fuselage as already noted. It was "twisted at a slight left angle and separated from the dorsal fin by impact forces."

The mud-covered condition of the horizontal stabilizers, elevators, and trim tabs, vertical fin, rudder, and elevator trim tabs was pointed out. It continued:

"The rudder assembly remained intact at all attachment points. There was slight scorching of the paint on the right side but the left side was undamaged. The rudder was trailing free as the cables were severed."

The landing gear was examined and found to be completely salvageable. It had been retracted, up and locked, into the nacelles and exhibited only minor fire damage; all tires remained inflated. Obviously Ambulance Driver White's "firsthand information" was incorrect.

The left outboard wing tip and panel were located along the flight path 290 feet northeast of the main wreckage.

There was no evidence that there was any structural failure before impact nor was there any evidence of fatigue failure (breakage due to constant vibration or flexing). No evidence was found that would indicate in-flight fire, explosion, or collision with foreign objects. All doors, emergency exits, flight controls, and their attachments were accounted for.

After examination at the accident scene, the two engines were moved to Mohawk's maintenance facility at Oneida County Airport in Utica and the Power Plant Group of the investigation team convened there on July 8 and began the tedious task of tearing down the engines for detailed examination. Serving on the team with the chairman, J. H. Lewis, were members from Mohawk, the FAA, ALPA, and from the engines' manufacturer, Pratt and Whitney Aircraft Corporation.

Those mysterious mechanical footprints in the mud told much about the plane's demise. A set of slashes made by the left propeller blade was found about 148 feet from the left side of the runway and about 250 feet from the main wreckage; another set of slashes from the right blade was found 72 feet away from the first set of slashes about 178 feet from the left edge of the runway. Although many people had observed one of the blades shortly after the crash, the other could not be found for four days. It was finally located about 550 feet from the main wreckage. The left engine was found about 190 feet from the left side of the runway. It exhibited a moderate amount of fire damage on the right side; ground fire damage was slight because of the rain and the rapid action by the emergency crew. But the engine was a total wreck with pieces torn free and scattered about. Almost every component was crushed, bent, or damaged in some way.

The comparably damaged right engine was found separated from the wing about 242 feet to the left of the runway. The top rear portion of this engine was severely fire gutted with most of the hose coverings burned off down to their exposed metal cores.

The parts were all brought back to the Utica hangar and intricately measured. From impact markings on the propeller blade shim-plates, which gave the pitch or angle of each blade, and the setting of the engine-speed governor, engine speeds could be calculated at the moment of impact: left engine—2,720 rpm, and the right, 2,740 rpm. From these figures and the spacing between the slashes in the mud (the left engine hit first and was taken as being more indicative of speed at impact; the spacing was measured at about two and a half feet between slashes), the ground speed of the aircraft at impact was calculated to be ninety-two knots or about 106 miles per hour.

All inner parts of the engines were minutely inspected. Whatever could possibly be tested, was, even if it meant substituting parts, wires, or whatever. The parts tested all proved to be normal. The group concluded that the engines had behaved normally in every way and that there was no pre-impact failure of any kind. Each engine had developed its rated takeoff power and propeller pitch was properly set.

When Francis Mosher of the CAB's New York office had received the call from Lamb to head up the Records Group, he immediately telephoned Mohawk in Utica directing them to seal all records relative to the plane and mark them "Hold for CAB." The records were pulled in the Mohawk chief inspector's office and so sealed. At 11:45 P.M. that same night, Mosher arrived at the Mohawk shops in Utica and took charge of them. The following morning he was joined by representatives from both the FAA and Mohawk and began reviewing them, starting with the present and working backward chronologically to December 1961, noting the mechanical troubles the plane was heir to. The record added up to the following:

12/23/61 Aircraft has a pre-stall shudder which appears about ten knots faster than is normal—corrected.

2/16/62 Elevators are very stiff in flight—corrected.

3/15/62 Gear handle must be returned to neutral manually on gear retraction—corrected.

3/16/62 Repeat on gear—replaced and corrected.

4/9/62 Flight 773—number one propeller feathered on reversing at SSI (Sea Island, Georgia)—Golden Isle mechanic found loose can-

116

non plug #1 prop. Now turns 2900 rpm. Note: takeoff rpm reset
—corrected.

5/18/62 Flight 432 air turnback. Service door warning light came on
in flight. Stewardess and passengers reported banging in vicinity
of lower rear cargo service. Pressure began dropping off. Returned to Baltimore. Checked lower rear cargo door for security.
OK—corrected.

12/21/62 at ATT—Airframe time of 29,768:89 hours the plane was
sold to the Charlotte Aircraft Corporation (North Carolina).

6/4/63 Left engine and propeller were replaced.

6/6/63 Discrepancies were corrected as follows: escape chute was
packed and installed; anti-icing heaters were repaired and
checked; main oxygen bottle was replaced; nose wheel assembly
was replaced; a defective right auto-feather warning switch was
replaced; #2 pitot heat ammeter was removed.

From June 7 to June 21, 1963 the aircraft was put through
a one-hundred-hour inspection in the Mohawk shops. The aircraft was also weighed. One hundred and ten discrepancies
were noted with corrective action taken on all. Fifty two of
these discrepancies were actual defects in air worthiness. The
most significant was: "Dress out crack at tip of number one
propeller blade—corrected."

The weighing of N449A indicated that the basic operating
weight of the aircraft was 32,617 pounds which included a total
of 410 pounds of permanent ballast. The ballast was stored in
five olive-drab-colored canvas bags, each holding approximately ninety pounds of sand. These were added by Mohawk
to compensate for the weight of the galley equipment and
supplies originally carried when Eastern Airlines flew the aircraft. The ballast was kept in a compartment just aft of the
copilot's bulkhead. The actual aircraft weight differed from the
basic operating weight of 32,560 pounds listed in the company
operations manual. However, this figure was the fleet operating
weight for both of the Martin 404 airplanes that Mohawk
leased.

On June 21, 1963, the plane made two scheduled flights.
Nineteen maintenance items were noted including indicator problems and pressures. One item read, "Capts.' A/H
[artificial horizon] reads 40 right wing down in level flight
and horizon bar has a constant vibration making the bar

appear fuzzy and twice as thick.—replaced A/H."

The plane was flown on six more days prior to the crash with the following maintenance record:

6/23/63 On schedule three flights—five items, all minor—corrected.

6/24/63 On schedule two flights—all minor—corrected.

6/26/63 On schedule three flights—five items—gen/glide slope/ADF, not homing—corrected.

6/27/63 On schedule two flights—five items—corrected.

6/28/63 On schedule two flights—two items—air conditioner problem.

6/29/63 On schedule one flight—four items—2 radio/capt's. side window/idle mixture #1 engine/hole in duct heat exchanger/duct screen to secondary tubing repaired.

This was the day before the crash. At the moment of the crash, the plane was 29,817:58 hours old.

Billy Hopper was the group chairman for systems investigation. He was assisted by a member of the FAA and an ALPA member who was also a Mohawk employee. This group examined all of the hydraulic equipment, pumps, etcetera. One fuel pump was found to be quite worn, but there was "no definite evidence of operating distress." As a matter of fact, they discerned no malfunction in any of the systems.

Both the pilot's and copilot's windshield wiper control valves were found to be full open.

The systems team also checked the electrical systems. No damage was found that was not caused directly by the crash itself. The pilot's circuit-breaker panel located on the forward side of the bulkhead directly behind the pilot was found in the wreckage completely intact. However, all circuit breakers were turned off; they were not in the "trip-free" position, but were definitely off. This was confirmed positively by testing the circuits with an ohm meter. This panel contains such important circuit breakers as propeller rpm control, propeller feathering control, nacelle bus power, and water injection power and control. A placard attached to the panel states that the breakers are to be on at all times. In view of the lack of damage to this panel, no explanation could be found for the positions of the breakers.

The main circuit-breaker panel, located on the aft side of the same bulkhead panel behind the pilot's seat, was also found completely intact despite the damage to the bulkhead itself and the surrounding fuselage structure. A similar placard gives notice that these breakers, of which there are many more, are also to be on at all times. Examination disclosed that all but eight heavy-duty breakers were on. These eight included fuel-pump control, hydraulic pump, landing light power, attendant's bus, and air-conditioning recirculating fan. No explanation could be found for these breaker positions, either.

This group determined that the post-crash fire occurred in the left-wing fuel-tank area and the right engine nacelle. The forward fuselage was torn apart, extensively crushed and collapsed from the top downward, worsening progressively in a forward direction to the nose section. There was no fire in this portion of the fuselage.

All available wiring was examined for indications of electrical arcing, burning, or overheating, but none was found. Examination of broken wire strands disclosed no indication of electrical power at the time of separation.

All radio communication and navigation equipment had remained in the rack aft of the copilot's seat. There was a moderate amount of damage to this equipment, but there was no indication of electrical distress. The radio selector panel was found separated from its normal location on the central control pedestal; the various control heads were examined to determine the frequencies at which they were set. The report of the group tabulated their findings, shown in the diagram on the following page. All radios were carefully checked to see if they would receive at the proper frequencies. The ADF receivers were checked at the Page Aircraft radio shop at Rochester airport, but could not be made to work because of dirt and foam resulting from the crash. All but three instruments remained intact on the instrument panel. These three were found back along the wreckage path.

Other navigation equipment was recovered and checked at Page Airways. The VHF navigation instrumentation unit (omni bearing indicators) number one VHF Nav. (upper indicator) was set at 200 degrees; the Number two VHF Nav. (lower indicator) was set at 271 degrees. Also checked were the Num-

SELECTOR	FREQUENCY	REMARKS
No. 1 VHF Communication	118.15 Mc	Close to 118.3 Mc; Rochester tower frequency
No. 2 VHF Communication	131.2 Mc	Close to 130.0 Mc; Mohawk Company frequency
No. 1 VHF Navigation	120.0 Mc	Nothing close to this frequency in the area; Rochester VOR frequency is 110.0 Mc
No. 2 VHF Navigation	108.7 Mc	Close to 109.5 Mc; Rochester ILS frequency
No. 1 ADF	385 Kc	Nothing close to this frequency in the area
No. 2 ADF	259 Kc	Nothing close to this frequency in the area

ber one and Number two ILS glide slope receivers and the marker beacon receiver.

The fuel system controls were checked. They were set with the left engine selector at "CROSS FEED TO L. H. ENGINE" and the right engine selector at "R. H. TANK TO R. H. ENGINE AND CROSS FEED." The valves themselves were set differently than the selectors probably because of the control cables pulling in tension during the crash, changing the valve positions.

The fire-protection system consists of two mounted pairs of carbon dioxide bottles (pressure cylinders) controlled by a common cable. There are rupture discs which indicate the type of discharge: a yellow disc is broken when the bottles are intentionally discharged by the crew; a red disc is ruptured due to heat from fire. The yellow discs were missing and the plungers extended indicating that both pairs of bottles had been intentionally discharged into the system; both red thermal-indicator discs remained intact.

The emergency oxygen system consisted of one high-pressure bottle for both the flight crew and the passengers. The tubing from the bottle broke and the oxygen had discharged.

The air-conditioning system, which consisted of two 100,000 BTU surface combustion heaters and a secondary heat exchanger located in the under-floor compartments of the forward fuselage section, were intact and undamaged.

Ice prevention and elimination systems are provided for the wing and empennage leading edges through a pair of 100,000 BTU surface combustion heaters located in each wing in the engine nacelles. Heated air flows inboard to a mixing box in the wing fuselage center section and is then routed out through the wing leading edges and aft to the empennage leading edges. These were all undamaged.

The propellers and carburetors are de-iced by means of alcohol from a single tank located in the aft end of the right wing fillet. Each carburetor is supplied by a separate pump and both propellers by a single pump. All were intact and the alcohol tank was nearly full.

A listing was made of all instrument settings. These were grouped under various headings: "Captain's Instrument Panel," "Center Instrument Panel," "First-Officer's Instrument Panel," "Fire Control Panel," "Pedestal Controls and Other Cockpit Controls," "Radio Communication and Navigation Frequency Selector Panel," "Captain's Audio Selector Panel," "Overhead Switch Panel."

The captain's altimeter was set at 29.74; the spare altimeter was set at 29.87; the first officer's altimeter almost matched that of the captain's at 29.75.

And the clocks were still running.

The landing gear handle was in the "down" position, although all three main landing gears were up and locked. The wing-flap handle was in the takeoff position.

The engine throttles showed the right engine closed and the left engine 80 percent open with the right engine mixture control set at auto-lean and the left engine at auto-rich.

The elevator trim tab indicator was set at "4 degrees nose up" and that of the aileron at "6 degrees right wing down."

Most important was the finding of the pilot's checklist scroll which was set at the *beginning* of the "Before Takeoff Check List."

The rotating beacon was in the "on" position, a fact corroborated by a ground witness. The fire warning bell switch had the switchguard down, exposing the switch which was in the "on" position.

Bruce Hoch's operations group was manned by two Mohawk representatives: Walter J. Ferrari, assistant to the vice-president, flight, and Robert G. Harrar, acting director of flight. There were two other Mohawk employees on the panel, one representing ALPA, the other representing ALDA (the Airline Dispatchers Association), and a representative from the FAA, George L. Howard.

Their investigation showed that the aircraft made initial contact with the ground 4,670 feet from the takeoff end of runway twenty-eight and approximately 2,250 feet south of the centerline of the runway.

Digging into the muddy morass in the cockpit area, the aircraft documents were recovered. These included:

Aircraft log for N449A.

Martin 404 Flight Manual.

Weather sequence with date time group "02 1800Z" which included the Rochester sequence July 2, 1963, 2:00 P.M. EDT.

Mohawk Airlines Flight 115 Flight Plan for July 2, 1963 covering the flight from Ithaca to Rochester.

Mohawk Airlines Daily Flight Time Record for July 2, 1963 for the crew.

Copies of the fuel requirement records for July 2, 1963.

Pilot Navigation Kit for Captain Dennis including portions of the Company Operations Manual, Company Schedules, Jeppeson Charts, a pair of clear-lens eye glasses and his FAA medical and pilot's certificate. A second set of clear-lens glasses were found in the mud.

Pilot Navigation Kit for First Officer Neff which contained his personal flight log, Company Operations Manual, Jeppeson Charts, Flight Equipment Manual for the Martin 404 and flashlights.

The Operations Group investigated the history of the flight. Examination of the fuel slips for July 2 gave evidence that fuel consumption for N449A was normal for a Martin 404 and fuel planning on the flight-plan form was within safe operating limits. Thirty-five gallons of fuel were taken on board in Rochester bringing the total fuel load up to six hundred gallons.

The cargo was recovered and examined and compared with the cargo manifest. There were twenty-one pieces of carry-on baggage; seven pieces of checked baggage, including a large corrugated carton containing materials that I had used earlier in my presentation, still in almost pristine condition; one piece of air freight; and one piece of mail, a package that did not appear on the load manifest as it had been boarded after the engines had started. It weighed only one pound.

The five olive-colored canvas ballast bags were recovered, but they were torn and the sand ballast was dumped out so that it was impossible to accurately check the ballast weight. A review of the weight chart in the company operations manual indicated that each bag held only fifty pounds of sand for a total of two hundred fifty pounds instead of the weight indicated earlier.

The weight of the plane on takeoff was determined after the crash as follows:

	COMPUTED	ACTUAL
Basic Operating Weight	32,560 lbs. (Fleet basic operating weight)	32,617 lbs. (taken from analysis of weight and balance)
Fuel (3,600 lbs. less 114 lbs. for taxi and run up)	3,486 lbs.	3,486 lbs.
Passengers (40) all seats occupied	6,600 lbs. (using factor of 165 lbs. per passenger, 51 lbs. for carry-on baggage)	6,400 (using factor of 160 lbs. per passenger)
Cargo	176 lbs. (using an average baggage weight of 23.5 lbs. per bag	280 lbs. (recovered baggage)
Lift-off Weight	42,822 lbs.	42,783 lbs.

According to the company operations manual, the maximum allowable takeoff weight for a Martin 404 on Rochester Airport's runway twenty-eight is 44,900 pounds up to the critical temperature of 84 degrees Fahrenheit. The temperature on the weather sequence for the hour previous (4:00 P.M. EDT) was 94 degrees Fahrenheit. The temperature correction factor for each degree above the critical temperature was to deduct thirty-seven pounds. Thus for ten degrees, a total of 370 pounds would be deducted, reducing the maximum allowable takeoff weight to 44,530 pounds. Dennis had assumed a temperature correction on his flight plan of seventeen degrees which established a maximum allowable takeoff weight of 44,271 pounds, a more conservative figure. If the computed and actual takeoff weights are compared with this conservative value, both are safely below the allowable weight.

Detailed calculations of the center of gravity (hence, balance) of the aircraft using either the basis of 410 pounds of ballast or the actual 250 pounds (based on only five bags being found in the wreckage) put this figure also well within the allowable limits.

The group reviewed all the records concerning the flight, the dispatch, and company operations procedures, and the past history of the crew, the plane, the company, weather and crash and rescue operations.

Air traffic control was investigated separately by a group headed by Robert Rudich, of the CAB, Walter J. Ferrari, Mohawk Airline's director of flight service, and Edward Rooney, the Mohawk captain who was representing ALPA.

They merely established the procedures used and the messages transmitted in clearing the flight. As was pointed out earlier, no provision was made for superimposition of a time signal on the recording tape to establish a correlation with a specific transmission.

Appended to their study were two drawings made by Air Traffic Controller Sufrin of the radar screen at 4:00 P.M. and 4:48 P.M. EDT on which the ominous storm is seen creeping amoebalike towards the center cross on the scope.

Corwin Grimes headed the Witness Group whose purpose it was to interview survivors and other witnesses. Two Mohawk employees, one representing the company, the other representing ALPA (the same Captain Edward Rooney who served on the Air Traffic Control Group) and another ALPA representative, Eleanor E. Schneider of Boston, assisted. This group interviewed all of the survivors except the five who were critically injured; I fell into that category. Twenty-five passengers and the stewardess were personally contacted and the interviews were tape-recorded. Five passengers were interviewed by telephone. Notes were taken in all cases. Fourteen survivors submitted written statements which the group included with its report. Forty other witnesses were also interviewed and thirty-two of these submitted written reports as well.

The report pulled out of context quotations made by the many witnesses in order to build up a verbal description of the events that transpired.

Three days after the crash, the witness group spent the morning viewing the trail of damage left by the storm as it had progressed through the airport and the adjacent town of Henrietta. Ten persons along its path were interviewed.

A concensus of the facts were taken for each phase of the takeoff and consequent crash. Ten persons on the ground watched the takeoff roll; ten saw the plane in flight; twelve saw it make impact with the ground; and fifteen witnessed the resultant explosion.

The Human Factors Group was the largest of the investigative teams. They were charged with determining the identification of all victims including the cause of death in every case, and determining or eliminating as possible causitive elements, inflight incapacitation of a crew member, or preexisting disease or other possible environmental causitive conditions. They were to determine the sequence of events of the accident and determine the conditions, circumstances, and environmental factors that might govern the survival aspects of the crash. They were further responsible for the identification, documentation, and reconstruction of the passenger seats at the crash site in an attempt to determine the sequence and kinematics—the failure of the seats and surrounding structure—during the accident.

The makeup of the group was heavily professional. In addition to John Carroll of the CAB as chairman, other group members included Major R. M. Chubb of the United States Air Force

Medical Corps on loan from the Armed Forces Institute of Pathology in Washington, D. C.; the Monroe County Medical Examiner, Dr. Greendyke; the Assistant Regional Flight Surgeon for the FAA out of New York City, Dr. John Moling; two representatives of AVSER, the acronym for Aviation Service Engineering and Research Corporation of Phoenix, Arizona, a division of the California-based Marshall Industries. (This company performs crash dynamic research, having taken over the work of AVCIR, Aviation Crash Injury Research performed under the auspices of Cornell University.) Three other group members were from the Civil Aeromedical Research Institute of the FAA in Oklahoma City; one was an M.D. The sole distaff member was an ALPA representative, Miss Iris Peterson from New York City.

The group examined the personal and medical records of the flight crew and interviewed a number of professional acquaintances and flight-crew members who had flown recently with Dennis and Neff. They determined that the bodies of the two pilots were found in the cockpit wreckage with Dennis's head and shoulders resting on top of Neff with Dennis to Neff's right. The location of the bodies of four of the five fatally injured passengers could not be determined because they were removed early in the rescue operations. It was reported, however, that they were found in and around the forward part of the fuselage that became known as the "death section." The fifth dead passenger was said to have been the occupant of seat 9A, which would be the next to the last row at the left window, which would seem at variance with the facts. In any case, he was found on the left side at the break in the fuselage.

In addition to evaluating the autopsies performed on the dead passengers, the group also looked into the nature and severity of the injuries suffered by the thirty-five surviving passengers and the lone surviving crew member, Stewardess Miara. The injuries ran the gamut from very minor to very severe. It was determined that twenty-six of the survivors lost consciousness as a result of blows to the head; two others probably lost consciousness for other reasons. The remaining survivors could not be interrogated because of the severity of their injuries.

Fifteen of the passengers were burned to some degree irrespective of where they were sitting in the plane; the seats of twelve of these passengers were determined and found to have extended over the entire length of the plane except for the fifth row. Eleven passengers had bone fractures of one or more extremity; seven suffered rib fractures. (I suffered a severely fractured clavical, but this was not discovered until months later when I finally explored my damaged body with my hand and discovered the protruding collarbone under the skin surface. It had already healed in a distorted position. Nothing was ever done to correct this and no problems have been experienced from it.) Four survivors had fractures of the spine. All survivors had bruises and minor lacerations which produced for some, considerable bleeding of disrupted tendons, large muscle masses or nerves. Conversely, six had injuries miraculously limited to contusions and abrasions or minor lacerations.

The Human Factors Group was particularly interested in the efficacy of the seat belts, but was only able to investigate the matter with respect to twenty-one of the survivors. They determined the presence or absence of contusions across the lower abdomen in the area normally underlying the lap belts of these passengers. All ten rows of seats were torn loose from their attachments to the aircraft floor during and following the principal impact. Some were displaced within the aircraft and others were thrown free of the wreckage. In all cases, however, the seat belts themselves withstood the impact forces and were none the worse for it when carefully studied later by the group. Ten of the passengers investigated reported that their seat belts were fastened snugly or tightly and seven of these suffered contusions, abrasions or lacerations in the belt area. Two reported that their belts were very loose and only one of these passengers had contusions under the belt. Four passengers reported that their belts were "not tight" and two of these had no marks, one had contusions, and one had a ruptured mesentery (the membrane that attaches the intenstine to the back wall of the abdominal cavity), although he had no external marks on his abdomen. Five other passengers could not recall how tight their belts were fastened and of these, two had no marks on the abdomen and two had marks on only one side.

A diagram was made of the location of each seat after the crash and an attempt was made to relate each one back to its original position (not always with certainty) inside the aircraft.

It was not determined whether the seats had been moved outside the aircraft by the rescuers. Each seat was minutely examined to ascertain the nature and extent of structural failure, which was photographed and described. Subsequently, a mockup of the reconstructed seats was made in the relatively intact floor structures of the three fuselage sections.

The pilot's and copilot's seats were found in their proper positions in the wreckage of the cockpit. The investigation indicated that during the initial compressive failure of the forward fuselage, these occupied seats were carried in the flight-deck wreckage in essentially their normal positions. During the ensuing rescue operations the flight deck area was dragged some fifteen to twenty feet to the northwest in an effort to determine if any victims were trapped in this area.

Although the seat belts fared quite well throughout this ordeal (one of them gave the appearance of having been sliced clean through as if by a knife; it was still buckled), the seats themselves proved less crashworthy. Many of them completely disintegrated with breaks at welds, and metal sections cracked, deformed or shattered. Seat-back frames were broken. Legs sheared off. Most were twisted if still intact. Some of the track structure to which the seats were attached was torn out along with the seats themselves. Many of the seats were covered with blood.

The Human Factors Group also made an examination of the wreckage to supplement the one performed by the Structures Group. They reported their findings from the standpoint of environmental damage. Their conclusions stated in part that

> due to structural disintegration from the nose . . . this forward section of the fuselage is considered a non-survivable area. The remainder of the aircraft . . . is considered survivable or partly survivable. The absence of major reduction of volume [crushing] of these occupiable areas, with the exception of the break in the fuselage . . . indicates that injuries may not be directly attributed to lack of structural crash worthiness, but to the injurious effects of impact-induced tiedown failure and environmental hazards produced by tearing of internal structures, cables, components, etcetera. The fuselage floor in the separated center section remained essentially intact, the major damage consisting of seat

failures at rows three and four. Metal trimming used to attach upholstery was ripped loose and blocked operation of emergency exits. The right front emergency exit was in place and operable but blocked by trimming. The left front emergency exit was inoperable due to the handle being broken off. The lock released from the outside but the exit would not operate because of deformation of the hull structure.

The major environmental damage to the aft section . . . consisted of seat failures at rows five through ten. The floor was essentially intact. The emergency exit at Row 5R was jammed by compressed fuselage structure and inoperable. The emergency exit at Row 8R was popped out. The emergency exit at Row 5L popped out at impact and was found west of the main wreckage. The emergency exit at Row 8L was found intact and operable.

There were two sets of double emergency lights which are activated by an impact in excess of one and one-half times the force of gravity. These look similar to the emergency lights mandated by law in restaurants and other places where the public gathers. One set was located on the forward side of the partition at the back of the cabin directed toward the aft emergency exits. These lights were operated by a battery powered lantern next to the stewardess' seat on the left side of the aft bulkhead. The battery was found after the crash in the baggage rack. When inserted in the lantern, all the lights came on, indicating that the impact-operated switch for the emergency lights had been activated. A similar lighting system in the front of the cabin could not be checked due to excessive damage.

The stewardess' fold-down seat, which faced aft against the left rear bulkhead, had not failed but the metal seat pan was deformed. Both hinges on the rear cabin door leading to the anal staircase were fractured; a deep gouge was found in the metal lockplate. Firemen were reported to have ripped this door out, although the failures noted appeared to have been induced by the crash.

The group summarized the crash kinematics with a couple of succinct paragraphs that wasted few words:

Shortly after takeoff from Runway 28 and after attaining an altitude in the order of 50-100 feet, N449A encountered low-altitude turbulence in connection with a storm described as violent. According to passenger descriptions, the airplane, while being buffeted, rolled sharply to the left, then sharply to the right then sharply to the left again—the left wing tip contacting a hard grassy surface of the airport adjacent to the takeoff runway. This initial contact point was approximately 150 feet to the left, or south of Runway 28 and east of the runway's west end. At impact the aircraft was rolling sharply to the left and was in an attitude of at best 45 degrees left wing down with the fuselage estimated to have been nearly horizontal. Progressing across the terrain, the bank continued to increase to the left with the left wing progressively disintegrating inboard toward the No. 1 engine nacelle area.

Approximately 150 feet beyond the point of initial contact, the No. 1 propeller followed by the No. 1 engine, dug propeller marks and a deep gouge from the engine with the aircraft rolled in excess of 90 degrees to the left. Continuing in its roll to the left to a nearly inverted attitude—the nose between level and pointing down twenty degrees in relation to the horizontal—the windshield and overhead portion of the upper left cockpit area contacted the ground, rolling counterclockwise, telescoping the forward fuselage and failing it in compression back to station 212 on the bottom of the forward fuselage; and to approximately station 290 on the upper portion of the forward fuselage. At approximately 210 feet along the crash path, the No. 2 propeller cut slash marks into the ground. The No. 2 engine failed at its mount and separated as the aircraft, now completely inverted, contacted the outboard leading edge of the right wing, as evidenced by compression damage in this area and green wing tip light glass fragments found in the dirt.

There then followed a brief description of the terrain in the impact area and then continued:

Compression damage inflicted in the fuselage at approximately station 505 during the compressive telescoping of the nose section substantially weakened the fuselage in this area. Impact forces sustained during compression of the nose and failing of the aft fuselage were responsible for initial failure of most of the passenger seats.

Following impact of the right wing, in an inverted position —with a counterclockwise rotation—the center fuselage with the inboard left wing section and No. 1 nacelle and essentially the entire right wing with the No. 2 engine nacelle bounced counterclockwise to an upright normal position while the aft fuselage from station 505 broke open on the right and "hinged" on the left side, swinging to the left to a nearly uprighted normal position. The aft fuselage before coming to rest at 90 degrees to the center section fuselage, impacted against the ground with the left horizontal stabilizer and elevator being progressively bent upward. The underside of the rear fuselage from approximately station 838 to station 892 impaced the ground approximately ten feet east of its final resting place. The aft fuselage came to rest, rolled approximately forty-five degrees to the left.

In addition to investigating in depth the aircraft and passengers, this group also reviewed the records of the crew members, noting their medical histories, logged time and flight experience. They did not fail to notice Captain Dennis's sordid flying history with respect to his several failures and infractions which, even in the briefest form, encompassed four pages of the report. First Officer Neff, who had a clean past, rated only a very short paragraph.

The results of these painstaking investigations were brought together at a hearing held on August 20, a month and a half after the accident, when all of the pertinent facts that were uncovered would be made known. But the verdict as to the exact cause of the crash would have to wait an additional nine months until the CAB issued its final judgment.

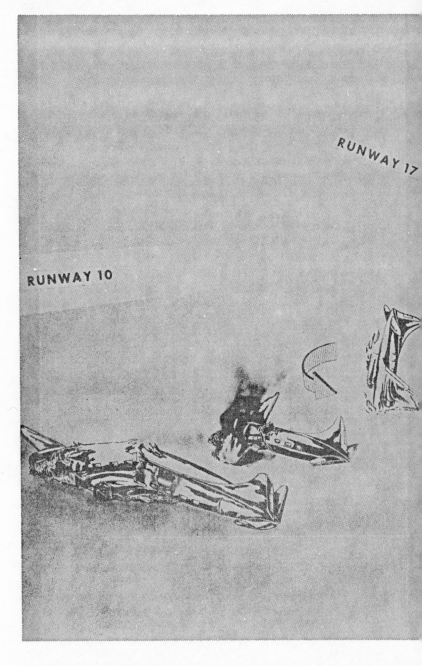

RUNWAY 17

RUNWAY 10

ATTACHMENT #1

CIVIL AERONAUTICS BOARD

CRASH KINEMATICS

MOHAWK AIR LINES MARTIN M-404, N449A

ROCHESTER, NEW YORK, JULY 2, 1963

HUMAN FACTORS GROUP ILLUSTRATION - drawn by AVSER

Part Two
The Anatomy
of
Survival

8

One of the reasons I consider myself lucky is that the crash took place where it did. If you have the misfortune to be burned, it is best that it happen in Rochester, close to Strong Memorial Hospital, which certainly is among the top five medical centers in America. If I hadn't crashed in Rochester, I might be worse off today: I might not even have survived.

The proximity of the hospital to the airport was a fortunate circumstance, although the traffic jam caused by the sightseers and the curious, and the fact that the crash occurred at the height of rush hour, had a delaying effect.

The hospital had no advance warning. The police had not thought to use the police-band radio to call ahead. Fortunately, the warning was triggered by the first victims who arrived—by taxi.

Dr. Lee Davenport had managed to make his way across the muddy airfield on foot to a cab in front of the terminal building while in a state of shock. The cabdriver asked him, "Where to?" Davenport mumbled something about "Mohawk."

The driver, thinking he had said "Mohawk Manor," drove him to the motel in Rochester by that name. Davenport was just disembarking when he sensed that something was not quite right, backed into the taxi, and finally got across the message that he wanted to be taken to the hospital.

The cab pulled into the curved driveway leading to the main entrance of the hospital. Davenport got out of the cab slowly and gazed up at the Palladian portico. For a moment he stared at the pediment above the four columns, where three marble panels were inscribed with the legend, "The University of Rochester—Strong Memorial Hospital—Medicine, Dentistry." Then he glanced down at his feet. A look of surprise washed across his face. He was standing ankle-deep in a puddle of water and wearing no shoes. Bobby Keene* assisted him up the long flight of marble steps, past the main lobby and into the emergency treatment area.

A yellow CAUTION sign warned the vehicles as they turned into the narrow driveway and entered the small emergency courtyard. As each ambulance arrived, flashers bobbing, it wheeled, executed a turn and backed in. When the extent of the tragedy became known, a doctor was put aboard each ambulance as it returned for another macabre cargo. As soon as the doors were opened, medical information was exchanged between the ambulance doctors and those waiting to receive the victims. Mixed in with the staff and drivers were Pinkerton guards, sheriffs' deputies and newspaper reporters. One of them, John Mullins, wrote about carrying in a man who kept moaning, "My shoulder, my arm" as his stretcher was laid on the floor. "I gotta have a shot of something," the victim said. When Mullins put him on a bed as directed, he noticed the man's hair was singed.

Bloody, mud-covered, black, burned, skin hanging, the victims continued to stream in. The hospital driveway now seemed

*who had driven her sister Becky back to the hospital and stayed on to help.

138

alive with ambulances—as many as five at a time, red lights flashing in a psychedelic display, were arriving, each containing two or three more victims. One came in with five patients slung on litters. The drivers pleaded that the injured be removed from the litters quickly so they could return for more victims, and stretchers on four-wheeled dollies were rolled along the pavement away from the Cadillacs. The stench of burned flesh and hair, of charred wet clothing, of antiseptics and medications filled the air in the crowded courtyard. Some patients had oxygen tanks lying between their legs, the plastic tube snaking up to masks that covered their tortured faces.

Inside, Mullins lit a cigarette for one of the survivors from the Human Rights Commission, who was sitting stupefied in the corner, his head cut. "Where am I? What happened? What day is it? What month is it?" he kept asking. "I'm completely disoriented," he finally admitted.

Several survivors lay on their original litters in the hallway, others more seriously hurt occupied the few beds that were available, while some chose to sit or sprawl on the floor and wait for more comfortable quarters. James Kirkpatrick, one of the few coherent patients, looked around the littered hallway and murmured, "It's horrible! What a terrible thing!"

Some sat alone, awaiting medical attention. Others called out to each passing nurse, intern or physician, asking for sedation or a comforting pillow or cushion. A doctor from the psychiatric department, who happened to be passing through the emergency area just as the first casualties came in, was pressed into service starting intravenous fluid setups. It was the first time in five years he had been called upon to perform this medical task, but, like riding a bicycle, once learned the skill is never lost.

All thirty-six of the surviving crash victims came to Strong —one way or another—within one hour after the crash. As they arrived, a triage team under Dr. John Morton sorted them out according to the nature of their injuries in order to enable the greatest number of patients to receive the best possible treatment. Triage is a French word that came into use during World War I, when there were not enough medical supplies to go around at the front. In practice, it meant that what was on hand was used to treat those patients for whom treatment would make the difference between living and dying, while those who could recover without medicine and attention did so and hopeless cases were permitted to die. Dr. Morton, who, I learned much later, had been a classmate of mine at Amherst during the 1940s, had set up priorities in anticipation of such an emergency. Top priority was given the group requiring urgent attention and with a chance of survival; those with acute but not mortal needs were to wait until the first group was under control; those requiring observation for potentially serious injury were to be attended to third; and the fourth group would consist of those with lesser injuries who could safely be transferred to other hospitals.

The emergency division at Strong contained two operating rooms and a plaster room for making casts and setting splints that could be converted into an operating room if necessary. There was, in addition, an entire surgical suite on the fifth floor with ten operating rooms. As luck would have it, none of the operating rooms were in use at the time of the disaster, and so were available for the many operations required. Five were put into immediate use.

The initial triage efforts rapidly disclosed five patients in need of urgent attention. Tracheotomies were performed on four of them. Tracheostomy is a dangerous source of infection and adds greatly to the problem of managing a very sick patient, who is usually the one in need of it. But it is also considered one of the best ways of treating respiratory burns, as was diagnosed in my case. An emergency "trache" was decided on at exactly 5:00 P.M., just ten minutes after the crash, and performed on me in the emergency ward without the usual local anesthesia because the burn trauma had destroyed the nerves and effectively anesthetized the area from the minor pain of the scalpel.

The emergency area was closed for three hours to all non-crash casualties, who were, except for emergencies in pediatrics, diverted to other hospitals. A separate emergency ward for children under fifteen was also set up.

The scene in the emergency division was one of organized upheaval. Virtually every foot of available space in the winding halls was taken up by equipment, oxygen tanks, mobile beds and stretchers. Patients were spread out on the floors, some-

times on mattresses, sometimes not, awaiting beds and treatment while ambulance attendants, like vultures, waited to re-
trieve every available stretcher for return trips to the airport.
Cries of suffering, shouted orders, puzzled queries from the
stunned casualties, all turned the ward into a living nightmare.
A half-blackened foot stuck out from under a sheet; an almost
totally nude man lay just barely covered by his sheet. An I.V.
setup hovered over his prostrate form, the needle held in his
arm by bands of adhesive tape. An intern ran his fingers over
the motionless body in search of broken bones. Two other doctors examined another partially draped form lying next to him
on a sheet-covered, thin pad of sponge rubber laid directly on
tile floor. There weren't enough metal I.V. stands available to
serve every patient so the Strong maintenance department
jury-rigged some from wooden two-by-fours.

The long corridor resembled a rush hour subway filled with
angels. The walls and ceilings were all shiny white; the angels
were packed in the train tightly, all dressed identically in the
same, pure, virginal color. The steel rods that held the various
intravenous-solution bottles rose above the mass of humanity
like TV antennae in a crowded neighborhood. Four medical
personnel now hovered around each of the beds or stretchers
that alternated from side to side down the length of the hall.
The beds were barely visible. Each nurse's cap signified the
nursing school she had graduated from. There was a fascinating
variety.

Although there was an initial shortage of medical personnel
available in the emergency division, that situation was quickly
remedied. Most of the 200 residents and interns on the hospital
staff were mobilized in record time. Everyone pitched in. Fortunately the emergency had come just after the change in shifts
and those few who had already ventured out into the deluge
heard the news over the radio on their way home and returned
to Strong. This lucky timing gave the hospital its full surgical,
laboratory, pharmaceutical, kitchen and other staffs, which normally would have been down to skeleton crews after the shift
change. The kitchen staff, on duty since 7:00 that morning,
remained until midnight to be sure that staff members and
visitors were fed. Doctors, residents, nurses, technicians and
other medical personnel who were due to go off-duty remained

on. In a short time, 70 doctors and 40 nurses were in the emergency room area alone.

Meanwhile, Strong had almost 500 non-crash patients, and to maintain proper continuing care of them during the emergency period, off-duty nurses from the staffs of other hospitals reported to Strong. Student nurses from the school of nursing were stationed as guards. One of them, Patricia Pierce, a short, chunky girl with a pretty, almost-cherubic face, had given birth to her first child just five days before. She was waiting in the maternity section for her husband to arrive with her clothes, so she could dress and go home, when a nurse supervisor walked into her room, handed her a ring of keys to the medicine and supplies, and said, "You are in charge of the maternity floor— an emergency has come up!" All the staff members rushed down to the emergency ward and Pat Pierce was left to her charges wearing only a nightgown and bathrobe—a shock, no doubt, to the patients. Months later, she would become a competent operating-room scrub nurse and would attend me during several of my surgeries.

The disaster was well handled medically. Because of the unusually large and varied staff that was immediately available, a definitive task could be assigned to each member involved, and they were able to carry on efficiently even in the face of such a major catastrophe. For the first few days, each patient had his own nurse round the clock in addition to the regular floor staff, even though the Fourth of July weekend would normally have depleted the supply.

In Dr. Morton's estimation, four people were so severely injured, myself included, that even if they had been admitted at different times as victims of different accidents, their chances of survival would have been only fifty-fifty. Yet they arrived together and the hospital was able to bring such massive resources to bear that all four survived; not one victim to arrive at the hospital died as a result of the accident. In fact, the response to a request by Strong for local physicians was so rapid and overwhelming that overcrowding in the emergency area became a problem, and the hospital's medical director had to ask some to go to other hospitals to see if they could be of any help there. The radiology department made 116 X-rays the first night, ninety in the first two and a half hours alone. The entire

Red Cross chapter mobilized and made contact with ninety blood donors the first night; when the blood supply dwindled nevertheless and the chapter's director became concerned about meeting blood demand for the Fourth of July weekend, the triage group decided that serum albumen would be liberally used as a blood extender, and forty-eight units of it were rushed to Strong, keeping supply ahead of demand throughout the emergency period. Afterward, with the cooperation of Rochester stores, the chapter was able to give clothing to all patients who could leave the hospital and "comfort" kits to all who could use them.

Not everything worked smoothly, of course; a number of weaknesses in the disaster planning were exposed. Patients entered the hospital through doors other than the emergency entrance where the triage base had been set up. They thus escaped initial evaluation and frustrated the operation of the disaster plan, which called for the other doors to be locked. The plan was correct; the execution was imperfect. The disaster committee had set aside a sufficient number of supplies and equipment for just such a major catastrophe as this in a special, locked closet in the emergency area. When the real thing happened—the closet was opened by a security guard—who then departed with the key. A punctilious nurse, attempting to keep everything shipshape, closed the closet door again, snapping its lock automatically, and it took an inordinate amount of time to find the guard with the key again. It was also found that much of the equipment was so poorly labeled, hospital personnel had to squeeze a bundle or minutely examine a printed label to determine a package's contents.

There were other weaknesses. There was no time initially to keep a written record on each patient and it became difficult later to ascertain what had or had not been done. For example, tetanus toxoid boosters were administered to some of the patients before they were removed from the emergency area, but when the first follow-up rounds were made some three hours later, it was impossible to be certain who had received the shots, and so a team was then delegated to give injections to all casualties, with duplication obviously occurring in some cases. And, since the hospital was not aware of the full scope of the disaster right away, the decision was made to postpone blood transfusions whenever possible. If a patient urgently required whole blood, it was decided to administer Rh-positive; it was in better supply, and since all the seriously injured were males it diminished the danger of the blood's producing antibodies to fight off a foreign substance. But one of the men was Rh-negative, and he had received four full pints of Rh-positive before shock from a massive hemorrhage could be brought under control.

Ultimately, the flaws in the planning were corrected and a number of technical and scientific papers were written and presented by staff members in order to make the knowledge and experience gathered by the tragedy available to others.

Later that evening, it was decided that the most efficient care could be given by grouping the casualties together into two areas—one for patients with serious burns and one for everybody else. Several non-crash-related patients were moved to other rooms or other hospitals in order to clear two areas and as soon as these were available the crash victims were quickly moved in.

Soon after this development, one of Strong's leading surgeons, Dr. Earle Barnes Mahoney, was making his rounds when he came upon a patient who was coated black almost from head to toe. Mahoney lifted the sheet to examine the patient and was startled to see the man garbed in nothing but a ludicrous pair of bright red shorts.

"What happened to you?" the doctor asked.

The patient was Mike Addante, a motel owner from Canandaigua, New York. Addante explained that he had been covered with hot tar from a tar tank truck that had caught fire in front of his motel. He had tried to be a good Samaritan and rushed to shut the valve on the burning tar truck. Instead, he inadvertently opened it further and the hot, liquid tar gushed over him, smothering and burning his arms. Since he arrived at the emergency area with the crash victims, it had been assumed he was one of them and he wound up in a room on their reserved floor. We got to know one another in the months that followed and I learned his story. When he was fairly well recovered, he would visit me in my hospital room and sit scratching the scars that covered both arms to assuage their incessant itching. I frequently experienced the same sensation with my own fresh scars and we commiserated with each other. Unbelievably, the truck driver tried to sue him for damages to the truck.

Business associates of some of the victims were among the first to arrive at the hospital. They congregated in the lobby tensely awaiting word from upstairs. My colleague Jerry Marrow was told at the airport by a Mohawk agent that all of the victims had been taken to Strong. Traffic by then was so unbelievably thick that the driver of the cab he was sharing had to go onto the sidewalk and across a field to reach the other side of the airport. When he arrived in the lobby at Strong, Marrow was in such a state of agitation the receptionists behind the counter took him to a room to lie down for a while, until he regained his composure and made his way back to the lobby.

There was as yet nothing to report. Marrow telephoned his wife Jean at their apartment in Manhattan and told her he was staying on in Rochester. She pleaded with him to call his sister and brother-in-law who lived there; he had a heart condition and she was concerned about him. Marrow had used up his last nitroglycerin heart pills in the first hour. He found a doctor wandering by and arranged with him to obtain an additional supply. He knew he was going to need them.

Marrow meandered over to the press section. There he learned that six or seven of the passengers on the plane had been killed. A priest walked by, spoke with one of the receptionists, and said he was going to the emergency area. Marrow chased him down and caught him at the head of the stairs. He took his business card, wrote Kurtz's and my name on it, and pleaded with the priest for any information about us. The priest told him, "I'll do what I can for you," and quickly proceeded downstairs.

At about 8:00 P.M. a dark, good-looking doctor entered the lobby wearing a white tee shirt and apron. He wore steel-rimmed eyeglasses, and his hair, cut almost to the scalp, was compensated for by a mat of dark hair growing all over his arms. Marrow wasn't even sure if the man was a doctor; with his blood-spattered apron he looked more like a butcher. But desperate for information, he approached him and asked about Kurtz and me. The young doctor answered that he didn't know anything about Kurtz, but he had just performed an emergency tracheotomy on me and he didn't think I would live because of lung damage from the fire. "We don't know how badly, but we believe his lungs were burned," the doctor explained, "and if there is enough damage done in there, there's nothing we can do. His condition is very, very critical."

The young doctor's name was Roger Breslau. We not only had the same last name, we were linked by other coincidences as well—we both came from the Bronx originally, both our fathers had been lawyers, we both had one sister.

When Jerry Marrow learned of my near-comatose condition, he asked his sister, who had finally arrived with her husband, to call my wife and break the news to her. He could not bring himself to do it.

Another doctor came up to the press section with the names of those patients who had been retained at Strong and those transferred to two other hospitals. There was a crowd around the doorway as the list was read aloud. Marrow knew he hadn't heard Kurtz's name.

"Doctor," he called out, "may I look at that list? I must have missed a name and I don't know what hospital he's at."

The doctor handed him the list. Kurtz's name was not on it.

Marrow asked, hoping against hope, "If his name is not on it, what does it mean?" But of course he knew in his heart it meant Kurtz was dead. He, his sister and his brother-in-law drove over to the medical examiner's office at the county hospital. Marrow was not even aware at first that this was the morgue; he was a bit rocked to discover that fact. His sister remained in the car while he and her husband went into the office to inquire about Kurtz. He was told that Kurtz was there and a manila envelope was brought out, its contents dumped on the desk. They were Kurtz's personal belongings: his watch, some jewelry, car keys and a badly waterlogged wallet. The examiner turned to Marrow and asked him, "Would you come downstairs with me and identify the body?"

But Marrow was afraid to face the unpleasant task, for fear that his heart could not take it. He had visions of finding Kurtz horribly smashed up and he turned to his brother-in-law, Ben Honigsbaum, who owned a Rochester clothing store, saying, "Ben, would you do that for me?"

The examiner wanted to know, "Does this man know him?" He looked pleadingly at Ben, his face pale. "Ben, you remember him—he has black hair flecked with a little white and gray. If you can honestly identify him, do it for me! If you can't, then I'll go downstairs." His voice trailed off forlornly.

To his great relief, Ben went downstairs and confirmed the identification.

Once again Marrow telephoned his wife. This time he asked her to call Connie Kurtz and break the news to her. The two women had been friends for many years. At first Jean held out and wanted him to do it, but finally she acquiesced.

Before they left the morgue, the medical examiner told Marrow the autopsy showed Kurtz's heart muscle had badly deteriorated and that he might not have lived much longer in any case. We already knew he was suffering from gout.

Marrow and his family returned to Strong. When he entered the lobby he heard himself being paged. There was a telephone call for him. It was Kurtz's widow, Connie.

"Are you absolutely sure?" she asked him in a husky, quiet voice.

"Absolutely," he replied and burst into deep sobs.

Connie Kurtz immediately made arrangements to go to Rochester and do whatever had to be done.

Dr. Breslau later told me that as he bent over me in the emergency area, examining my face, which resembled an overly toasted marshmallow, he asked, "What's your name?"

I was somehow able to whisper, "Breslau."

Thinking that I was reading the plastic name badge pinned to his uniform, he said, "Not my name, your name!"

We repeated this Abbott-and-Costello routine several times before its meaning finally dawned on him. Then, surprised and incredulous, he proceeded to cut a hole through my throat in the recess below my Adam's apple into my trachea so that I had a separate entryway for breathing. A rubber tube was pressed into the hole to maintain the passageway. Unable to cover the opening with my fingers because of my injuries, I could not divert the air back through my vocal chords to talk; I could not even whisper, and for some time after that I had to resort to other means of communication. That opening in my throat, the tracheostomy, became one of the most unpleasant aspects of my hospitalization. It remained in place and plagued me for almost four months. I was, in time, able to plug it so that I could talk, but I grew to fear it and hate it.

Once Dr. Breslau had finished the tracheotomy, the staff evaluated my injuries. Burns were estimated to cover 45 percent of my body—35 percent third-degree burns and 10 percent second degree. The third-degree burns were of my scalp, face, neck and chest.

That was almost the critical limit in those days. Survival was practically precluded with skin loss of over 50 percent, since there would not be enough remaining skin to cover the burned area with grafts, thus protecting the body from loss of body fluids and infection. Third-degree burns are so deep that skin grafts *must* be used; no viable epidermis remains and the skin cannot regenerate itself. But many of my burns could be classified as fourth degree because the underlying fat, muscles, and even bone were damaged by the fire.

Although the burn wound is three-dimensional, the surface area is very important in determining the severity of a burn, and to do so the method most commonly used is the so-called Rule of Nines. Using a chart of the body, the wounds are sketched in. The head and arms are each allotted 9 percent, the anterior and posterior trunk and legs are allotted 18 percent each, and the perineum (the region between the thighs) is figured at 1 percent.

The major damage involved my head, face, neck, upper trunk, left upper extremity (arm, shoulder and hand) and right lower extremity (thigh, knee, leg and foot). I was placed on the danger list and kept there for eight weeks.

My face was almost totally destroyed. My youngest children would be too young to remember what I had originally looked like except, perhaps, from old photographs. Although I had never been happy with my original nose—it was somewhat large with a bump at the bridge—I had grown attached to it in the course of thirty-seven years. In that single explosive flash it was completely burned away, exposing fragments of nasal cartilage and the mucous membrane. My lips had melted and spread from halfway down the chin to just below where the nose had been. The left ear was completely charred and would have to be removed. The right ear had been so badly burned that, though it could be saved, it would take on a cauliflower appearance. Both cheeks sustained third-degree burns. The lids of the left eye were destroyed, the burned lens was left with a permanent gray scar and there was nothing left with which to blink; on the right side the eyelids and eyeball had survived with only slight scorching but it could no longer close completely.

A part of the scalp was burned away. From below the eyebrows across the forehead to the top of the skull, the skin was completely destroyed all the way through to the bone—and beyond at the sinuses above the nose, leaving the moist, pink cavities exposed.

What flesh remained hanging on the fingers of my left hand was black char. The skin was seared off the back of the hand from the wrist to the fingernails, exposing the tendons and the skeleton. The muscles of the left shoulder broke through the redness that remained there of what had been skin. The burn penetrated to the collarbone and shoulder blade. The arm itself was a tortured mass of crimson flesh. So, from the groin to the heel, was the right leg. Two thirds of the burns here were third degree. They were deepest at the thigh, heel and knee, and at the side of the right knee the peroneal nerve, which compares to the funnybone in the elbow and which caused Joe Namath the worst pain he had ever experienced when he damaged it in 1971, was destroyed. The nerve is responsible for bringing the toes and foot into the air when walking, and losing it results in a peroneal palsy called drop foot. Two tendons in my heel were also burned through.

While I was still in the emergency area, intravenous doses of antibiotics were begun. So was fluid flow management: intake and output of fluids were monitored to detect loss of water, colloids, electrolytes, and red blood cells; a Foley catheter was inserted to obtain urine samples which were weighed and analyzed; blood samples were taken and tested for traces of acidosis. As soon as the flow was started between the two bottles of glucose and saline solution towering over my bed on a T-shaped rod and the needles taped to my inner forearm, I was rolled through a maze of hallways and swinging fire doors to the elevator, where the medical crew and their macerated cargo were whisked to the fifth floor and through another set of swinging doors into the surgical suite. There, a team was waiting and my gurney was turned over to the people in hospital green (white has long since been discarded as the operating-room color because it reflects too much light). They hustled me along a corridor into surgery. It was now 9:00 P.M., according to the large clock on the wall.

The proper fluid replacement in my blood had not yet been completed, and so I lay there for almost three quarters of an hour, the brilliant light beating down on my unfeeling face, tying up the operating room, before they could anesthetize me. Fortunately, there was no other demand for the room at the time, so no harm was done.

It has been found that the patient's speed in healing is in direct proportion to his desire to recover and his faith in the surgeon. This has been labeled the "acceptance concept." Although I had no inkling of it at the time, I was in the best possible hands.

The young resident in plastic surgery who was in charge of my fluid management, Dr. Elmer Theodore "Ted" Mitchell, Jr., had served at Brooke Army Hospital, the leading burn research unit in the world and the place where the formula for fluid therapy was developed. The surgeon in charge, who signed the authorization for my immediate surgeries in the absence of any of my kin, was Dr. Earle Barnes Mahoney, who had been associated with Strong since the early 1930s. Two eye specialists were in consultation for the initial procedures—Dr. Albert Snell and Dr. Donald Zehl. Dr. Zehl would continue to care for my eyes. Although he was still only in his early thirties, he had established a major reputation.

The senior surgeon assigned to me, a man four months my junior, was the most unlikely candidate you would pick out of a crowd. He was small and very slight of build, with a thin shock of straight, straw-colored hair neatly combed to one side. The thin, metal-framed glasses out of a bygone era that he wore gave his pale face a studious look. He would keep his lips pursed tightly together and his eyes focused studiously, grasping every detail. He almost never smiled, maybe to convey a maturity that was all but destroyed by his boyish look; but Dr. Lester Cramer came with impressive credentials. He had earned a rare doctorate in medical dentistry from Tufts University and his M.D. from the Columbia Medical School; he had already served two years in residence at Strong in one of the most difficult of all specialties, surgery of the hand.

Cramer worked directly under Dr. Robert McCormack, an equally short but huskier man with a pleasant and enthusiastic personality, who was one of the world's leading hand surgeons. Both men were active members and officers of the learned societies of their profession, both were recipients of countless honors and awards, both were lecturers and consultants all over the United States and abroad. As a result, Strong had become a mecca for plastic surgeons from all over the world, and I eventually became one of the star exhibits for these out-of-town dignitaries. They would be taken into my hospital room by the staff to demonstrate, with understandable pride, what the maestro had accomplished, interrupting my monotonous isolation and doing me a lot of good.

The day of the plane crash found Dr. McCormack out of town and Dr. Cramer nominally in charge, although McCormack kept in touch by telephone. Dr. Cramer advised Dr. Mitchell to overtreat me with the fluids, then cut back and make adjustments as I responded. Fluids were fed intravenously for almost the entire next four days. I was never aware of the catheter that had been inserted, even though it must have been in place several weeks. Massive infusions of antibiotics and whole blood were begun, and both the blood and urine samples were collected every hour to be tested thoroughly in the laboratory. Oxygen was fed to me through the tracheostomy and morphine was given for the pain.

The brilliantly lit, very cold operating room hummed with activity as preparations were made. Trays of equipment, covered in green towels or wrapped in white muslin, were placed on auxiliary tables. Figures in misshapen, almost silly looking green skullcaps that concealed their hair, and masks that revealed only their eyes, huddled and mumbled to one another their diagnoses and prognoses for the wounded body that lay before them. Muffled instructions to a nurse or resident calling for some extra instrument or adjustment, were being issued. Everything was smooth and efficient. All bases were touched; nothing was left to chance. They were professionals and they exuded the confidence of professionals. They knew what had to be done. Dr. Cramer's green eyes fixed on the black flesh that had been a face, waiting to begin another miracle of plastic surgery that would take a place in the annals of modern medicine.

Dr. Mitchell's team finally brought the I.V. management under control, and maintained the life-saving infusions while anesthesia was administered through the tracheostomy opening. Then the surgeons explored my raw body from head to toe, almost all of which had suffered some kind of damage.

Their examination revealed that the thinning hair and skin cover over the scalp had been destroyed. The burn had penetrated the delicate, flat, helmetlike membrane that covers the skull beneath the scalp, which connects the front and rear muscles of the head. The outer bone table of the skull itself was severely damaged and there were two openings the size of a quarter and a dime, respectively, into the front sinuses. The nose itself had completely burned away, giving my face the look of a skeleton. The remainder—cheeks, lips, chin—had been scorched rather badly.

The burns over the left shoulder involved the muscle and the joint itself. The burns to the left hand were totally third degree. The thumb and index finger were burned beyond the point of recovery. There was a total loss of skin and tendons on the back of the hand, and the bones in the three remaining fingers were charred. The deep red gashes perforating the black char of the hand could not be sutured shut because of the poor quality of the skin that surrounded them. The burns on the right leg extended into the knee joint.

The trunk was the least burned portion. Several areas on the lower chest and abdomen had sustained second- and third-degree burns, but my back and buttocks were hardly touched and my genitals, fortunately, not at all.

It was decided that since survival was uncertain, and even doubtful at this stage, little should be done until my vital signs were stable. The only area that required immediate attention was the left eye where all of both lids had been burned off, exposing the scarred eyeball. Emergency surgery was required at once or it would be lost.

My gold wedding band was removed from the shards of my fourth finger, left hand. The anesthesia took effect quickly and the teams began to debride as much loose and damaged flesh clinging to each burn site by cutting, picking or rubbing it away and to stitch any lacerations in the viable tissue. The extremities were bandaged in bulky dressings, but the main body areas were left exposed to the air. Then surgery began.

Two areas were involved—the left eye itself and a small square of unburned left thigh that was to be the donor of needed skin. The thigh was neatly shaved with a safety razor. Both areas were sterilized with a rough rub of germicidal solution and then draped with green sheets and towels, leaving the eye and the small area of the thigh the only parts of the body exposed. The green drapes were held together with scissorlike clamps.

One team performed a so-called split-thickness excision of the thigh skin, large enough to cover the entire eye. In a split-thickness excision the lowest of the skin layers is left intact so new surface skin can regenerate. The surgery was performed using a special knife called a dermatome that can be set to slice off a precise thickness of skin. In the meantime, Dr. Cramer was busy undercutting the skin around the eye, leaving the inner edges intact. These skin flaps were laid over the globe of the eye and the conjunctival surface was delicately stretched to cover the eyeball. Then the thin layer of thigh skin was laid over the eye wound—but not sutured into place. Instead, a dressing was spread over it, which would hold it in place until it grew together with the surrounding facial tissue. Another piece of the split-thickness thigh skin was placed in front of the burned-away left ear. The entire head was then swathed in massive layers of flexible gauze bandages with not even openings for the mouth or nose, since breathing could be maintained via the tracheostomy.

The entire operation took an hour and a half.

With the last stitch in place and my head, left arm and right leg completely wrapped in bandages, making me look every bit a mummy, the tension abated in the operating amphitheater, and the snap of rubber gloves being peeled off could be heard above sotto-voce discussions of treatment orders and prognoses. Dr. Cramer took time to neatly pen an entry on the bottom of my medical chart that read: "Prognosis: doubtful for survival because of the high likelihood of respiratory burns." He listed my condition as poor.

The recovery room off the anesthesiology corridor was large enough to handle eight gurneys, which could be isolated from each other by surgical green curtains. But the curtains were rarely used since the patients were usually unconscious and the staff could keep watch over them more easily if they were open, as they were now. Here, "Robbie" Warfield was the overseer. This strongly built, forty-six-year-old black woman had a heart of gold. She was reputed to be related to the famous Negro opera star William Warfield. Her husband died shortly after the elder Warfield's world tour of "Porgy and Bess" in 1960, leaving her with five children and twenty-two grandchildren. Not long after the Mohawk crash, one of her children died. She remarried a minister and he too died. Yet in spite of her own personal tragedies she was able to render each of the suffering patients who passed through her domain not only efficient service but as loving a tenderness as though each was her blood kin. Most of her charges were never in any condition to be aware of this tenderness of hers, but I came to know her and love her rare spirit.

It was about midnight and the hospital was very quiet when I was wheeled from recovery to the elevators that lowered me to the B wing of the second floor with the other badly burned patients from the plane crash. Dr. Cramer, meanwhile, whose day had begun at 6:30 that morning and his surgeries only an hour later, was going ice skating for an hour with his wife at a rink in the Rochester Institute of Technology. Skating had become his escape-all from the pressures of his profession—that and the weekly poker game with his cronies—and it engaged his entire family. His youngest son, Scott, has since placed second in the Junior Men's National Figure Skating Championship. The doctor even wore a tiepin of a golden ice skate (which he sometimes varied with one of a golden hand, symbolizing his medical specialty). After an hour of relaxing on the ice, Cramer returned to Strong to check on patients, working until about 2:30 in the morning.

Ted Mitchell, though, remained on duty all night, monitoring the blood transfusions and checking my blood and urine samples. I was beginning to develop complications.

One danger was the onset of the dreaded acidosis—increasing acidity of the blood stemming from loss of bicarbonate. The hydrogen-ion concentration that is taken in a blood test, or pH, measures acidity, and a patient whose pH drops below 7 on a scale of 14 is very close to death. The acidosis will weaken the pumping of the heart and cause constriction of the blood vessels. That in turn tends to send too much blood into the lungs and lead to pneumonia or, if too much blood is fed intravenously before correction of the acidosis, the swelling of lung tissue called "pulmonary edema." Yet another threat was hemoglobinemia, the presence of hemoglobin in my blood plasma.

With Dr. Cramer's approval, Mitchell began infusions of an experimental drug that Cramer and another surgeon at Strong were testing under a research contract to Abbott Laboratories of Chicago. The drug had the impressive title of tris- (hydroxymethyl) amine buffer and was to be marketed under the name of Telatrol. It was being tested for use as a supplement to standard intravenous (I.V.) therapy in maintaining kidney function and controlling shock. Telatrol is still not used very much for this but is confined mainly to open-heart surgery and deep-shock cases. But in 1963 the purpose was to gain as much clinical experience with it as possible.

I also began to develop serious lung problems, probably from smoke inhalation, which were controlled by repeated suctioning of accumulated mucus through my tracheostomy. A length of narrow metal tubing with a curved end, connected to a small vacuum pump and trap by a length of flexible hose, was inserted into my throat. The gurgling and crackling noises caused by the suction of the mucus were not the cause of any pain or even discomfort to me, but they were to become a constant reminder of the disconcerting existence of a less-than-normal opening in my body. Swallowing was a little difficult because a repulsive metal-and-plastic insert was pressed into the opening to keep it from resealing. I would have preferred to let the phlegm accumulate rather than have it suctioned out. I often pleaded with my nurses to let it be.

During the first night, a doctor noted that the "chest sounds were fairly clean."

I am told that by the time I was wheeled out of the recovery room, I was fully conscious and responding to questions. But I have absolutely no recollection of that. All I remember is a recurring nightmare of being tortured by the Nazis. These were my memories—my only memories. Yet, to all who came into contact with me, I appeared to be awake and lucid. Loss of memory after a trauma is reported to be quite a common occurrence.

I don't remember what they looked like in my nightmare. I don't remember ever hearing their voices. I don't remember if they knew that I was Jewish and were torturing me for that. I don't know where I was being held or how they were torturing me, just that they were inflicting pain, that it was all physical pain, that my mind was a whirl of just pain. I don't even remember what they wanted to know.

But I know I didn't tell. I wouldn't talk. It was a kind of game—"Tell us." "No, I won't." And when I refused to divulge the secrets the torture, however it was being administered, was renewed.

I arrived on the B-2 wing with my escort, my bandage-swathed head looking massive and grotesque, the trache tube in my throat set off against the soft white gauze. One of the nurses attending me said, "This one's out of it."

Her name was Annette Hancoski. I didn't get to know her that first night, but she was very quiet and rarely smiled in those days anyway. Though she looked like a girl of twelve she was in her late twenties, married, the mother of a beautiful son, and in the process of getting a divorce. We met again on Thanksgiving Day of 1964 when I returned to Rochester for further surgery, a period that was the most critical four months of my surgical recovery. She "specialed" me every day, and we became quite close. Later she remarried and moved to Oklahoma.

The other nurse was Linda Hart. A sharp contrast to Annette, she was effervescent, outgoing and very empathetic. She disapproved of talking within earshot of a patient with the assumption that he could not understand what you were saying. "I always felt deep down," she told me years later, "that the patient may be hearing and not responding."

Linda bent over the lump of gauze that represented my head and said gently, "Mr. Breslau, can you hear me?"

The white, faceless lump nodded: yes.

Linda then explained that I had been in a plane accident, that I was in Rochester and that I had a big bandage on my head and arm—she hadn't seen the leg yet—but that I was all right. Then she asked me, "Are you a Catholic?"

With the white mass of my bandaged hand (my good right arm, which I would normally have used, was restricted by the I.V. connections) I traced the six-pointed Star of David, two overlapping triangles, on my chest.

Linda understood. She, too, was Jewish, and she asked, "Would you like me to call a rabbi?"

I slowly shook my head: no.

Linda then generously asked if I would like her to leave the Star of David she wore on a chain around her neck, and I again nodded no.

When I was finally settled into my new room, dressing changes of the burns on my legs and chest, a standard treatment for burns, was begun. This is the worst aspect of burn therapy and probably the most agonizing pain that can be experienced. It must have been what caused my Nazi nightmares. By then it was about 1:00 in the morning.

I indicated with my hand that I wanted to write, and Linda placed a pencil in my restricted but undamaged right hand. She held a pad below it.

Using only my fingers, I wrote in an illegible scrawl, "Am I dying?"

Hoping to dissuade me from thinking of death, Linda pretended that she could not read my writing.

I tried again and this time wrote, "Am I going?" She assured me I was not.

Then I wrote, "Arm sleeping," for it felt completely dead, as though it were not even there.

I can't remember being scared. All I wanted to do was the correct thing—to get a message to my family, the last words, just to be fastidious, to leave everything orderly. I wanted them to know my last thoughts were of them and to leave some loving message for them to hang onto.

Then I brought my hand to my mouth, to indicate that I was thirsty and desired something to drink. But Linda could not decipher my charade and so did nothing about it.

At 8:30 P.M. two blood donors walked into the emergency ward, while a young couple, embracing their new baby, walked out into the cool, clear evening.

As the night wore on, patients were transferred from the emergency area to rooms upstairs. I and some of the others were taken directly to the operating rooms; others were taken to the X-ray division. By 9:30 the emergency section was clear of plane crash victims. Only the blood donors were still there, standing by in case they should be needed. By 10:00 even the operating rooms were empty.

Gradually, throughout the hospital, the pressure subsided. Everything was quiet.

As that first day passed into night and regenerated again into morning, with the anesthesia still coursing through my body, I lapsed in and out of consciousness. I didn't notice the gray dawn expand into daylight in my hospital room.

9

As the story of the crash spread across the nation via the wire services, it was disseminated by all the media—radio, television, newspapers—in special bulletins and on front pages. Grace heard a bulletin about it on the kitchen radio and her heart froze. I hadn't called all day, but she knew I'd be coming home on an evening flight. So she had a feeling.

She picked up the phone and called our friend and neighbor, Joan Shifter, and said, "I know you'll think I'm crazy but I have a feeling that Alan was on the plane that just crashed in Rochester." Joan tried to assure her that her worries were groundless and then hung up, thinking the matter had been resolved.

But Grace called right back and repeated the same conversation word for word. Then she telephoned the nearest Mohawk Airlines office, which was in Philadelphia. They referred her to company headquarters in Utica. Reaching someone there, she was told that there was no record of anyone with my name on board the plane. In a daze, Grace hung up. Soon after that the call she had been dreading came in. It was from Jerry Marrow's sister. She told Grace that I was in the plane crash, that I was very badly hurt and that they were not sure I would live.

Grace immediately swung into action, notifying several of our friends, and a mobilization was underway. Saul Chavkin, a man with a clever sense of humor, came to the house immediately with his wife Lil, and told Grace to throw some things into a bag. He picked her up in twenty minutes and drove her to Rochester, while Lil stayed with the children; Grace just told them that their father had been in an accident.

They drove all night, stopping only once, for coffee at a diner in Syracuse. Saul, using the pretext that he was going to the restroom, surreptitiously telephoned the hospital to ascertain that I was still among the living. He wanted to prepare Grace for the bad news. But I was holding onto life with all my power. Saul returned to the table, relieved to be the bearer of good news instead.

They pressed on. Saul never ceased his patter of clever jokes and army reminiscences in a futile attempt to keep Grace's mind off things. The trip took nine hours. It was still dark when they turned off the New York State Thruway, paying their toll and getting directions to Strong.

On Elmwood Avenue they noticed a large building looming in isolated grandeur on an extensive, flat lawn. Taking this to be the hospital, they headed up the driveway. It was a hospital, but it was too dark for them to notice that it was not Strong —it was a state hospital for the insane. Rushing up the steps to the front door, Saul gave it a jerk only to find it tightly locked. They walked a few steps to a basement window where a lone light pierced the gloom. Inside, they could see a white-capped nurse sitting at a desk and the two of them rapped excitedly on the windowpane. The nurse jumped in terror.

The figure in white opened the window. Saul and Grace explained why they were there and the nurse told them how to get to the correct hospital, only a couple of blocks away. They got back in the car, easily found their way to Strong, parked and, though exhausted by now, raced into the quiet hospital lobby.

Again they explained their presence, and this time they were directed to an elevator that took them to the dimly-lit corridor on B-2 where the more serious victims were. It was almost deserted here too, except for a pair of nurses at their station and an intern filling in a patient's chart on a clipboard. Grace told the nurses who they were and they were asked to wait while one of them fetched Dr. Mitchell.

Mitchell was tense as he stepped out into the hallway and met them. He told Grace that he was very pessimistic. I was critical and could go either way. The extent of damage to the lungs was not known and they wouldn't know anything definitive for a while. In a low voice he quickly summed up my condition. My face was burned, he said, and I would be disfigured. He didn't give the extent of my injuries.

Grace asked, "Can I see him?"

"Of course," Mitchell replied, and, with him on one side and an intern on the other holding Grace's arms for fear she would faint, took her through the door into my room. Saul followed.

But Grace is no fainter. She was very strong and prided herself on being that way. She shook herself free and walked up to the bed. In her most cheerful voice she said, "Hi, darling."

I lay stretched out on the bed, fully exposed. All the dressings had been removed to allow two young doctors to perform whatever debriding they could, and also to allow air to dry the exposed tissues. The whole center of the face, particularly the eyes and forehead, was a gaping black mass. The skull showed through, dry and blackened. What remained of the nose closely resembled pictures of undraped Egyptian mummies, the bridge high and blackened, the nose gone. The remaining edges of the left ear were black. The solid skin graft over the left eye removed the last semblance of features from that side of the face.

The left arm was blackened all the way from the protruding shoulder muscles to the skeletonized hand, totally devoid of any skin covering. The finger bones looked like overcooked frankfurters. They were swollen to twice their normal size; the index finger and thumb looked gangrenous and had fused together.

The skin had been almost completely stripped off the right leg from the groin to the pad of the foot, leaving mottled areas of black, brown and white behind. The rest of the body sported deep gouges as though made by a blowtorch.

There was a soft thud behind Grace. Saul had passed out and hit the floor. He was revived with spirits of ammonia, escorted to the visitors' room and told to lie down on a couch. He did, for a while, and when he felt sufficiently recovered, poor Saul said his good-byes, got in his car again and started on the long trip home.

Before she had left for Rochester, Grace had notified my only sister, Helen, and my brother-in-law, Milton Myer. They, in turn, notified Grace's father, and the three of them started out from Long Island, Helen doing most of the driving while Milton napped after a long day of work and my father-in-law Irving Tauscher tried not to let his worry show as they sped along the nearly empty Thruway. Their presence later in the morning helped to steady Grace even further. She filled them in with the facts as she knew them and they made their way as cheerfully as they could into my room.

I apparently had periods of consciousness. At one point I issued instructions to my brother-in-law: "Milt, make sure they take pictures!" I vaguely remember doing that. I was thinking already of the legal ramifications. An attorney friend of ours had told us about a course he took as part of his continuing education that taught him how to take medical pictures for better legal presentation. I knew there would have to be a suit, and I wanted to make sure they photographed me at my worst. I didn't know then that photographs would hardly be needed to show the extent of my injuries. My appearance would speak for itself very eloquently.

In order to feel that he was doing something worthwhile, my father-in-law had Milton and Helen drive him out to the crash site to look for my gold Omega wristwatch that had not been among the victims' items already collected. Milton was very familiar with it; he had worn the exact same model and we used to jokingly compare time with each other. Even though they didn't find it, they felt a little less helpless trying.

On the morning of July 3 my mother heard the news of the crash on the radio. The newscaster gave the names of the dead and my mother recognized the name of Jerry Kurtz. She had no inkling I was on the trip with him. With this bit of gossip, she called long distance to let Grace know what had happened. But it wasn't Grace who answered; it was our friend and neighbor Loretta Elkin, who was baby-sitting. Loretta told my mother to call my sister for information, which she hurriedly proceeded to do. But my sister and brother-in-law were long since gone. My nephew Don answered the telephone and merely said his mother was out. He did not pass on the bad news. My mother's heart by now was in a knot and she knew something had to be wrong. She called Mohawk in New York City and they referred her to Utica, which repeated its erroneous listing of no one with my name being on the flight. It took my mother two days to learn that I had in fact been a passenger, and how badly injured I was. She didn't find out, I guess, because everyone wanted to spare her the pain until my condition took some definite direction. She could not bring herself to view the damage done to her only son and she could not find the courage to visit me the entire time I was in the hospital.

One of our closest friends, Dr. Melvin Krant, was told of the accident and immediately headed for Rochester from Brookline, Massachusetts, where he and his wife Mimi lived. Mel was the head then of the department of oncology—the study of tumors—at Lemuel Shattuck Hospital in Boston, where most of the patients were terminal cancer cases, a situation which led him into thanatology, a specialized field of medicine dealing with death and dying.

Mel's arrival at Strong bolstered the members of my family. He was introduced to Dr. Cramer and got the complete diagnostic rundown from him.

Dr. Cramer was always very pessimistic, and the complete opposite of Dr. McCormack, who would always smile and say, "Don't worry! He's going to be fine." But Dr. McCormack was not there yet, and Cramer said I was probably not going to survive. Mel then took Grace to an isolated room and just as solemnly laid it on the line to her: "Grace, you have to steel yourself! Alan is not going to make it—you have to accept that!"

But Grace would not accept it. She had faith that I was

going to survive—not a religious faith—it simply never occurred to her that I wouldn't.

We never discussed what I looked like. It never really came up. When we talked, it was about external problems, about other people and our children. She never intimated she would leave me and I never thought that she would. Without talking about it, we didn't worry about it.

She may have had problems at first but I don't think so. If she cried, she cried in private, not in front of me. She became more involved with helping me and other patients and other visitors to make it easy for them.

On the morning of July 3, a new private-duty nurse was assigned to my case. She was a large woman, with short, black hair and a rather round face. She had received her training at Columbia University, Kings County Hospital in Brooklyn and the University of Rochester. Her name was Florence Greenhouse Jacoby.

Florence was a very outspoken person and a crackerjack nurse. She would frequently advise the doctors as to the best treatment to employ, or corrected what they were doing—an unheard-of procedure in a hospital. She did this, not too sotto voce, particularly with the young interns. They sometimes resented this, and didn't always take it good-naturedly. The trouble was that Florence was usually right.

She went to work on me immediately. Dressings had to be changed continuously as they became putrified with the oozings from my burnt body. The tracheal secretions had to be suctioned. Intravenous solutions had to be monitored and adjusted. Blood and urine samples had to be taken and sent to the laboratory for analysis. Fresh, sterile bedding had to be put on without disturbing me. A metal frame was erected to prevent the sheets from coming into contact with my wounded flesh. The work was constant, and Florence went about it in her customary high spirits and booming voice. In her free moments she raided the supply closets throughout the hospital, requisitioning most of the sterile bedding and bulk bandages which she then stuffed into the dresser drawers in my room. From then on, when any other nurse had need of those supplies, they sooner or later found their way to Florence, who doled them out very grudgingly.

During this entire shift, Florence never learned my real name because, as a carry-over from the airline's flight manifest, it had been listed erroneously. That night, she went home and made dinner for her husband, Marvin, and their three sons. After a quiet evening's relaxation, they went to bed. Florence lay reading the evening paper while Marvin began to doze off. He was shocked awake when Florence bellowed in that inimitable voice of hers, "Maar-vin, do you know who my patient is? It's Alan Breslau from Pennsylvania!"

Instantly awake, Marvin sat up and said disbelievingly, "Nooooo."

Several years before, when I was the technical director for a firm that manufactured machinery used to produce polyurethane foams, Marvin Jacoby had been one of our customers. At the time, he was a manufacturer of rubber latex pillows and wanted to switch to the more desirable polyurethane foam. Florence, doing only occasional special-duty nursing, was acting as his office manager. He bought a large, complex machine from our company and came down to our Philadelphia plant for a week to learn how to operate it. While he was working alone with the machine, one of the high-pressure steel lines broke loose from its fitting and Marvin was squirted in both eyes with a caustic chemical capable of inflicting severe tissue burns.

I was the first to encounter him. I flushed his eyes at once with water, and rushed him to the emergency room of a nearby hospital. We waited for what seemed like forever without receiving any attention because of the backlog of patients. So I looked up the name of an opthamologist in the telephone book, called him and explained our problem. He told us to meet him right away at Temple University Medical Center, and we raced there in my car, running every red light, hoping to attract a police escort. Of course, not one policeman was in sight.

When we finally got to the hospital Marvin was examined and treated quickly; the prognosis was good. But he was temporarily blinded and would remain so for several days. I drove him to his motel, fed him his supper the way one feeds a small child and helped him to bed. I picked him up every morning, fed him his meals and took care of him until he was in condition to make it on his own power back to Rochester. Later, I met Florence and the family when I went up to help with the machine we had installed.

It seemed more than coincidence that Florence now had a turnabout opportunity to minister to me as I had ministered to Marvin. Her constant, impeccable care lasted without letup for four months.

My night nurse was a young, attractive black girl. She had a warm, bright smile and a nice manner and I felt very comfortable in her care; she anticipated my every need and never let me sink into the abyss of my injuries. But she appeared to be having problems at home with her mother and boyfriend and one day she took off for parts unknown. No one I knew heard of her after that.

The third shift, from 7:00 in the morning to 3:00 in the afternoon, was handled by an attractive girl in her early twenties. Her sparkling personality tied all the interns, residents and staff around her little finger, but that did not prevent Joan Burak from being a very good nurse.

Early in the morning I could recognize the squeak of her rubber-soled shoes as she came bounding into the room with a smile and a lilt of "Good morning, Sunshine" while she unpinned her nurse's cap (against regulations), shook out her black pageboy and daubed at it lightly before coming over to my bed for my morning ablutions. Since I was totally immobile, I was forced for many weeks to use the bedpan to relieve myself and just positioning myself was difficult and painful. I made a practice, I can recall, of holding off till after Joan's shift was over. She was young and attractive, and I felt we both might be embarrassed by it. Florence, though, was more of a mother-figure to me, although our ages could not have been far apart; I didn't mind her assistance.

A massive burn has been called the most severe injury a human being can suffer. It throws almost every system of the body out of kilter. Nurses and doctors hate the odor of the burn room. They find burn-scarred bodies nauseating to look at. One nurse admitted, "I have to grit my teeth every time I enter a burn patient's room." But I experienced none of that.

The worst thing I had to face, initially, was the dressing changes. They took place with great frequency and the pain was excruciating. Usually they are performed under anesthesia.

But because of anesthesia's peripheral risks and the fact that I would be exposed to much of it during my projected surgeries, it was decided to reduce its use to a minimum and most dressing changes were performed without any anesthesia at all.

The second day after the crash, the fifth floor of the C wing was set aside for all of the burn patients, because it was adjacent to the surgical suite. One of the patient rooms was set aside for dressing changes. My bed was wheeled in there, and a large staff was generally in attendance to watch—Dr. Mitchell, other residents, interns, nurses, students, on occasion even Dr. Cramer. I was an interesting case study because of the extent and nature of the burns I had suffered.

The memories of the horror are quite vivid. As the soiled bandages were slowly peeled from my charcoaled flesh, taking dead skin and tissue along with them, I could hear myself screaming as though my mind was separate from my body. The constant removal of the dressings was the recommended burn treatment even though the exposure of the nerves when taking away the skin sears and smarts and resembles the flaying of nonbelievers' flesh during the Spanish Inquisition. But every precaution was taken to minimize the tearing of my nerve endings. Gauze pads dipped in hydrogen peroxide or saline solution were squeezed over those areas of bandage that refused to release their hold on the scabrous skin underneath. Sometimes I was lucky. If there was sufficient notice given as to when the dressing change was to take place, this softening process was begun in my room before I was brought to the dressing-change room, and the hardened scabs had more of a chance to soften before the flaying began.

To take my mind off the pain I tried at first to concentrate on what seemed to be the clever, gay repartee between Dr. Mitchell and either Joan or Florence, depending on who was on duty at the time. There was a lot of joking going on around me, including an incredible flow of sexual innuendo between the doctors and the nurses. This was not only an attempt to cheer me up, but also to cheer themselves up. They had a big problem, too. They had to look at me. Fortunately, they were able to divorce themselves emotionally from the task at hand, an important trait for both them and their patient.

I tried to take my mind off the pain, and discovered, as if by a miracle, I could actually do it.

On a tall vertical rod at the foot of my bed was taped a little Danish troll doll, a rubber one with bright eyes, a pointed nose and a bright orange Afro that would draw the envy of any hippie. It had been sent to me for luck by my ten-year-old niece, Jane. The troll looked like Leopold Stokowski. While I lay in my bed waiting for the next dressing change, I came up with an inexplicable name for this doll—Stokowski Seven. Then I made it my personal god, and began to worship it. And the next time I was wheeled next door for more of the Spanish Inquisition, I prayed to little Stokowski Seven as hard as I could. Not a scream made it past my lips. I had hypnotized myself. After the hypnosis was successful, I was jubilant.

When the next Inquisition was over Dr. Mitchell bent over me and beamed, "We did it without hurting you this time, didn't we?"

I said, "No. It hurt just as much, but *I didn't feel it!*" It was true, and I discussed my marvelous feat with anyone who would listen.

I had to use self-hypnosis because the pain was so severe; I had no alternative. Nobody taught it to me. I didn't have time to learn it. The technique is used in some burn cases, and I asked about it. But the man who had taught it at Strong was not there anymore. They had to do the treatments and I had to suffer the pain. There was no way of putting that off, so I had to suffer or help myself.

Self-hypnosis is a kind of concentration. You don't count. You don't fall unconscious. You just divide your mind mentally and separate the pain from your mind. I needed a focal point to get away from the pain, to start helping me separate my mind from it. That was my Stokowski Seven.

Because the pain is so severe you must divorce the sensitive nervous system from the rest of your body. You screen out every thought; you have to force that separation. You know the pain is there, but you just don't feel it.

The use of hypnosis with burn patients is similar to its use in childbirth. The principal objective is to block sensory perception by diversion. Today, the approach has taken on an official name—biofeedback research—and a rash of new proponents and practitioners. It is surrounded by fad and fancy, spiced with a touch of the occult and garnished here and there with more than a trace of charlatanism. But it still follows the ancient concept: mental control of the physical world. And it works.

Dr. Breslau had also remained on duty all during the first night of the crash. By the morning of July 3 a note of optimism was in his prognosis: "Seems to be doing better than predicted when admitted. . . . He is rational, very cooperative and communicates well by hand signals. Major complaint is severe thirst and rotten taste in mouth."

Dr. Breslau cut a window in my head dressing to expose my lips so they could take in liquids. A drinking straw was too painful, so I suggested we try a piece of soft rubber tubing, which worked well enough but was still somewhat painful, especially to my tongue, which must have been burned, although this was never officially acknowledged. Coke was soothing to my dry palate as Florence squeezed it into my mouth from gauze sponges, but I preferred crushing little bits of chilled watermelon between my teeth.

Later that morning, when Florence returned from one of her foraging expeditions, she found me sitting on the edge of the bed with my bandaged feet dangling and my arms outstretched. All wrapped up, I was doing exercises! I vaguely remember doing that, too. Somewhere I had learned that exercise would prevent crippling skin contractions from setting in, would prevent bed sores and keep my blood from thickening. Being impressionable, compulsive and eager to survive, I just went right at it. Florence could not believe her eyes, but she just suggested that I not overdo it.

July 4 was, of course, a holiday, but business went on as usual in the hospital. My eyes were examined. Dr. Zehl recorded on my chart that "the cornea and globe [of my left eye] appeared grossly negative."

The next day a rubber plug was pressed into the tracheotomy tube in my throat, sealing it off. This enabled me to speak normally and breathe through my nasal passages. It was a great relief, except when the stopper was on occasion inserted while the tube was still moist and it popped out again. I was instructed to do deep-breathing exercises and to blow through a device with the impressive name of a Dale-Schwartz tube. I examined it. It turned out to be a plain, hollow tube, about three feet long and an inch or so in diameter. But there was nothing inside of it. It was just a tube. When I saw what it was, I said, "You must be kidding," and I refused. I thought they were putting me on. I was also regularly forced to take the antacid Maalox, which I detested. It was prescribed to prevent ulcers due to hyperacidity, a not uncommon occurrence among burn patients.

Finally I was authorized to sit in an easy chair, covered with sterile sheets, at mealtime. Meals were only clear liquids, high in calories and protein. Shifting position was a slow, tedious process. Crawling back into bed always a welcome relief. Two days later, my diet was advanced to soft foods, mostly baby food, particularly the "junior" meats, which I refused to eat. Even in critical condition I was being picky and choosy. Two weeks had elapsed, but at no time did I consider my condition critical. In spite of the official hospital listing, I wasn't fighting to live; I just never conceived of dying.

10

All thirty-six survivors had been brought to Strong, and the twenty-two most seriously injured were kept there. The other fourteen were transferred to two other hospitals nearby.

Nine patients in all were delivered to Genesee Hospital. IBM's Karl Schink had been moved there because he was thought to be in good condition; upon arrival, he was found to be suffering from a cerebral concussion and put on the critical list. He also was found to have scalp lacerations, minor burns of the face and left arm, multiple contusions, a foreign body in his right cornea and breaks in his jaw, leg and collarbone. Within two weeks he was in satisfactory condition and able to go home.

The others brought into Genesee were in considerably better shape. H. W. McCalley had only a slight arm injury and Robert Christopher suffered only minor shock. Connecticut salesman Gary Higgins cut his legs and his partner James Kilpatrick had some mild injuries, but both were able to be interviewed. So was gun promoter Richard Baldwin, even though he needed a plastic brace, like some futuristic turtleneck, for pinched nerves. Jane Nixon had numerous bumps and bruises plus two cracked ribs, but was still in good condition. Charles Yelin of Hickock Manufacturing had a broken leg, and Edward Rutledge of the Human Rights Commission a brain concussion. Both recovered rapidly. The five patients at Highland Hospital —Robert Bernstein, Thomas Mayer, Daniel Schwester, Nathan Shippee and young Alan Crandall—were all only slightly injured.

The twenty-two left behind at Strong fell into the first three triage categories. Seven were placed on the danger list, and one, Charles Wright, was listed as poor.

The other fourteen were in fair or good shape. Dr. Lee Davenport of GT&E was treated by a local physician for a minor knee cut and discharged the next morning. Mary Ann Miara was able to leave the hospital within three days. She sustained fractured ribs and a badly bruised right leg; her whole right side was painful but undamaged. Morris Housel, one of the IBM people, was discharged the same day with a head injury. Lloyd Trent, the newlywed member of the Human Rights Commission who came to, mired in the mud, went home after four days, with broken ribs and cuts on his right forearm. So did Stephen Kissel of IBM, who had internal injuries. Andre Nys, another from IBM, stayed less than a week with head injuries and first-degree burns.

Gene Beare of Sylvania and Charles Martin of Kodak shared a room. Beare was in fair condition with multiple fractures; Martin was in a body cast for a year with a broken vertebra. They left together after a week. Architect John O'Brien, whose skull had been fractured, went home at the same time. Henry Fetz, whose arms were burned and his head cut, left on the ninth day. IBM's Louis Wirtz had a head injury and broken ribs; he left three days after Fetz.

Charley McAdam's clothes were cut off him in the emergency room and two attendants began to bathe him with medical soap. He saw two nurses and became embarrassed by his nakedness. In an effort to regain his composure he cracked,

"Hey, where are we anyhow—at a Playboy Club?" One of the medics laughed, "This one's all right; he'll live!" McAdam's injuries were multiple fractures of the right shoulder and four ribs, and burns over his hands, forearm, back and leg. His intuitive gesture of slapping his hands over his face as the plane's cabin burst had saved his eyes and cheeks, but still the fire singed the tip of his nose, gave an involuntary crewcut to his red hair and burned his eyebrows off. He spent seventeen days in the hospital and rested four days more before flying home to Connecticut in a Gannett company plane, another Martin 404. He teased the pilot, "Think we can do it again?" He returned to Rochester for the CAB hearing, and departed once again for home on *another* Mohawk Flight 112 at 4:45 P.M., he traveled with Miss Miara. Once they were airborne, he broke their tension by saying, "Well, anyhow, this is farther than we got last time."

The same day McAdam flew out of Rochester, the last patients to leave for a while checked out of Strong. Advertising executive Laurence Johnson, who had broken his right leg in two places, checked out. George Bossi, stranded with burns of the face and hands and a fractured shoulder blade until his wife could fly over from Italy, flew back with her. When he was first brought to the hospital he took one look at the nurse assigned to him and stretched his English to the limit: *"Mama mia!* With you take care of me, I soon get better." Donald Carney also flew home with his wife. He had fainted at the hospital and undergone emergency abdominal surgery to stop internal bleeding. When he flew home, he was using a cane, not for physical support, but for emotional support; it was filled with whiskey. As he started to pour himself a drink on board from this marvelous instrument, another passenger across the aisle saw him and said, "Hey, it's too early for that!" Carney explained why he was drinking so early. The other passenger said, "If you don't mind, I'll join you."

Carney had been on the danger list the first night. Three others on it preceded him home—Walter Rappoport, fractured ribs; Donald McCauley, broken ribs and arms; Joseph Crimi, first-degree burns and a broken ankle.

Four of us remained behind.

The injuries suffered by fifty-seven-year-old John Sullivan, of the New York State Human Rights Commission, were at first markedly underestimated. He was diagnosed as having scalp and facial lacerations, first- and second-degree burns on his arm and hands, and a fracture in his upper arm. In a few hours it was obvious he had something more serious than that. His breathing became heavy and labored; an X-ray revealed a collapsed lung.

A fine rubber tube—a chest catheter—did not significantly improve his respiration. Neither did a tracheostomy until a so-called Bennet respirator was attached to it. While that was working, he developed pneumonia. More X-rays showed eleven undetected rib fractures. An electrocardiogram showed he had a prior history of myocardial infarction—a blood clot in a heart muscle. Then the tube from his bladder closed up and he couldn't urinate without a catheter.

As Sullivan became able to move about, it was evident that he had still another complication, a protuberance, called a gibbous formation, of his upper thorax. A new set of X-rays showed that he had three broken bones in his spine, perceptibly bending it. To correct this condition and to prevent further damage, Sullivan was fitted with a brace that stretched the length of his spine. At the time of his discharge from Strong in September, Sullivan outwardly was suffering only from a partially paralyzed forearm. But his ordeal had caused him to appear depressed, and some of the priests at St. John Fisher College near Strong came to try to lift his spirits. A year later, he still could not make it to his office, but was working and convalescing at home.

David Elwell of Sylvania had been brought in with major fractures of the bones in his face and a nose not just broken but crushed into many pieces. He, too, was having trouble breathing and underwent a tracheotomy. Because his left leg was totally incinerated from the knee down, it was amputated just above the knee. While the surgeons were occupied with that, there was major bleeding from his mangled face and fingers, and he needed almost ten pints of whole blood.

A second team of doctors turned their attention to his face and his fingers even before the first team had finished, stitching the lacerations, wiring the jaw together, repairing the nose.

Elwell underwent subsequent skin grafting and reconstructive surgery. A congenital deformity in his jaw was corrected, silicone implants were inserted into his eye sockets and the bones in his face were wired together so that his face was completely restored. If you were to look at him now for the first time, you would never suspect that he had been through any ordeal at all.

Elwell spent the tail end of his four months at Strong in the room next to mine. It was then that I got to know him, as he raced up and down the hall from the solarium to his room to the swinging doors of the operating suite at the other end, balanced on his new crutches, raising morale in every room as he made his own daily rounds. Elwell was a yachtsman and kept a pitcher of martinis in his room, contrary to all hospital rules but with the staff's covert knowledge and consent. He designed his own artificial leg with a method for quick disconnection, and later used it to resume his sailing career (his son sailed on the yacht *Columbia,* which won the America's Cup). He was an inspiration to me, and I secretly envied him and his popularity as he made his way around the hospital while I lay silently on my back in the next room. Chuck Wright, on the other hand, was even worse off than me.

Wright, the IBM research chemist, then thirty-nine years old, was out of it when he entered Strong, occasionally groaning and trying without success to speak. He was placed on the danger list—for fractured ribs. He also had a deep scalp cut and a burn on the right hand. But a short time later the attending staff was horrified to observe him trying to move his jaw and tongue and lift his shoulder. There were no movements below the neck, and deep tendon reflexes were absent in the arms and legs. When doctors jabbed his shoulder and neck with a pin, he felt nothing. It had been missed in the initial diagnosis, but Wright was paralyzed from the neck down. He would probably never move again.

Shock had overwhelmed him. He could not remember anything about the crash; he couldn't, for that matter, recall what he was doing in Rochester. A tracheotomy was performed and he received a blood transfusion. An X-ray confirmed the paralysis.

Cruel-looking Crutchfield tongs were installed on Wright. They pierced his scalp, screwed into the skull, and arrested movement, thus preventing further crushing of the nerves. Only then was it safe to move him. During the first week he needed a catheter, and when his tracheotomy gave him trouble he was placed in a sandwichlike bed, which could be rotated in any direction, called the Bradford frame. Whenever it turned him into a prone position his skin turned blue for lack of oxygen. The next week, there was evidence of pneumonia in his lungs. Antibiotics gradually cleared the pneumonia, but his breathing would still periodically fail and it made him irritable, restless and confused. By the second month, with his lungs clear, Wright improved mentally. Some motion returned, too: he could stretch his left arm, flex the elbow, rotate the forearm slightly. But he could not move anything else and neck surgery did not change the situation. After two and a half months, Wright was moved by ambulance to the famous Rusk Institute of Physical Medicine and Rehabilitation in New York to make the adjustment to his new, supine, motionless world.

Compared to Chuck Wright, I consider myself lucky. I'd rather be able to get around than be beautiful.

A week after the crash, my life at the hospital had settled down to routine. I was to undergo a complete dressing change and evaluation with the entire department of plastic surgery in attendance. I was wheeled next door and given narcotics for analgesia intravenously. Then the dressings were removed to reveal all my wounds in full, glorious, gory color. The skin graft over the left eye appeared to be taking, but my nose, forehead, left cheek and left thumb were described as "mummified," while the left ear and temple were "grossly purulent," as was most of the rest of me. The right side of my face was one big infection. After a cleansing and anointment with antibiotics, Dr. McCormack trimmed off the degenerating portions of my left hand while Dr. Cramer cleaned off the exposed scalp.

My relatives didn't know anything about Rochester. They just stayed at the hospital or the motel, not planning to leave it until Grace knew I was stabilized. Other victims' relatives arrived, too; IBM brought whole families in by company plane and limousine. At that time there was a large, attractive motel just around the corner from Strong called the Towne House Inn. Mohawk booked a whole block of rooms there for people coming to see their relatives and picked up the tab. Various airline personnel, including Robert E. Peach, president of Mohawk, paid visits to each relative.

Peach made it a point to visit each of the survivors and reassure them as best he could, too. At that point he had been with the airline for eighteen years, joining it as a flight captain and taking it over from its founder in 1954. This crash was by far the worst blot on their record since its inception, and he was personally upset. Several years later Peach, citing ill health, stepped down the very day in 1970 that Mohawk was absorbed into Allegheny Airlines. The following spring he put a gun to the side of his head and shot himself.

For several months Mohawk continued to pick up the motel and travel expenses for the survivors' relatives and to give them priority on Mohawk flights between their homes and Rochester. Only when the airline received notification from legal counsel that they were being sued did they halt this generosity.

Most of the male relatives of the victims had come and gone, back to their breadwinning, leaving behind mainly a contingent of women. Friends and relatives were by now beginning to get acquainted. One of our neighbors, Joan Shifter, came to stay awhile. Grace, my sister Helen, and Mimi and Mel Krant stood around as she unpacked. They couldn't believe it. Each item Joan removed from her suitcase was individually wrapped in its own plastic bag. Both Joan and I were often teased at home about our compulsive organizing and squirreling habits, but this was ridiculous. Everybody laughed.

One day the hotel operator called Grace and said that a man was there to see her. She went to the lobby to meet him. He was a complete stranger, a Rochesterian who identified himself as Frederick S. Forman, a lawyer. He was wondering if there was anything he could do to be of help. The conversation got around to asking him what he did for a living and Forman said, "I own a shop in town." Grace naturally assumed he meant a small shop. She later discovered that the "shop," which bore the family name, was probably the finest department store in the state outside of New York City. Though we never met, he sent me a handsome AM/FM portable radio and, when he learned what my musical tastes were, he had the radio station he owned broadcast a list of my favorites each day. Forman's interest in us may have stemmed from the fact that I was the only *landsman* badly injured in the crash—he and his wife were very active in their temple. They even invited Grace and Helen to their house outside Rochester for dinner. A few years later, we were upset at the news of Fred Forman's fatal heart attack.

The day after Forman paid his visit to Grace, Linda Hart watched as Dr. Breslau slowly peeled the bandages from my eyes and had me read the print on the side of a box of cookies, and she was too overcome to hold back her tears. The left eye could see nothing, but Dr. Breslau noted that the right one "reads fine print well at fifteen inches, has clear distance image." The bandages were not removed, however, until—at Grace's insistence, and without my knowledge—all mirrors had been removed from my room.

She didn't know how I would react. I didn't either. I still had no inkling as to the full extent of my injuries. There were no sensations to indicate what the damage was. You don't feel it when a part of your body is missing; quite the opposite, it often feels like it's there even if it isn't. I couldn't see anything because of the damage to my eyes, and even when they got better the bandages blocked my vision.

Nor had I brought myself to ask how badly I was hurt. And I didn't speculate. I didn't want to know. What you don't know won't hurt you: that's the basis under which I operated. As long as I didn't know and they took care of it, eventually everything would be all right. I was in good hands. I'd leave it up to them.

On July 12 I underwent a thorough physical examination. A thick greenish-yellow exudate with a foul odor covered my left hand and parts of the left arm, chest and abdomen. The infection turned out to be the dreaded *pseudomonas aeruginosa*, the major cause of death in severe burn cases. Massive doses of antibiotics were prescribed. Two days later another checkup disclosed that the right eyelids still did not close completely, and I was treated with methyl cellulose solution to protect the eye from the irritation and conjunctivitis that continued exposure to the air was causing. The right cheek and chin had healed somewhat, but the all-but-gone left ear and the left eye were discharging pus; my forehead was beginning to split because of the deep char; my left hand, right leg and chest were degenerating.

Two days later there was another major debridement and dressing change in the room next door. Some of the dead tissue was beginning to come off. The graft over the left eye had taken well. But contractures, the disfiguring pulling-together process that burn scar tissue undergoes, had begun in the fingers of the left hand. In order to counteract this, the fingers were stretched apart and gauze pads were wedged into the webs between them. The right knee had also started to contract and had stiffened at a thirty-degree angle. A plaster cast was molded to hold the leg straight while lifting the foot back into its normal alignment.

Calorie intake is very important to burn patients. Someone as severely burned as I was needs between 7,000 and 10,000 calories daily, but it is common for burn patients to suffer loss of appetite and distaste for food. That was certainly true in my case; my weight dropped from 145 to below 90. It has since been found that loss of zinc in the patient's body is the cause, but at the time my loss of appetite was attributed to emotional problems. Mel Krant gave me daily pep talks on the importance of eating. Relatives and friends sent me ample supplies of gourmet delicacies. I tried to comply, but I only ate a little. Four months of constant nibbling on my storehouse of "goodies" did little good for Nurse Jacoby's already ample figure. It was Linda Hart's mother who ultimately sent me the real medicine that I am sure was responsible for my recovery—chicken soup with knadles, which, for the uninitiated, are like dumplings made with matzos, eggs and chicken fat. Creating them is culinary art at its highest. They can either float through the heavens like balloons or sink like lead cannonballs. Bea Hart's knadles flew. I come from a long line of gourmands, but I was never served the likes of that marvelous masterpiece of hers, that panacea, that Jewish penicillin, Mrs. Hart's chicken soup. She is dead now, but I am forever grateful.

One of the attending physicians made note of the fact that I was eating poorly, but his opinion was that my appetite would pick up with better food, which is what eventually happened. Nevertheless, he also wrote down that my "mental status appears to be one of slight depression at the moment."

I knew I wasn't depressed. I almost never get depressed, and I never was the whole time I was in the hospital. I've always adjusted well. One summer my cousin and I were sent to a camp that was actually a military academy. He hated it, he had a terrible time, he was miserable, he had all kinds of problems and finally his toe got infected. To his relief his mother came and took him home. To me, it was fun. I loved it. I had a marvelous time. Here we were, two relatives, and we reacted completely the opposite. I thrived then because I've always prided myself on being able to adjust to almost any situation. It's a matter of temperament and personality, and I think it's what saw me through.

Nobody said, "Alan, you're depressed," but they worried that I might be. So they had a psychiatrist come and spend time with me.

My emotional condition was supposed to be handled by a staff psychiatrist that Dr. Cramer had called in because he felt, as he put it, that my family and I would need help "because of the severely mutilating injuries" and "the long traumatic period of hospitalization and surgical care" that lay ahead. They agreed that this doctor would be more effective if he came for rehabilitation, rather than present himself as a psychiatrist who was there for formal psychotherapy. But after he had come to my room on several occasions without apparent reason, I became suspicious and asked my nurse what he wanted. She told me who he really was, but I never let him know that I was aware of his real mission. Instead, I tried to help him as much as I could. He seemed nervous and tense himself, and was a heavy smoker; I tried to get him to quit, as I had done the moment of the crash, and there is no more persistent a crusader than a converted sinner. We also played chess quite often during his visits, as I did with several of my regular visitors. I don't think I needed this therapy and what there was of it made little or no difference; I had enough emotional support already. Had I known I was going to receive a bill for what I thought were his friendly visits, I'd have stopped them at once.

For the next four days I had daily dressing changes and blood transfusions in preparation for major surgery planned for July 22. Dr. Donald Zehl, who now took over the care of my eyes, examined them. With great effort, I could draw the shrunken right lids together. I could count fingers accurately at six feet. The right cornea was bright and clear, but antibiotic ointment and methyl cellulose were still continued. That same day my own exploring fingers located a sharp protrusion at my collarbone with the broken ends overlapped. But nothing could be done about it. The ends had knitted together in this position, and some concern was expressed that the bulge would eventually break through my skin.

On July 21 Dr. Mitchell brought in a "Consent for Operation" form that I was now able to sign myself for the first time with my good right hand. The signature was wobbly, but distinctively mine. Next morning a nurse gave me a couple of injections in the buttocks and one hour later I was wheeled into the operating suite, relaxed and almost unconscious. Once I was on the table, general anesthesia was administered via a tube passing through the trache in my throat, since my face was so damaged it could not be covered and sealed with a mask.

While I was still awake my left hand and face were unbandaged. The face, left arm and hand were prepped by rigorous scrubbing with germicidal solutions, and then I was draped to expose only those two areas to the blazing overhead lights. Before the last drape clamp was in place I had succumbed to the anesthesia.

A team headed by Dr. McCormack began to remove the dry, sloughy eschar crusts and devitalized tissue from the left hand. The mummified thumb had already sloughed off by itself and the team now amputated the second joint since it was beyond saving. The entire index finger was amputated, and part of the long hand bone connected to that finger was removed with a heavy-duty forceps called a rongeur. Had this been almost any other hospital probably all the fingers would have been amputated. But Dr. McCormack and Dr. Cramer were two of the finest hand surgeons in the world, and for whatever they were worth those three remaining digits, damaged and grotesquely distorted as they were, were saved. Neither the doctors nor any of the staff were aware at the time that I was an accomplished pianist.

The extensor tendons on the back of the three saved fingers were either burned through or devitalized and had to be cut out to allow the remaining portions of finger to retract. After all of the obviously damaged tissue was removed, the remaining fingers were fanned by placing gauze pads between them, and, with the wrist bent upward, the whole hand was wrapped in a bulky gauze dressing. The amputated pieces, meanwhile, were examined macroscopically and microscopically by a staff pathologist who made a detailed report on his findings.

The surgeons finished up, directing their attention to my face. The burns on the right side were mostly second degree, so they were left alone. But the severely burned skin on the left side was sharply debrided. So was the grossly necrotic tissue around the nose and forehead.

I was given two pints of blood during the procedure, which lasted eighty minutes. In the recovery room, my vital signs were stable. But my temperature shot up to 103 degrees and remained there three days. A decision was made to use an ice blanket in an attempt to lower it. An elaborate machine, designed to pump ice water into the balloonlike sections of a rubber blanket, was wheeled into my room. Ice was not in plentiful supply at Strong, so Florence and Grace had to raid refrigerators on every floor to assuage the machine's voracious appetite. My temperature finally did return to normal, though periodically after surgery it would jump again.

The eschar on my chest and left leg was coming off, the right side of my face and chin were well on their way to healing, and the granulation tissue, needed for skin grafts to take, was beginning to form. The doctor who had diagnosed me as being depressed before now decided that I was in good spirits and only slightly depressed. The right eye improved steadily. Dressing changes continued on a daily basis. So did self-hypnosis.

On July 30 I received a major debridement and a transfusion in preparation for surgery the following day. I was again asked to sign a consent order, when I noticed that the bottom half of the form was an approval for a circumcision. I was careful to restrict my signature to the upper half; to sign the bottom part would only have been redundant.

11

The plastic in plastic surgery doesn't refer to high polymer materials—that's my specialty—but to the pliability of skin and tissue. Its beginnings have been traced to Hindu texts predating Christ that describe the use of a skin flap from the forehead to replace noses that had been chopped off either as punishment (to set an example to unfaithful wives) or in battle (a rather common result of swordplay). For the time, that was an extremely advanced procedure, and daring plastic surgeons ever since have developed and refined procedures that stun the imagination. I was fortunate that the skill had developed to where it was when I found myself under the surgeon's knife.

The more than six thousand plastic surgeons in the United States are builders or rebuilders of body parts that for one reason or another have been damaged, lost, eroded or congenitally deformed. A lot of plastic surgery is cosmetic in its nature, but the most daring and valuable advances have been in the reconstructive and rehabilitative aspects of the specialty.

The first of August marked the real beginning of the major reconstructive phase of my surgeries. Preoperative medication and general anesthesia were administered as before. My left leg, which had suffered only minor burn damage and was in fairly good condition, was carefully draped while the rest of me was submerged in the usual green sheets and towels. The exposed leg was shaved and scrubbed relentlessly with germicidal and saline solutions.

With the use of a special knifelike device known as a Brown Dermatome, long slices of the outer skin layer were shaved off the leg and laid on a sterile glass plate for later use. The newly exposed donor areas on the leg were treated and bandaged, and then it was submerged in the expanse of green cotton while the left arm and the head were brought to the surface. The white dressings there were taken off and the exposed areas were washed. Drs. Mitchell and Cramer lifted each strip of peeled flesh by holding the corners with forceps, and laid them over the exposed muscle tissue of the left shoulder and upper arm. Other strips of skin were placed over spots on the face that were ready for grafting. None of the skin grafts was stitched in place. Instead, they were held by Vasoline-coated dressings and two-way-stretch gauze pads. A plaster cast was then molded around the entire upper left arm to keep it immobile long enough for the graft to take.

Grafted skin can take on muscle tissue but it cannot take on bone, and that was the problem the skull now presented. The skull has two layers of bone separated by a spongy core. The voids of the core are filled with a form of bone marrow. Marrow is tissue you can graft to. So the decision was to fenestrate—to drill little holes all over the skull until the marrow flowed out and covered the head.

Dental drill bits mounted on the end of a flexible shaft and attached to a high-speed motor were used to drill over a hundred holes through the outer bone into the marrow cortex. The holes were spaced so closely together my skull looked like the kitchen colander my mother used to drain water from spaghetti. Not all of the holes could be drilled during this one operation because there was a great deal of bleeding, because the drill would overheat, and because Dr. Cramer's hand would tire.

It was important that the holes bleed because as the blood clotted granulating tissue would form. When some holes did not bleed because they had been drilled over the nexus of the bone, adjacent bone was chiseled away until marrow was reached. When others bled too much, or refused to clot, a small plug of sterile beeswax was pressed in until the bleeding stopped. These plugs, being foreign bodies, had to be picked out within a day or so or the body's natural rejection mechanism would begin.

Dr. Cramer was disappointed with the amount of my bleeding, and stopped for the time being. Vasoline gauze was spread on the skull to prevent sticking and I resumed my mummylike appearance.

Beginning then, and covering the period of the next three operations, I was subjected to a procedure I found distasteful and depressing. A plastic-surgery resident would come into my room ahead of the other plastic surgeons on their rounds and poke into each of the skull holes with sterile cotton swabs, trying to induce bleeding and pick out any bone chips he could find. This was not really all that painful, but just the thought of what he was doing chilled me (pardon the pun) to the bone, and I would moan as if in terrible pain every time he tried to touch me. I suppose I hoped my moaning would deter the torturer from his evil practices.

I began to think of this doctor as just that—my torturer—because he was given the onerous duty, as junior doctor-in-residence, of doing the proverbial dirty work. He was the one who had to remove the painful dressings and clean out the burr holes in my skull, and so I took my hostility out on him. I convinced myself, in spite of any intellectualizing I might do, that this dark and sullen man was indeed a sadist.

One day he was taking off a dressing that had been taped to the back of my neck with a wide, sticky piece of adhesive. Slow removal was terribly painful, and for some reason there was no suitable solvent to unstick the hold on my skin. He relied on the time-tested remedy—he ripped it off in one fast sweep. Unfortunately, he also ripped a large piece of skin, of which I did not exactly have a surplus at that point, off with it. "You hurt me!" I accused him, and he apologized. When the rest of the staff came into my room on their rounds he made no mention of what he had just done, and I was too scared to, for fear of what he might do to me the next time he got me alone. I waited until I was finally alone with my nurse, Joan. Tears came into my eyes for the first time since the accident and I pleaded with her, "Please keep that sadist away from me!" She promised me she'd stand by and make sure he wouldn't hurt me again.

Eventually, the revolving residency took him elsewhere, to my relief. The wound he left was an area of constant, excruciating pain and did not heal for several months afterward. When it finally did, I had another scar to add to my extensive collection.

I cried only one other time. One morning, a particularly gloomy one made more so by the limited vision of my damaged eyes, Dr. Cramer came into my room and pulled up a chair close to my bed. I didn't know him well yet, but I could tell that it was a difficult moment for him. Without too many preliminaries and in very little detail, he described, in a very soft voice, the extent of my injuries. I learned, for the first time, that I had lost my fingers, my nose and my ear. The doctor indicated that, in time, much of the damage could be repaired. He asked me if I had any questions.

I asked him, "How long will it take to repair and rebuild me?"

He replied, "It could take the rest of your life, but you will want to stop before I do."

Then I asked, "Will I ever be able to play piano again?"

He looked me squarely in the eyes, didn't blink and said "no."

Quietly, Dr. Cramer got up and left the room. And I began to cry, silent sobs wracking my body. I carried on crying this way for about fifteen minutes, getting it all out of my system. After that I never cried again. I never again felt a twinge of self-pity.

It's a horrible feeling at first to know that you've lost your ear and your face. The loss of my fingers bothered me more than anything else. It wasn't so much that I wouldn't have the use of them but that I was a snob, I admit it, and I associated misshapen hands and missing fingers with stereotypes—the lower classes, blue-collar laborers, motorcyclists, the uneducated.

I felt the same way about tattoos.

I never met an educated person in my life who was tattooed, and I had read somewhere that, statistically, people who have been were more likely to have prison records.

Genteel people never have disfigured hands, I thought. Now I felt a certain amount of self-loathing and I imagined that others would look at me with the same sort of distorted prejudices I had adopted.

On August 6 the next plastic surgery was performed. Once I was anesthetized all dressings were removed and the appropriate areas were prepped and draped. The skin grafts this time came from both legs and the rib cage, and the slices of donor skin were laid over the granulating tissues of the right leg and chest. One patch was placed over a part of the left shoulder that still lay exposed; the earlier grafts there had taken well. The front of the right thigh, from the knee to the groin, was covered with strips of donor skin. So were parts of the knee and ankle. Between being used as donor sites or being grafted, almost no part of either leg remained untouched. Both legs were treated and wrapped in dressings. Then additional burr holes were drilled in the skull, drawing more blood. Next, the last damaged tendons and exposed bone were removed from the left hand with the rongeur forceps. Meanwhile, Dr. Zehl made a horizontal slit in the skin graft covering the left eye, exposing it to light for the first time since it had been covered on the night of July 2. The pupil was fixed and dilated; there was an opaque, cloudy gray scar on the cornea. It would require several days of medication before it began to perceive light or even blurry images.

Surgery took a little over ninety minutes, and when I was in recovery, I was still so groggy from anesthesia I lapsed back into unconsciousness. Then I began to react to the anesthesia in a new way: I got chills that made me shiver uncontrollably. My chattering jaw was vibrating so severely I was in terror my teeth would be knocked out. My temperature dropped to 96 degrees. I shook for another hour and a half until the steel bed itself shook and I was scared I was going to damage it as well as myself. Florence found six blankets for me but they did no good.

Grace tried to find an electric heater, but the hospital had none. Someone notified the Fred Formans, and once again they came through. They rushed two heaters from their home, which were quickly plugged in and directed at me. After a while, more I suspect from the anesthesia wearing off than the heat, the shakes began to subside, and along with them the panic I was in.

Florence was the only staff member at Strong who seemed concerned with the reaction I had just had, but I learned later that sometimes under anesthesia the body's thermo-regulatory mechanism stops working and the temperature of the body drops or rises to that of the surrounding atmosphere, which in the operating room is quite cold. It had been standard procedure to strip me at least partially during preoperative prepping. Prior to every surgery after that, I gave explicit instructions to the attending staff that I was to be kept covered and warm during surgery. I would add other instructions as other complications arose.

Before surgery again on August 9, Dr. Richard Burton, a resident, took measurements on my legs. The right one needed 168 square inches of skin and the left 127. This time surgery took over two hours, and I received two pints of blood transfusion. Both a Brown Dermatome and something called a Humby knife were used to shave skin from the unburned portions of the legs, which was then laid in place over third-degree-burn areas. Leftover pieces of donor skin went on the left shoulder, abdomen and forehead.

Two days later, a consultant on infectious disease was called in because the *pseudomonas* infection was spreading over some of the burn areas. He concluded that the use of broad-spectrum antibiotics might be spreading rather than reducing the infection and recommended they be discontinued. Six weeks after the crash, I was still on the danger list.

I was fortunate that I had been in excellent physical condition at the time of the crash and that I was a quick healer. All of the grafts had taken. Unfortunately, they formed thick scars on healing. I was under the incorrect assumption that the scars could be buffed down later on and so was not concerned. What I found out was that buffing works only in cases of shallow pits like acne and that if my scars were buffed they would simply return. However, with the passage of time most scars tend to become more supple, less raw-looking and pronounced.

During a two-hour operation on August 20, Dr. Cramer drilled more holes in the skull and Dr. Mitchell debrided more burn scabs. Grafts from the left thigh were placed over the right leg, the chest and a spot on the left shoulder. More bones in the left hand were rongeured down to the marrow. The right leg and the left hand were put into splints so grafts could take.

The week before, my Torquemada had briefly turned savior. The resident issued instructions to remove the trache tube for all but one of my waking hours to give the opening in my throat a chance to relax back to a closed wound. And on August 21 he found something very important: granulations had developed at the bases of the burr holes in my skull. Grafting could be done there. But there was bad news, too. For one thing, the order about removing the trache was rescinded after only a few days.

For another, both ears had developed pus-filled areas and had to be soaked with saline-solution compresses. I was forced to remain immobile for long periods so as to not disturb the wet dressings draped over them. I didn't realize how much damage there was to my left ear; it didn't feel any different from the right. The only sensation I felt on either side was stinging pain. Meanwhile, Dr. Zehl noted that my burned left eye could make out fingers a foot away, but that the right eyelids were contracting, would not close completely and might need an operation known as an *Elschnig tarsorrhapy* to join them together, plus a skin graft. He held off the decision to operate in order to keep up my morale.

In another two-hour operation on August 24 the fenestration of the skull was completed. The left-leg grafts had taken so well no further dressing was necessary, but the right leg was redressed and a splint was made to keep the right ankle from contracting. The last bone fragments on my left hand were debrided; all that remained of the hand was the front of the fingers and their survival was still in doubt. The back of the hand was redressed in its wrist-up position, and I was returned to my room—still on the danger list, but more now to continue my family's unlimited visiting privileges than from fear for my life.

Three days later, a new experience intruded on my routine. Two orderlies appeared in my room. One, named Arthur Steve, was short and heavyset with wiry gray hair. The other was a lean black man who wore glasses and had a prominent gold tooth. His name was Shirley Tyler. Tyler and I had met before. One of his major duties was to shave patients' hair just before surgery. He would have before him front and rear diagrams of the nude body, with the area to be shaved shaded in by the surgeon. He would proceed from there with an ordinary double-edged razor. This time, the two of them wheeled in another ordinary instrument—a white-enamel steel bathtub—on noisy casters that wouldn't stop squeaking.

They held a long discussion as to where to place the tub and how to fill it and how they were going to get me into it. I found it a little hard to believe they had never done this before, which is the way it seemed. Finally, they used a garden hose to run lukewarm water from the room sink until the tub was half-full, and added plain old Joy detergent to the water. With each taking a side and with Florence at the foot, the sheet on which I was lying was lifted like a hammock and I was lowered into my Joy bath.

Once I settled in the water, naked except for a towel over my midsection, the bandages soaked loose and I relaxed. Florence placed a plastic-covered pillow right in the water under my head and sat at the edge, dripping water from gauze sponges onto unsubmerged areas and cutting away the freed bandage, often pulling at them—intentionally—a little extra hard in order to remove them with the least amount of trauma, producing shouts of pain from me.

Removal from the tub was accomplished in reverse fashion except that now the sheet was soaking wet. Somehow Florence managed to remake the bed without disturbing me and the Joy baths became part of my regular routine. Whenever Arthur Steve would announce himself with his "Hello, there" it brought a smile to what was left of my face.

Another new procedure at the hospital, one so sensuous I took advantage of it whenever I could and enjoyed more and more as it was extended over other parts of me during later stays at Strong, was ordered for me by Dr. Burton: massage of my healed graft sites with cocoa butter. Cocoa butter is used mostly to make chocolate, but it has a smoothing emolient effect on the skin. The nurses rotated a block of it in their hands like soap until it melted and gently applied a coat of oily residue by sensuously (it seemed to me) massaging the skin (and never underestimate the value of sensual pleasure in aiding recovery).

The splint for my right leg was now put on only at night. I didn't mind it. I can remember how proud I was at being able to hold the leg up in the air for long periods without support while lying on my back as the nurse wrapped an Ace bandage around the cast. It was pure pretense, but it did me physical good besides raising my morale. When the splint began to irritate my heel, the hospital came up with a genuine sheepskin lining to pad it. I was impressed that they would have such an exotic bandage on hand in a hospital.

Strong's ear, nose and throat specialist was called in. He was John Frazer, a redheaded Scotsman whose own nose had in his youth received a flattened groove below the bridge that detracted not at all from his elegant good looks. The doctors had left my open sinuses exposed; they didn't know what they were going to do with them or whether they were healthy or not. Dr. Frazer examined them to see if the ducts that connect the sinuses to the nasal cavity were blocked or open.

His recommendation was to drop blue dye into the sinus cavities to trace whether it drained to the nose or the eye. I had great fears about this procedure, but they proved to be unfounded when it was done during surgery the next day.

The preoperative shots were so powerful I was unconscious by the time I reached the operating room and needed no general anesthesia. Frazer's test was tried; it showed that the right duct was open and that the left one was blocked by the burn. The tentative conclusion was that surgery would be necessary to either reconstruct or obliterate the duct, but luckily a final decision was put off and the condition ultimately corrected itself. Three other surgical teams went to work on me during the same operation. One numbed my wrist with shots and then rongeured the bone from the fingers, reducing them to half their original length but leaving the nails intact. When they were through, the fingers swelled from the surgical trauma until they looked like paws or sausages, but in time the swelling subsided. Another team was using grafts from both legs on the left hand and right ankle. The third team, after applying the test dye, extracted a dead mucus membrane and sent it to pathology for evaluation. Luckily for me, the sinuses turned out to be healthy. They had survived all the trauma and exposure.

I was becoming more active socially. The hospital installed a television in my room, which helped to pass the time. I also had a parade of visitors: my wife and sister and a throng of friends were always there. Both Grace and Helen would visit other crash victims on the floor, and their families would visit me. A camaraderie built up. Gerhard "Gett" Elston, a neighbor and the husband of one of my son Leigh's teachers, visited Rochester on business for the National Council of Churches and learned that I had developed a compulsive interest in the history of the Mamalukes, the Russian slave-rulers of Egypt. He spent hours at various libraries doing research and finally came up with a list of books to satisfy my curiosity for a long time to come.

I had round-the-clock private-duty nurses, and floor nurses checked on me several times a day. The plastic-surgery staff dropped by often not only to examine me but to sample my array of gourmet delights. Besides the senior staff surgeons, residents, interns, orderlies and technicians, there were medical students and student nurses, all of them identifiable by the uniform or cap they wore that indicated their school or what training they were in. Becky Keene, the public-relations director at Strong, made it a point to visit once a day, and hospital volunteers would stop by. I always tried to be cheerful with my visitors. By now I knew how tough it was for them just to walk into my room in the first place, and I wanted them to feel no discomfort or unpleasantness. After a while I could sense that they no longer "saw" my disfigurement but only the real me underneath, and because of their backgrounds I found them intellectually stimulating. Their constant attention was as important to me as the fluids being pumped into my veins or the rearrangement of my flesh. I never once lacked for company, and I never once had the chance to sink into despair.

In fact the visits could tire me out, because I was being kept unbelievably busy. I was awakened early in the morning (much earlier than I like, since I am a night person) to have my temperature and blood pressure taken. Morning ablutions followed. For a long time I could not brush my own teeth. The nurses had to do it using a child's toothbrush, and just getting it past my lips was painful. Shaving was also done for me, and that was painful too until the arrival of my electric razor from home. Then came breakfast. This was followed by a sponge bath in bed performed by a nurse, another source of sensual pleasure. The end of the bath usually signaled the arrival of the first wave of visitors. Mail was delivered by the floor secretary, and I awaited it eagerly each day. I could recognize the click of Grace's heels down the hall as she made her entrance looking vibrant and beautiful. She would read the mail to me and then read books aloud, which she enjoyed doing as much as I enjoyed listening. Since she knew I enjoyed Michener and we had a great interest in Afghanistan because I had a cousin living there writing a book about it, she read *Caravans* to me. But I can remember the anguish I felt at the vivid descriptions of blood and gore so close to my own.

Lunch was served before noon. The doctors made their rounds just beforehand or in the early afternoon. I usually took naps after lunch because I had lost so much strength along with the weight.

Most of my chess opponents in the past had been male, but I found a couple of female partners in the hospital. Joan, my afternoon nurse, played. So did another nurse, Carol Bachman, a strict fundamentalist from the coal regions of my state whose only aim was to beat me and who almost never did. Chess was a marvelous tonic; with the time I had to devote to it, I became a real aficionado.

Late afternoons were edgy periods as the sun began setting earlier and earlier. The room was quiet then. Television was meager fare, though I found some of the morning comedies amusing. Dinner was served before five, earlier than I was used to eating, but after a while, like Pavlov's dog, when I heard the rumble of the dinner carts down the hall my digestive juices started flowing. After dinner I was ready to relax, with the evening TV shows killing a lot of endless time, unless I had more visitors.

One moment I especially cherished came every evening at exactly 6:00 when I made a long-distance call to my three sons and to Grace, once she finally went home to care for them. Strong's communications department had rigged up a speaker phone for me so that I only had to push a button with my bandaged hand to get the operator. I spoke with each of the three boys in turn, learning what they had done that day and telling them what I had done, never complaining to them of any pain or discomfort. Leigh, the eldest, was only seven then, but he was very mature and empathetic; we would have serious and lengthy discussions. Three-year-old Cory would be excited when he got on the line. "Hello, Da-di. How are you today?" he would ask, sounding genuinely interested. He had to fend off his little brother. Tod, who had just turned one, fought for his turn at the telephone, his blue eyes wide as saucers while he listened to me. He could not quite mouth intelligible words, so Grace prompted him.

My telephone bill was astronomical, but it was one of my best investments.

I had always been an excellent sleeper, so at night I rarely took the sleeping pill offered me. More often than not, I refused the pain medication too. I just never believed in taking medication unless you really *needed* it, and most of my pain I could bear.

In addition to having my days punctuated with dressing changes, medical treatments, linen changes, and the taking of blood pressure, pulse and temperature, and being photographed and X-rayed and sponge bathed, I had to contend with each new intern, resident and student who, for the benefit of training rather than my welfare, wanted to conduct an examination or take yet another medical history. I became quite expert at supplying the newcomers with the facts of my case, and everything was dutifully recorded and added to my ever-growing file, which would eventually be more than a foot thick.

September 3 found me back on the operating table for two hours. Again the I.V. of Demerol was enough to put me out. The holes in my forehead were cleaned; my leg and hand were trimmed of excess grafted skin, redressed and splinted. The slit over my left eye was enlarged to almost the full width of a normal eye and the edges of the newly created lids were stitched together.

A week later, about fifty square inches of skin were shaved

off still-untouched areas of the right leg while a second team, with rongeurs and a chisel, removed the outer skull layer in those areas still without any granulating tissue on which to graft. The bone over the left front sinus was removed completely, fully exposing the healthy mucus membrane. Then the moment that had been awaited with trepidation for weeks arrived: a skin graft from the leg was placed over the entire skull area. Other pieces went onto the left side of the face and the left hand. With the sinuses still left open, the skull was gingerly dressed.

Subsequent examination of the skull graft site was very encouraging. The take was good, with only small areas where further grafting would be needed. The pale skin was bumpy and pebbled, matching the perforated and unevenly chipped skull it covered. The dressings remained clean and there was no odor.

Dr. Zehl had discovered, however, that because of the skull graft the right eyelids now would not close completely, and he performed corrective surgery on September 16. The idea was to join the lids together until they had been permanently stretched enough to meet naturally.

One would think the procedure a matter of simply being able to sew carefully, but sutures can remain in only so long before the body starts rejecting them. They can also leave disfiguring marks. The lids will grow together only if the outer skin layers on both of the surfaces in contact are taken off.

Even after Demerol put me to sleep, the injections of Xylocaine to deaden my eye were torture. I could feel myself wince and hear myself scream each time the needle penetrated the skin. But once the Xylocaine took effect, I sank back in to the Demerol-induced sleep and the pain became just another fading memory.

Dr. Zehl began the Elschnig tarsorrhapy by making four tiny incisions with his scalpel on the edge of the lids, two in each lid. The skin and muscle of the eyelid was separated from the tarsus plate, the fibrous connective tissue that gives the eye its stiffness, and the conjunctiva. Four tiny triangles were cut— once again, two on each lid. Small rubber pegs were then put in place over the lids and four sutures were threaded through them, drawn tight until the four triangles were properly aligned, like a key in a keyhole, and knots tied. Except for the four fine punctures made by the sutures, the skin of the eyelids was not damaged in any way, so from a cosmetic standpoint a good recovery could be expected. At the center of the eye the lids had not been touched at all, so that within a few days, when the post-surgical swelling went down, a peephole over the pupil sufficient to see with would form. Meanwhile, an antibiotic petroleum jelly was liberally squeezed over the eye and a gauze eyepad Scotch-taped over it.

The numbing Demerol still held sway and was not to be wasted. Drs. Cramer, Mitchell and Burton removed the dressings from the head and hand, washed and debrided, rolled out pus-soaked material with cotton swabs from under the grafts and redressed.

Next day the gauze eyepad was removed. The lid was a little sore, but the eye itself felt okay. I could not see with it yet; the other eye was starting to make out shadowy images on TV, but not much else. A few days later the eye opening began to form as planned, though it seemed that the triangular adhesion next to the nose side might not take.

Just sitting up in an easy chair for meals was a major effort. I was afraid that any movement I made might do some damage —a stitch might come undone, bleeding might start from stretching the scab-covered skin. The stagnant muscles, unused for three months now, had also atrophied. I either could not or would not stand up straight. On the other hand, I could get around fairly well. Only the drop-foot seemed to be a problem, and sleeping with the leg cast seemed to be of some help there. Other help came in the form of a freckle-faced redhead by the name of Peggy Welch.

Peggy was a young, heavyset physical therapist. A little shy but always with a smile on her face, she started to show up in my room each day, usually after lunch, on the seventeenth of September. Slowly, she forced me to sit up in bed and swing around painstakingly until my feet dangled over the edge of the bed. Then, supported by either Florence or Joan, she helped me to a standing position. With their arms around me, I was able to walk—only a few faltering steps at first, but after a while to the door of my room and back to the bed.

It was on one of these strolls around the room that I caught the first glimpse of my face. As I walked past the stainless-steel paper-towel dispenser next to the sink, I saw, out of the corner of my eye, a hazy, distorted reflection of my face. I did not dwell on it for long.

I just didn't know how I would react to the knowing, and because I didn't know I didn't have the guts to look. The looking was nothing. It was the fear of looking, and the fear of seeing my face. The anticipation is always the worst part of anything. I suppose I thought the sight of myself would bother me. Maybe it was *too* awful, and I didn't want to react suddenly, become shocked by it and pass out. So I had to sneak up on it slowly. I think the nurses knew I was avoiding looking at myself, but I didn't discuss it openly with them and I didn't discuss it with them this time. I didn't even know they'd taken the mirrors out of the room. I just didn't think there were any, and I didn't find out there were until after I'd seen myself, in the stainless steel and again afterward. At some point I had to start shaving myself and, when I did eventually start to do things for myself, they brought a mirror back in.

Attempting to walk in itself was neither painful nor uncomfortable. It was simply that the muscles were not there. So Peggy trained the nurses in "passive exercises" while she worked at stretching my leg muscles. I would lie on my back while Peggy raised my leg in the air, held it by the ankle and pressed down again and again on the knee in an attempt to straighten it. Another maneuver was to hold the ankle and push up on the bottom of the toes to stretch the muscles and tendons in the heel. These passive exercises were repeated three times a day and were not particularly unpleasant, though when Peggy held my left arm and tried rotating it around my shoulder, which was very tight, I resisted out of fear that any locomotion would cause the grafted skin to separate from the muscle to which it had so recently been attached.

Peggy Welch monitored these exercises for five weeks, until, little by little, without any help from anyone, I could miraculously move my arms and legs all equally well.

An examination at the end of September indicated that the whole back of my left hand, the fingers too, had been covered with skin grafts. I was able by now to sit up in a chair and feed myself. Dr. Zehl removed the sutures and rubber pegs from the right eyelids and, though sure enough only one of the two adhesions had held, a second operation proved unnecessary.

The night before my next scheduled surgery Dr. Breslau came to my room to prep the donor site, my left thigh this time. He suggested that rather than shave the area we try out a new depilatory cream he was researching for a drug company. He applied the cool, pearly white cream over the thigh and, after a suitable wait, wiped it off and washed the area thoroughly. All of the hair had come off with the cream, as was its purpose, but in a short time the treated area began to sting, swell tremendously and turn a raw shade of pink. I presume that Dr. Breslau suggested to the drug company that they go back to the laboratory.

In surgery the next morning, October 2, the donor skin from the puffed-up thigh was used to cover scattered spots on the skull and hand. The sinuses were still left exposed.

On October 5, I was able to go outdoors for the first time. I was bundled into a wheelchair, covered with a blanket and taken by a circuitous route up and down elevators and along unending corridors until we got on an elevator that could take us to the rooftop solarium. It was a chilly autumn day, but the sun was bright. Only a couple of other patients and nurses were there. With its polished red ceramic tile floor and a handsome set of matched redwood and gold-anodized aluminum outdoor furniture, the solarium was quite attractive. Laboriously, I got out of the wheelchair and, holding on to the railing that surmounted the parapet wall, made a tour of our sixth-floor aerie. The view in all directions was breathtaking. Joan pointed out the sights, giving me my first inkling of Strong's geographical relationship to the airport, the university and Rochester itself. We sat for a while, bundled up against the wind and the chilly air, and then returned to the room with a whetted appetite for dinner.

The trips to the solarium continued and a pair of lightweight plastic sunglasses were prescribed for me because I had been diagnosed as having photophobia—the sunlight striking the scar on my left cornea would dazzle me, hurting and interfering with my vision. Since there was no nose on which to rest the glasses, they were held on with a little tape and a little ingenuity. On one occasion we took the sun downstairs instead of up. One of the hospital courtyards was like a monastic sanctuary: old red-brick flooring, moss-covered fountains, shrubbery. I could see this courtyard from the window of my room, and its one tree whose delicate gray-green leaves stretched out like some fairy tale umbrella—a Russian Olive. Florence and I sat under this beautiful tree and when I eventually returned home, I planted several in our garden.

One day a hospital volunteer who had learned that I had some artistic talent stopped by with oil paints, brushes, canvas and other supplies, and encouraged me to paint a picture. My hand was not too steady and I could not see as well as I might have liked, but it was good therapy and whiled away some hours.

I was beginning to enjoy the social life at the hospital. I had developed a craving for spaghetti with red clam sauce, a dish that has always been a favorite of mine, and as luck would have it, Joan's father had a friend who owned an Italian restaurant in Rochester where this was the *spécialité de la maison.* As a favor to her, a batch was made up for us. One of Florence's secret ambitions was to be a caterer, and the two nurses prepared an Italian *festa* in my room. Florence moved a bridge table in from the floor solarium and covered it with a red-and-white-checkered tablecloth. We had a beautiful centerpiece arrangement of assorted flowers requisitioned by Florence from patients' rooms, in most cases without their knowledge or consent, and a candle stuck in an old bottle of wine as our lighting. We also had a large raffia-wrapped bottle of Chianti (alcohol is permitted in the hospital only for medicinal purposes, so of course this occasion qualified), a long loaf of Italian bread, a salad, and freshly cooked spaghetti prepared *al dente* by Florence and Joan in the kitchen down the hall, topped off with the most delectable red clam sauce.

It wasn't easy feeding myself. My arm tired quickly. I didn't eat as much as I thought I would, either. But the experience was totally enjoyable, and the expressions on the faces of staff members who came upon this scene was worth the price of admission alone. As we held more feasts, we added guests to our exclusive club.

The rest of October and November was taken up with dressing changes, debriding and examinations, except for one skin graft done right in my room. My left thigh, that never-ending source of good skin, was disinfected with "pHisoHex" and then numbed with injections of Procaine. Dr. Mitchell, using all his strength—I felt him shuddering with his effort—squeezed the thigh taut. I could hear the mechanical whir of a precision instrument as Dr. Cramer, using the electrically powered dermatome, shaved off skin from my upper leg. The skin was then divided into smaller pieces and placed over areas of the scalp. I couldn't see what was happening, but only because I didn't dare to look. I held my breath during the entire procedure and didn't breathe again until the slicing was finished and a dressing placed over the donor site.

This was the first of many times that I was completely awake during a surgical procedure. I was amazed I tolerated it so well, considering that as a youngster I used to faint at the sight of blood.

I was beginning now to renew my contact with the outside world. The first memorable trip outside the hospital was arranged for me by Becky Keene. She obtained tickets for a concert at Rochester's elegant Eastman Theatre on the night of October 31. Joan and Florence were to accompany me.

I was very concerned, before we got there, over how the audience was going to react to my appearance. In the hospital, disfigurement was the norm, but this was something else. I was amazed at the concertgoers' aplomb; they barely seemed to notice me.

Wearing street clothes over my bulky bandages, I was wheeled into a private elevator that went up to the loge, where I sat in one of the ornate antique easy chairs in the last row, said to be the one used by George Eastman himself.

The cacophony in the pit suddenly hushed, a circle of light hit the curtain at the end of the stage and there appeared my little troll, now gray-haired, full-grown, and very much alive—Leopold Stokowski. He was conducting the Rochester Symphony that night in a memorable performance of his own arrangement of Mussorgsky's *Pictures at an Exhibition.* The evening was a very strenuous one for me; the eighty-one-year-old maestro held up better than I. When we returned to the hospital, I was absolutely exhausted, physically as well as emotionally.

Just pulling off my shirt sleeve over the bandaged hand was a job.

At another time Joan took me to the Italian restaurant that had been the source of our clam sauce. It was located in a seedy part of town, run down and all but deserted at night. We found a parking space right next to the building. The restaurant was dimly lit, and broken up into small private dining rooms so that we easily found a remote location away from prying eyes. They were out of clam sauce that night, but we had an excellent meal anyway, and I began to feel human again. We followed dinner with a movie, *Lilies of the Field,* starring Sidney Poitier. It was like being on a date—dinner and a show with a young, attractive girl. Joan drove me back to the hospital and dropped me off at the emergency entrance, since it was on street level and I wouldn't have to climb any steps. I made my way to my room unassisted for the first time, and managed to undress myself and prepare for bed. This was progress!

A little while later, a New York psychiatrist and his wife, close personal friends, came to visit. Florence joined us for lunch at a so-so Cantonese-Polynesian restaurant. Then, on one of Grace's frequent visits, Florence took us to a kosher delicatessen near Strong for corned-beef sandwiches, pickles and soda. She had been using this eatery as a standby to occasionally supplement the institutional food. Bagels and lox had become routine on Sunday mornings and many staff members were being introduced to this delicacy for the first time. As for me, I was regaining my lost weight, in no small part because of these supplements to my diet.

The expense of burn treatment in a hospital can become astronomical because of the long-term treatment, the constant care, and the quantities of supplies required. All of the Mohawk victims were fortunate in that Strong decided to cancel all charges for the first two weeks of hospitalization, partly because so many doctors, nurses and departments had been involved that it became impossible to assign the proper charges to the proper accounts. In spite of this gratuity on their part, my medical costs skyrocketed to $75,000. But I was nevertheless in reasonably good financial shape. Rico Internationale, my firm, continued to pay my salary for the first four months of hospitalization. When it was bought and merged into a division of Revlon, the new owners agreed to continue my salary as an interest-free loan for which they would eventually be reimbursed from the settlement with the airline. So, from a financial if not from a physical standpoint, I had no worries.

Jerry Marrow, my business associate, called to find out if I felt up to doing a little work. I'm sure he felt this would be good for me psychologically, and he was right. The project that had brought us to Rochester in the first place had bogged down. An attempt to construct a working model of the spray gun we had invented was at a standstill because no one could instruct the model-makers as to how to proceed. Jerry wondered whether I felt up to receiving the model-maker, who would come up from Pennsylvania. I said I did. I was looking forward to some kind of productive activity.

One dreary overcast morning the model-maker arrived as expected. We had a brief preliminary meeting and he asked to be excused for a moment. He never returned. My nurse came in and informed me that the man had fainted and could not bring himself to return. The project was resumed by long-distance telephone.

Once my condition had stabilized and my survival was no longer in doubt, I had no further requirement for a private-duty night nurse. All my needs could be readily handled by the floor nurses, so Florence and Joan alone attended to me during all the months of my first incarceration, except for a night nurse after some operations and on their few, occasional days off. On those days, I had the company of other delightful nurses. One of them was a tall and very attractive blonde, Dorothy Sauer. One afternoon she took Grace and me on an outing to Lake Ontario. We bought hamburgers at a little shack near the lake and sat in the car in a pine-wooded area, looking out at the water. It was a cool fall day—too cool to get out of the car after becoming so acclimated to the heat of the hospital. My exposed sinuses and thin skin covering at the forehead were particularly sensitive to the cold.

During these early excursions I was concerned that people would stare at me and be shocked by my appearance. To my relief that didn't happen. At other places and at other times, it would. But by then I didn't care.

12

I needed to replace the missing parts of my body. Strong had its own prosthetics laboratory, and in fact it made several of the casts, braces and supports I had to use. But it did not make cosmetic prosthetics, so Dr. Cramer suggested that I pay a visit to the laboratory in New York City considered by him to be the best in the field.

Arrangements were made for the trip to New York on November 4. It was agreed that I should go by train; I was not yet ready to fly. Florence would accompany me. After many tedious hours on the old New York Central we pulled in to Grand Central Station, where Grace was waiting for us with the car. The laboratory was in the East Bronx, in one of the most dangerous crime prone areas in the city, but the owners had invested a great deal of time, money and creative effort in their facility and could not bring themselves to give it up, even when it had become unsafe to step outside the door. As we drove there and parked in front I was a little shaky about it. I didn't know what to expect.

The owners were a sweet, middle-aged couple, Milton and Adele Tenenbaum, who lived next door to the laboratory with their little dog and a constantly chattering Mynah bird. It was a converted home, a Victorian brownstone. Actually, it was two homes, one in which they lived and one in which they worked, with a large arched doorway connecting them so that they did not have to go outside to get from house to house. The Tenenbaums were charming people and put me at my ease immediately. Adele, who has since died, was a sculptress; he was the technician. They were used to my kind of problem for that was their business; they had seen a lot worse.

We talked a little while, and then Milton took me into the front parlor, which was the fitting room, and sat me in a barber's chair in the center of the room. Here was he going to measure me, photograph me, and make a mold of me.

Florence removed the dressing over my missing nose and unwrapped the bandage around my head, which was now on mainly to conceal the missing ear. Milton studied me for a while, then set up some very elaborate photographic equipment and lights, and took photographs of my face. He was particularly interested in recording the appearance of my right ear to use as a model for the destroyed left one. Unfortunately, the good ear had abcessed from the burns and bent over as it healed (the same thing happened to our cat) and was thus a rather poor model. The photographic equipment was removed and Milton went to work mixing chemicals—silicone resins and fillers—into a thick paste. Then, while I breathed through my mouth, he carefully pressed the paste over the center of my face until it was smothered with a thick resinous mass. I sat there rigidly, my pulse beating rapidly, until the chemicals solidified into a flexible elastomer that easily peeled off my skin. The impression made was a perfect mold of the gaping lesion on my face. Plaster of paris, cast into the mold, created a *moulage* which reproduced my face in exact detail.

The same procedure was repeated on the left side of the head where the ear was to go. Once both molds were done, it would be up to Adele to model in clay a new nose and ear right on the plaster itself. From these finished replicas Milton would, in turn, cast new molds into which he would pour a liquid vinyl resin that would solidify into a finished prosthetic that would fit my damaged tissues exactly. There remained only to paint the prosthetic parts with vinyl inks to match my skin color, using an airbrush. But this process would take some time; only the *moulages* were made in my presence. These prosthetics were expensive and fragile. They were glued in place with theatrical spirit gum, the way actors use to hold mustaches and beards on. The vinyl plastic discolors, shrinks and hardens with age so the prosthetics must be replaced every few years.

We were finished with the casting now, and Milton took me on a tour of the laboratory. First we went to what was once the dining room to sit under a bank of lights he had devised which reproduced the entire spectrum of the common artificial and natural-light frequencies. Here he could control the switches to see what your prosthetic looked like and how it matched your real skin under different lighting conditions. From here we could see his workers brushing the prosthetics, painting on hair and capillaries, and carving the swirls of fingerprints into a mold of a man's hand. (Hands are Milton's specialty.) We could also see the factory area, where he had big ovens to cure the plastics. In one storage area, box after box, containing the molds for each customer, was stacked to the ceiling. "People parts" in various stages of production were piled everywhere. Milton even showed me an erect prosthetic penis he had made for a man in California who had lost his (for a reason I have long forgotten) and was about to go on his honeymoon. It was a depressing place, and quite shocking to see for the first time.

My mother also lived in the Bronx, and when we were finished at the Tenenbaums we were expected at her house for dinner. Although she could not bring herself to come to Rochester to see me in the condition she knew I was in, she kept in frequent touch. She wrote often and sent a steady supply of goodies.

When she opened the door of her apartment to let us in, she did not betray any shock. Florence bandaged me up before we left the Tenenbaums, but whatever skin on my face remained uncovered was red, raw and disfigured. Most devastating, she told me later on, was the fact that I could not hold my head erect; the burned tendons on the left side of my neck had contracted and pulled my head to one side. I walked with a hesitant, slow gait and my hands trembled. Altogether I did not make a pretty sight to greet a loving mother. But as I walked into her apartment, she held up like steel. My aunt and uncle were there, and reacted even better.

Dinner was excellent, as my mother's dinners usually were, and we talked of many things—the accident, the hospital, the prosthetics. Florence gave my mother a very reassuring prognosis. (Later, when we got back, she wrote my mother a letter commending her for the way she handled the situation.) Finally we had to take our leave. After we left, my mother and her sister took one look at each other and burst into tears. I reluctantly said good-bye to Grace at the station, and Florence and I retraced our tedious way back to Rochester.

After my return to Strong I was being seen less and less by the staff. There was no more surgery scheduled for awhile. From now on it was a matter of regaining strength and healing properly, so that the major reconstructive surgery could begin. I had only to wait for the prosthetics to be finished before I could go home. In my last eye examination in Dr. Zehl's office, the left eye had only blurred vision and still could not read even the top letter on the chart, but the right eye had improved to 20/40, close to normal.

About this time I began watching a new series of programs on the National Educational Television network. The shows were produced by the American Medical Association specifically for doctors. Every week the series presented a different operation, carefully showing all its gory details in clinical close-ups. Tapes were shipped by the AMA to stations around the country for showing, where they were introduced by a small panel of local physicians who then commented on the procedure for about five minutes at the end of the program. Despite my squeamishness as a youth, I really enjoyed these shows and learned a great deal about surgery from them; after watching each one, I felt qualified to set up a private practice specializing in that procedure alone.

One program dealt with surgery of the hand and just before it went on the air Dr. Cramer walked into my room, looking tired for so early in the morning, to relax and share my breakfast of bagels, cream cheese and lox. We watched as the panel was introduced and who should appear on it but none other than Dr. Cramer himself. Although he never said so, I can only assume he knew the program would be on and wanted to watch himself—and surprise me as well. The operation, a tendon transplant, was fascinating.

The Joy baths in my room had stopped since I was now able to walk to the bathroom at the other end of the floor. Joan was in charge of giving me my bath. She would scrub out the tub thoroughly and fill it. I would get in, covering my private parts with a washcloth. After she had bathed me I used a towel to cover myself as I got out again. It was a little ludicrous, I know, but I had gotten to know Joan so well as a person and not just a professional during five months of being together with her that, like Adam and Eve, I began to feel embarrassed. This was a sign, surely, that I must be getting better.

These daily trips up and down the hall gave me a better opportunity to visit the other patients, nurses and staff members and talk with them. On one trip back, however, everything seemed to have changed. The date was November 22, 1963.

As we passed the floor nurses' station there seemed to be unusual agitation there. A nurse asked us, "Did you hear the news? They just shot President Kennedy!" Joan was stunned. I was in shock. I heard myself mumbling over and over again, "I can't believe it . . . I just can't believe it." They kept repeating it and I kept saying, "I don't believe it . . . It can't be!"

We hurried to our room and turned on the television. I stayed pinned to that TV set every minute of each day as the events unfolded. The guard of honor at the coffin was on TV all night and I don't think I even went to sleep. I watched everybody coming by, paying their respects.

The welcome decision was made that I would be discharged on Tuesday, November 26, so that I could be home with my family for Thanksgiving. Dave Elwell, the last of the plane-crash victims, had left the hospital more than a month before and I was champing at the bit. But there was much to do before I left. First and foremost, I wanted to say thank you to everyone who had been involved in caring for me; that involved invitations to over a hundred people from the staff and the city to a cocktail party I threw for them in my room. Florence and a friend of hers arranged scrumptious platters of cold cuts; Becky Keene produced an elaborate silver coffee-and-tea service; we had cakes, pastries and a well-stocked bar.

We chose two-thirty as the start of the party to take care of staff members coming off duty or going on at three. It took only a little while before the room and the hallway outside were mobbed. Groups of young men and women came in who were complete strangers but who knew me well; they were the scrub nurses and aides from the operating suites whose domain I always passed through in an unconscious state. After a few hours of this, the one Scotch-and-soda I was nursing began to take effect. I was really tired, and sat out the rest of the party in a chair with Joan at my side. It was an emotional letdown, too.

Joan and I were driven to the dilapidated Rochester railroad station just in time to catch the 10:00 P.M. train. We had adjoining compartments, and played chess with her portable set before turning in. I was beat.

That party ended my first surgical chapter at Strong. In 148 days I underwent 14 major operations, 37 dressing changes, innumerable sutures. I required untold units of blood and intravenous fluids, cartons of dressings and bandages and tapes, massive quantities of antibiotics and other medications, plus hundreds of man-hours of attention by highly skilled, very expensive practitioners. I also made many new friends.

And this was not the end; it was only the beginning.

We arrived at Grand Central early the next morning and were met by my father-in-law shepherding a wheelchair obtained from the stationmaster. He also had a very convenient parking space right at the station, which he got by tipping the cop on the beat a few dollars. After a few of these trips through his domain, the policeman got to know us and became quite solicitous of our welfare. But each time he accepted the money we offered him.

We drove straight to the Tenenbaums' laboratory and spent the rest of the day being fitted with the new body parts. The ear worked out marvelously well; the nose prosthetic was another story. It looked like a real nose when viewed in isolation, but when glued into place the line separating the plastic from the skin was quite obvious, and the nose had trouble staying on. I found it very grotesque, and if I hadn't invested so much money in it I'd have settled for wearing bandages until the real replacement nose had been reconstructed.

After my parts had been trimmed and perfectly fitted, the vinyl inks to match the color of my skin were airbrushed on. I marveled at the pores and subsurface capillaries that were reproduced. Then Milton photographed me fitted out with my new facial features, and Irving drove us to a surgical supply house in downtown Manhattan where I bought two eating utensils designed for one-handed persons.

It wasn't until after we finished shopping that my father-in-law gathered up the courage to tell me the news: my sister Helen was in Mount Sinai Hospital. Breast cancer had been detected and she had had a radical mastectomy. She would also have to undergo radiation and chemotherapy.

I could not believe what he was telling me. It was dark as we drove to the hospital, the same one where Grace had undergone major surgery and where our first son Leigh was born, but I didn't think of those times, only of my sweet, kind sister who did not deserve this. To see her in this state was overwhelming.

Cancer scares me. I dread the thought of it—more than fire. I had two uncles and an aunt who died of it. And my grandmother had succumbed to breast cancer, which I'm sure was on Helen's mind as it was on mine. I would have suffered thrice what I had just to spare her this now.

When Helen finally tired of our visit, we left our distraught mother and my inconsolable brother-in-law Milt Myer, and headed out on the New Jersey Turnpike to our home in Pennsylvania and my first encounter with my three sons.

They had not seen me since the crash almost five months before, even though we had spoken over the phone almost every day. I didn't know how they were going to react to me and I was apprehensive. I didn't want them to be hurt by the way I looked. I didn't want them to be scared by it. I didn't want them to be shocked.

It was past 11:00 P.M. when we arrived home. The younger boys, Cory and Tod, were already asleep, but Grace had allowed Leigh to wait up for us.

Joan, Irving and I came in the door. I had the bandages around my entire head, covering even the sinuses. My left hand was all bandaged. Leigh was in his pajamas. He had grown taller and serious looking. He was getting to be a big boy.

He said, "I'm so glad to see you. It's so great for you to be here." I thought he was going to have a negative reaction, to cry or shake, but he didn't. Then I put my arms around him and felt his head next to my chest. He was afraid at first to really hug me, or really wrap his arms around me. He hung back. I asked him why, and he said he didn't know where he could touch me, that he was afraid he would be touching some injury and hurting me. When I told him it was okay, he hugged me with all his strength and everything was just great. It took no more than twenty seconds before we both sensed everything was right between us. I think I was more nervous about the encounter than he was, but it took me only a moment to calm down once I saw how well he was taking it. It was as though I had never been away.

I think part of what eased it for him and for me, too, was the fact that I had spoken to him every day. I had been describing on the telephone what had happened to me and I guess Grace had told him many things about it too, so he knew what to expect. He told me that he wasn't afraid or concerned about how he was going to react or what I looked like, just concerned that I would be in pain. He was always very mature, very adult at every age and when he said, "Daddy, how are you?" he really wanted to know how I was.

We stayed up late and talked and when he saw that everything was fine and the reactions were good, he was able to go to bed comfortably. So was I.

The next morning, Cory and Tod reacted as well as Leigh had. I had missed them desperately, and they were an instant tonic for me—flexible, adjustable, adorable. Those little guys were really great. After the initial contact it was like nothing had changed, and they were concerned about me, wanting to know what they could do to help me, to comfort me. In a moment, we were a family again. It was Thanksgiving Day, and our family had much to be thankful for.

13

The first night home, I was awakened from a deep sleep by someone walking about in the dark room. Having been away from home for five months, and still in a daze from my heavy sleep, I naturally inquired in the dark, "Joan?" But it was not Joan who answered. It was Grace, and I could tell she was upset by my query.

Joan remained with us only a few more days, ministering to me, changing my dressings every day and flushing the still-open sinus cavities with pHisoHex from a large glass syringe. (pHisoHex is the trade name for the germicide hexachlorophene that was widely used in hospitals and in hundreds of commercial products, and that was finally identified as a cause of abdominal cramps, vomiting, convulsions and, in a number of cases, death. I was exposed to copious quantities of the chemical, both in my baths and in flushing my sinuses, over a long period of time, and can report no symptoms or problems from using it as far as I know. Of course the monkeys who developed brain lesions after repeated washings in it appeared outwardly normal, too. I think about that once in a while.)

To be sure that nothing would go wrong during my convalescence, at home, I asked our local general practitioner, Dr. Bernard Broad, to come in and check me over. We also arranged for a group of nurses from the local public-health department to come in so Joan could give them and Dr. Broad a live demonstration and instructions as to my medical care, including the daily flushing of the sinuses. The public-health nurses somehow seemed less competent than the ones at Strong, but they were very sweet and very interested. I must have been their most seriously injured patient and they approached me with awe; much of their normal work consisted of assisting the elderly and the incapacitated. In my case they had to wear sterile rubber gloves and use antiseptic techniques, and they seemed to enjoy it.

They provided my daily care until I returned to the hospital. They would come into the bedroom and take off the bandages, flush the sinuses, make sure the wounds were clean and rebandage them. They came every day including Sunday, and a girl who lived across the street and was a nurse volunteered to learn what to do in case of an emergency. Grace must have seen me at those times, just as she had seen me the first night, and I guess she just got used to it.

The bandages were kept on because I had to protect the exposed sinuses. I would put the prosthetic nose on myself. Catching a cold had now become a burden. The prosthetic nose, held on by the narrowest of glue margins to begin with, sometimes came unstuck and I would get a little unsettled and have to retreat to privacy so that I could dry it and reglue it on. I carried a spare glue tube with me at all times.

Because I was mostly bandaged, I never really saw myself without some kind of protective covering, and I still had no idea what my head or hand really looked like. I never really saw my fingers until long, long afterward. When the bandages were changed I avoided looking. I never saw my open sinuses, except later in the medical photographs.

Another reason I considered myself particularly lucky is that I was not affected sexually at all. My genitals were untouched by the flames. When I fainted and fell over in the plane, I instinctively protected that part of my body. The burns went up both legs to my groin and from the top of my head to my waist and stopped; I don't know how. I considered myself most fortunate.

Grace had been forced into the role of head of the household for a while. In the beginning she was often in Rochester, and we had friends who volunteered to take care of the children. Then we got a nice elderly woman to come in and stay with the boys and do whatever had to be done while Grace commuted between home and the hospital. Grace was always very efficient—before she would go she would store the necessary food for everybody and see to their special needs. She's always done it that way—she takes great pains in being sure everything is set up for the children, that clothes are laid out for the next day, and that instructions for each job, even if unnecessary, are given. But now I was home and despite my handicaps I was learning to do everything once again for myself; I refused to be a burden. My attitude seemed to bother Grace for a while. I think she wanted me to lean on her a little. But I wouldn't.

I wondered what limitations I would have—physical limitations, doing things around the house. Especially at first I had a period of wondering about my not being able to play the piano and what else I could do with one hand. I began to think about that one hand—concert pieces for one hand. I was discouraged at the thought.

That first Thanksgiving weekend I sat down at the piano to see what I could do. My right hand was not affected at all, and I just hit the appropriate keys with the bandaged side of my left hand. I started to play one of my old favorites, "Night and Day." It wasn't hard at all. The piano-playing fingers of my good hand had lost little of their dexterity, and with the half-sized remaining digits on my wounded hand I would "one-note," moving just a little faster with the good hand to fill in. The result was not half-bad. There were, I soon discovered, a number of professional one-handed pianists throughout the world.

One-handedness has few other limitations for me. I quickly

learned to tie shoelaces with the one hand although I replaced all my shoes with buckle shoes or step-in loafers. There are elastic shoelaces on the market that permit laced shoes to be used as step-ins, but I've found no need for them. I was faced with the problem of buttoning the right sleeve of my shirt cuffs, but I found I could force my hand through the cuff after I had buttoned it. If the cuff was too tight, I devised a simple expedient: I had Grace loop a piece of elastic through a spare button. I then put the loop over the shirt cuff button and buttoned the cuff to the spare button. The elastic allowed the cuff to expand as I pushed my hand through it. Lo and behold, I discovered this simple device sold in a store for people who were outgrowing their shirt collars. I also discovered that Christian Dior had designed an expanding cufflink for use with French cuffs.

For eating I had the two implements I had purchased in New York. One is called a fork-knife, or sometimes, as it was called when we bought one years later in Dublin, a Nelson knife, after Lord Horatio, who lost an arm at the Battle of Santa Cruz de Tenerife in 1797. It is shaped like a cheese knife; curved at the end, scimitarlike, and terminating in three flat tines. Rocking the knife over food cuts it with a shearing scissors action rather than with the sharpness of the blade. After cutting the blade is rotated, tines pointing downward, and used as a fork. The other implement was just the reverse: a knife-fork. It looks like an ordinary fork except that one edge bulges outward. It shears just like the fork-knife, but unlike the fork-knife it can contend with peas and spaghetti. I recommend them even to the nonhandicapped; they are easy to use, especially for cocktail parties when one hand is holding the plate.

I also found a device enabling a skier to grab onto a rope tow with one hand with sufficient force to prevent slipping on the way up a steep slope. I took up the sport with my sons and found slipping on the rope to be a problem sometimes. I use only one pole when skiing. My service form in tennis is not all that bad. I balance the ball in the palm of my bad hand before tossing it up and serve normally. I am not conscious of any shortcoming other than threading a needle—a task I rarely encounter. Even then, I stab the needle into an upholstered chair and manage to thread it. Driving with one hand and one eye is no problem on the open road, though I usually park at least a foot from the curb because of difficulty in judgment; I installed knobs on the steering wheel for one-handed driving, but with power steering it turns out even they are not needed. Four of my closest and most successful friends also have the use of only one eye and do not suffer for it. Some of the devices developed for the handicapped (or the "inconvenienced," as some prefer) boggle the mind, but I used only the ones I mentioned until I phased most of them out.

Shortly after Christmas I received word that my stepfather had died of Parkinson's disease and related complications at Bronx Hospital. He was alone at the time since the rest of my family were with my sister, still recuperating from her mastectomy at Mount Sinai, and because of this funeral arrangements were minimal. Almost no one was there. My stepfather, Vitale Della Penna, "Del" as we called him, was an architect with a small practice in the East Bronx, a bumbling, good, kind man, with no trace of malice in him. He was elderly, very bald and, to say the least, rotund—eating was his pleasure second only to playing gin rummy, especially with my late uncle, whom he could never beat no matter how hard he tried. His remains were shipped to his children, by his first wife, in Florida. Their mother had died when they were very young. Now they were grown, married and had children of their own. They had seen very little of their father when he was alive; now he returned to them for eternity.

How my mother survived these multiple tragedies to those she loved the most I will never understand. In the midst of all this some unknown stranger took it upon himself (or herself) to send her a poison-pen letter, which aggravated her problems. But she summoned up her inner strength and survived. We all did, in our own way. My sister, after undergoing all the horrors and discomfort of the radiation and hormone treatments, was completely cured—and, in spite of her amputated chest muscles, became as fanatic about tennis as Grace and I.

At home, life was achieving some normalcy. We began receiving visitors and going out to restaurants and movies. We spent a pleasant holiday season with the family. On New Year's Eve we went out for dinner, dancing, champagne and a party afterward. It was great to be alive.

Even before the crash, as far back as adolescence, I had

considered plastic surgery to correct the bump in my nose, so that I was looking forward to the cosmetic improvements I was led to expect would be forthcoming. I believed in the miracles that could be performed with plastic surgery, and when Dr. Cramer told me to think about the kind of nose I would like to have, I had every hope of being more handsome than I was before the accident.

But little by little I became aware that it wasn't going to be like that at all; when all was said and done, I would be unpleasantly disfigured. Soon, I began to discern some satisfying advantages to this condition.

For one thing, recognition is instant and total. As a result of that plane crash, I have become a personality; I am no longer anonymous. When most people return to a place after a few days, they generally are unnoticed nonentities. But now when *I* return even a year or more later I am greeted with "Hey! Where have you been?"

Wherever I go I get the feeling that a red carpet is being rolled out for me; the receptions I get are warmer and more friendly than any before the accident. This familiarity makes people feel more comfortable and makes it easier for me to form bonds of friendship with them. The more frequently a person comes in contact with me, the better I look to him even though I am not changing. Even my own relatives will invariably greet me with "You're looking much better" or "You look marvelous." They're just getting more and more used to me, until they finally no longer think about the way I look at all.

Elsa Maxwell once made the wry observation about overweight women that "men do not suspect them and other women do not fear them as competition." The reverse of that applies to me. Since my disfigurement, men are considerably more open and friendly with me. They accept me more now because they think that since I'm disfigured I'm not a sexual threat to them.

Women, I find, are more receptive to me since the accident than they were before. It isn't fair to say that they find me more or less attractive now than before, but they notice me because I am disfigured. Once they have picked me out and we get to know each other in a more informal way, they see what they want to see. Since they know this is not me they're looking at, the only real me they see is the one in their mind's eye. They paint that picture themselves and they react to my personality rather than my appearance.

Maybe they are more sexually receptive because of sympathy. I can't tell. I find that many people do feel great pangs of sympathy for me and tend to go out of their way to be nice to me. And I let them. I know that beauty is only skin deep and that's the theory I operate under. And since it is only skin deep, once you've seen the skin you get over it and you go deeper and you see what's beneath that skin.

I can't say I really prefer looking like this, but I guess I do. I know I sound like an idiot. But I find it more effective in many ways to have this face than to have the old one. The identification factor is a very helpful thing. I stand out in the crowd. It's no disadvantage to look this way. On the contrary, socially and psychologically, it's an advantage. It's just worked out that way. And, as long as it has, I don't mind.

14

The hiatus at home lasted a little over four months. It was marvelous to have been with family and friends again, especially since I was in no real physical discomfort or distress. I had even enjoyed the daily ministrations of my visiting nurses. But it was time to start the long rebuilding process, and I looked forward eagerly to going back to Strong again.

Grace and I started out for Rochester by car on March 30, 1964. We took two days to travel the 350 miles between home and the hospital. We wanted to avoid the superhighways and explore the secondary roads that threaded between the Finger Lakes. The trip was not unpleasant. We discovered an excellent motel, and ate at an outstanding steakhouse on our overnight stop.

When we got to Rochester Grace checked into the Towne

House, where she was by now a familiar and honored guest. Then we drove around the corner to the hospital. Each of my return visits to Strong was like a reunion. Becky Keene was my hostess and saw to it that I received the red-carpet treatment. I was overwhelmed by it. There was something very comforting about being back in the sanctuary of the hospital. Everyone knew about me and the accident, and I had no feelings of self-consciousness.

Becky had arranged for me to have one of the nicer rooms on the fifth floor of the Q wing, which was a private pavilion. I undressed and put on the shorty nightgown supplied by the hospital, with its opening in the back to make physical examinations and removal in bed easier, and stowed my gear, setting up the little portable TV I had bought mainly for use in the hospital. I knew it would be more economical to have my own than to rent one from the hospital, and though the practice is frowned on it wasn't questioned in my case.

The routine that I would follow each time I was readmitted to Strong began. A floor nurse took an inventory of all my valuables, allergies and food problems. She took my temperature, blood pressure and pulse, pointed out the features of my room and equipment, and departed. She was followed shortly thereafter by an intern who examined me from head to toe and wrote a case history for the record as a part of his training. Sometimes a senior medical student also stopped by to get practice in taking a history, or even to conduct a complete examination. I realized I was not required to submit to these practice sessions if I did not want to, but I felt that it might help if these young students were exposed to my unusual trauma, and it was an education for me to observe their different methods and personalities in interviewing me.

Next, an aide, usually a young girl, arrived from the blood laboratory with her sanguine tray, to take a blood sample and other tests. A little prick on the tip of the finger was enough to fill a tiny glass capillary, smear a microscope slide and discolor a solvent in a small test tube.

Then the anesthesiologist—in this case, the head of the department—came in to talk about any problems we might have in surgery the next day. Research has shown that a quiet talk with the anesthesiologist (or for that matter a doctor, family member or religious counselor) just before surgery results in the need for fewer narcotics to dull the pain after the operation is complete, which in turn lessens the chances for complications like pneumonia and shortens the hospital stay.

After the staff's visits were over I was wheeled down—patients are always moved in wheelchairs, since this reduces the possibilities of an accident—to Dr. Zehl's eye-examination room off the main lobby. He noted that the newly created left eyelid had shrunk over the past four months so that, even though the eye rolled upward in the normal reflex, the cornea was not completely covered by its blinking. A few days later, without apparent reason, the lids became inflamed and the eyeball reddened with conjunctivitis. There was no pain, tenderness or discharge, however, and Dr. Zehl's opinion was that it was a local condition stemming from use of eye ointment, soap or pHisoHex in surgery. After a few days of salt-water compresses the inflammation went away. After his examination I was wheeled to the medical photographer's studio for more mug shots, to be added to my file. Throughout all my stays, the well-equipped hospital photography department at Strong continued to take pictures of me—in their studio and in my room, even in the operating room. Their complete photographic record would be used by the medical and nursing staffs in lectures, articles and books, and my attorneys would have access to them, too.

Grace returned to the motel late in the evening and I relaxed in bed reading and watching television. Finally, the maestro himself, Dr. Cramer, put in an appearance. His day never seemed to be done. We talked a little bit and then, squinting through his metal-rimmed glasses, his lips tightly pursed, he studied my face and neck, poking me gently here and there, asking me to bend my head in various directions. Then he took a small metal ruler from out of his pocket and held it in front of my nose and sinuses, first vertically, then horizontally, to measure the areas involved. When he departed I settled down for the night, refusing the proffered sleeping pill but sleeping well nevertheless.

Breakfast was not brought to me the next morning. I was not allowed food after midnight before any surgery, as is usual practice—the patient might vomit from the anesthesia and choke.

My surgery was to be performed under local anesthetic so nausea would not be a problem, in any case. A nurse came into my room, raised my nightgown and jabbed a needle containing the preop medication into my buttock. An hour later I was wheeled into surgery semiconscious. I could feel myself being lifted from the gurney to the table; someone began tapping my right inner forearm to raise a blood vessel for the I.V.; other hands were quickly stripping me and roughly scrubbing my face, neck and torso, all the way down to my abdomen. In spite of my near-stupor, I could sense that I was chilled. My arm was strapped to the board extending from the table. A large needle was painlessly inserted into a vein and held there with a wad of adhesive tape. The numbing infusion of Demerol began. In moments I was asleep.

The usual green sheets and towels were draped over the areas that would be exempt from this procedure. Then the surgeons went to work. They rolled me onto my right side and supported my left shoulder blade with a pillow. The left side of my chest was given several injections to desensitize it. Dr. Cramer shaved off a thick layer of skin there and the raw donor site was covered at once with a layer of fine mesh gauze and a dry, sterile compression dressing.

I was rolled onto my back again. The surgeons directed their attention to the scar tissue between my neck and jawbone that had contracted and pulled my head to one side. If I tried to straighten it out, it would stretch, making the tendons underneath the skin appear too short (which they might have been) causing them to bulge and pulling the bottom of my mouth into a distorted, grotesque position. It also prevented the use of an endotracheal tube, which would have been necessary if general anesthesia had to be administered. For this reason, operation was being performed under local anesthesia.

The scar was released by cutting into it using a technique called a Z-plasty, or transitional flap. Z-plasties relieve tension or distortion of a scar by lengthening the line where the skin closed. One long incision was made. Two shorter, parallel ones were made at each end so that the incision resembled the letter Z. Skin hooks were placed along the edges of the cuts and the skin was gently raised by cutting under it with a scalpel. Then the edges of the main cut were drawn apart.

The points of bleeding were clamped and the two end flaps were transposed and sutured into place. They were tied off with plain catgut, which was to be absorbed by the body as the wound healed. Since this was a rather large area, some raw skin remained exposed. That was what the chest graft was used to cover.

The surgical team then moved to the area running from my right shoulder, close to the neck, across the collarbone to the breastbone. This was the beginning, unbelievably, of my new nose. Dr. Cramer had concluded that this was the closest match of skin to my face that was still available. The hard part of his decision was which arm to use for a wrist attachment in the later phases of the rebuilding. If it was my right arm then I would be without the use of my only good hand for perhaps a year. But the left arm was almost completely covered with grafted skin, so the decision was really made for him: it would have to be the good right arm.

The building of a new nose requires the use of a large, hanging piece of skin called a pedicle flap. It would be obtained by cutting three edges around a long rectangular area on the chest, in stages, and interrupting the blood supply. This cutting is called a delay. What they did in the delays was to make two parallel slits, undermine that skin on both sides and then re-place it in its original position. What that does is cut blood vessels, forcing the skin to get blood nourishment from other areas that were not undermined. At the same time they didn't lose that skin because it was put back in a bloody area and nourished with sufficient blood supply. Through eight separate surgeries, this rectangle would be undermined more and more until its only source of nourishing blood was one uncut edge at the upper end.

But today was only the first delay in the long process. Dr. Cramer measured a three-by-four-inch area at the base of my neck and made the first two parallel incisions with his scalpel. Gently, he elevated the edges with skin hooks, clamped the bleeding, stitched the edges back in place. A dressing was ap-plied and I was returned to my room in good shape. The entire surgery had taken three hours.

Several days later the dressings came off and the areas were cleansed with cotton swabs. The Z-plasties and the graft on the neck had both taken 100 percent. To prevent discoloration and disfigurement if they were left in too long and rejected by the body, the sutures were taken out of the pedicle flap. I would groan as usual in an attempt to force the doctor to exercise greater care as he took them out. The Z-plasty stitches were left in a little longer because they were exposed to greater tensions.

I was allowed to return home on April 9. Grace and I drove along Lake Cayuga, taking a short detour through the campus of Cornell University.

During the next month I made two quick trips to Strong by train. On the first I was accompanied by my father-in-law; he was too concerned to let me go by myself. We stayed overnight at the Towne House and the following morning we reported to the outpatient clinic. In the treatment room there, a pretty young blonde nurse, Helen Surline, was waiting. She asked me to remove my shirt, got me settled onto a complicated-looking treatment table and started to scrub the area around the pedicle flap. It was then that I noticed she was missing the same two fingers on her left hand that I was missing. I was startled. Her handicap was no impediment to her; she was extremely competent.

Dr. Cramer entered wearing his white laboratory coat and got down to the business at hand. After examining the flap area, he issued a terse set of instructions for the sutures and needles and assorted odds and ends he would require. The sterile green sheets were then laid over me, leaving only the torso exposed. Over the torso went a green towel with a hole cut in that, so only the ends of the scars on the chest were visible. The drapes were clipped together with a rasping sound; Dr. Cramer knocked out the local area with anesthetic. When pin pricks determined that the flesh was ready, he began cutting, joining the ends of the parallel scars in a U arc. Now all the blood was flowing from my shoulder toward the flap. It was a careful, precise procedure. Unhurried. I was not on any medication for anxiety, but I was unbothered by it, rather intrigued. It seemed so simple. In the middle of it, Dr. Cramer's secretary walked in and he introduced us, although my face was totally covered by the sheet. And even while he was stitching me up he dictated a letter to the renowned Dr. Harry Royster, of the University of Pennsylvania's Ravdin Institute (Ravdin was the doctor who operated on President Eisenhower for ileitis in 1956), requesting an appointment for me to go there the following week to have the sutures removed.

A small bandage was placed over the area. I dressed, said good-bye, and my father-in-law and I made it to the railroad station barely in time to catch one of the rare trains back to New York.

The next time I returned to the hospital I was unescorted and much less apprehensive. I knew what to expect. The surgeries and the visits had become routine. Surgery was once again in the clinic, extending the parallel incisions three more inches. They were now a full seven inches long.

A little more than a week later I returned again, driving up with Grace, stopping overnight and checking into Strong on May 10. This was to be major surgery and the admission procedures were the same as before, except for a complete cocoa-butter massage the floor nurse gave me with only the illumination of her flashlight. This was quite sensuous and, to say the least, distracted me from whatever fears and trauma I might have had about surgery the next morning.

Fear and trauma are certainly what awaited me. I was wheeled to the operating room under preop sedation. Since I could straighten out my neck now I was to receive general anesthesia. The anesthesiologist tried to insert an endotracheal tube down my throat and administer general anesthesia. But the tube kinked. He tried again and again. He tried different tubes. None of them could get past the thick scar that had formed under my Adam's apple during the four months of the tracheostomy. It was well over an hour before he succeeded. Finally, the anesthetic was administered and I mercifully went out.

The plan was to transfer one end of the pedicle flap from my chest to my wrist as the next step in the nose-building procedure. But it was not to be. When the flap was raised, its skin, particularly at the separated end, turned purple. This meant poor blood circulation, and it worried Dr. Cramer. The nourishment wasn't good enough; he would have to put it back and let it develop more. Other procedures were planned, but with so much time lost forcing the tube down my throat, he canceled the rest of the surgery.

I woke up with my throat throbbing. I don't think it was lacerated, but I know it felt that way. It was badly swollen and badly irritated—the worst sore throat you could imagine. I couldn't swallow. I couldn't even move without feeling worse pain than when I was sitting still. The pain was a deep pain, because the tube had gone all the way in. Pain-killers didn't do anything for it. I developed a fever that persisted for two weeks. Test after test was given in an effort to find what was causing it. Cultures were taken from every body fluid available—blood, urine, mucus. I was X-rayed. Every resident and intern tried his own thing. Finally, after a week of suffering and misery, they decided to use the broad-spectrum antibiotic tetracycline. It took another week for that to turn the trick.

There was a great deal of uncertainty, meanwhile, about saving the pedicle flap. It had turned black and blue. Finally, it appeared that it would survive, and the last sutures were taken out on May 22. I was discharged the following morning and sent home, still feeling pain in my throat despite the assortment of lozenges, aspergum and pain-killers I kept taking for relief. If surgery had proceeded normally, I would have expected to leave the hospital in a week. Instead, the surgery was unsuccessful and I had to suffer for two weeks afterward both from the pain in my throat and the knowledge of a wasted operation.

Because of this experience with the endotracheal tube all my future surgeries were performed under local anesthetic with heavy preop sedation to make me drowsy and insensitive to pain. I didn't complain, especially when I considered that ten thousand deaths a year are related to the use of general anesthesia.

In a little over two weeks we were back at Strong, but when Dr. Cramer examined the flap in the outpatient clinic he decided it was not yet ready for further surgery. Rather than waste the trip he agreed to operate on some contracted scars that were pulling my lower lip down considerably to one side. The following morning I got the usual two needles in the buttocks and lay in bed waiting for the drugs to take effect when the phone rang. It was a volunteer, who had become a close friend—the wife of one of the young doctors at Strong—who was calling to wish me well. Then, when she hung up, Florence walked in to pay a social call.

By the time the floor nurse and an aide came to take me to surgery on the gurney I was wide awake. In surgery, even with my eyes tightly shut to try to get to sleep, I could tell the lighting overhead was quite brilliant. One of the surgical nurses came over, cheerful and talkative, to ask me how I was. I answered her, with my eyes still closed. I could almost count the number of hands that lifted me onto the operating table. My faulty eyelids had even more trouble screening out the extreme brightness of the light overhead, and I knew that the room was frigidly cold. The pHisoHex solution felt like ice water. I could sense the anesthetist working on inserting the needle in my right arm and I made some little joke. Mentally, I followed every needle into my flesh. The needles started going into my thigh, which was to be the donor site.

I seemed to sense one especially deep jab going through the back of my leg and hitting my thighbone, or at least that's what it felt like. In any case, the shock, real or imagined, must have caused me to faint. The doctors and nurses thought I had gone into cardiac arrest and they went into panic. My left leg and trunk convulsed repeatedly. I stopped breathing for twenty seconds, turned white, then blue. An oxygen mask was quickly slapped over me. Breathing began spontaneously.

I overheard the nervous conversation: " . . . into cardiac arrest . . . he's coming around. . . . Is anyone still sterile?" There were murmurs of "no," then a dejected, "Well, I guess that's it." For the second straight time my operation had to be terminated.

Robbie Warfield was at my side as I was wheeled into recovery, in a conscious state for the first time, talking to me softly, gently wiping my face and lips. More oxygen was administered to me. I kept staring at a woman lying next to me, completely unconscious and oblivious of my presence. They kept me there for five hours in case a new emergency arose. Then I was wheeled back to my room. I was kept two more days for observation. Grace and I headed home disappointed—another wasted trip!

Nothing had been accomplished, but inwardly I felt happy and relieved. I was not to be cut up this time. It is a natural reaction—no matter how frequently you go under the knife you never get used to it. It is always something you shun, dread and want to avoid whenever you can.

While we were waiting for the train at Rochester, a reporter for one of the two Gannett papers in Rochester, Desmond Stone, stopped to talk to us. Stone was a tall, handsome New Zealander with a Down Under accent who later became an editor of the paper. He was also a close friend of Becky Keene and he took more than a professional interest in us. He told us he wanted to come down to our home in Pennsylvania and interview us for a feature article to appear on the first anniversary of the crash. Had it been that long already? I told him I would have to get my attorneys' approval. But they vetoed the idea because they felt the publicity might cause our case against Mohawk to be delayed. Nevertheless, on July 2, 1964, a page-and-a-half recap, with photographs of the crash, ran in the paper.

Three weeks later I was back, but Dr. Cramer still felt the pedicle flap was too dusky to be safely lifted and once again turned his attention, as he had the last time, to the lips. I was not taking any chances this time and gave my own orders to the staff: before I received my preop injection my phone was to be disconnected; I was to be lying in the transport gurney *before* the injections were given; I was to have no visitors; the shades in my room were to be drawn, the lights out; no one was to speak to me, nor loudly to each other. I also requested that I be kept as warm as possible in the operating room. I issued these instructions so that I would hopefully be asleep by the time I arrived in the operating room from now on and avoid any more premature terminations, and I repeated them before every surgery from then on. I was being a prima donna, of course. Patients are and should be. It's good for them to be treated as special people, and the fact that I was treated as one was very important to my recovery.

I was placed on my stomach on the operating table, scrubbed, draped and given the local anesthetic. Ten square inches were shaved off the right side of my back—another scar for the collection. Next I was rolled onto my back, onto the freshly dressed wound, but I felt nothing. Now my face was scrubbed, my body draped and the anesthesia was injected to knock out the nerve that passes through a channel in the jaw below the teeth. This was followed by smaller, no less excruciating, injections around the lips. These needles are probably the worst pain in surgery; after that the only pain is in your mind.

Dr. Cramer excised the large lip scar neatly and cleanly. The chin tension was released almost instantly. Bleeding vessels were clamped and the wound sutured and packed with saline gauze. Then two small Z-plasties were carved on the line that underlines the lower lip in order to prevent another scar from contracting. The surgery progressed very slowly; the cutting required more precision and care than usual. Two hours into surgery, while Dr. Cramer was slicing off pads of thickly scarred tissue, the effects of the shots started wearing off. I came out of my drugged state long enough to mumble this fact to him, careful not to move my lips and make his scalpel slip. He directed that more needles be administered to me, but they didn't have any effect. So, for the next hour and a half, I lay there and felt every cut, every stitch, as it perforated my skin. The pain was not excruciating in itself; it was my awareness of what was going on that disconcerted me. Because I had been so heavily sedated I was able to tolerate it, though. I had gotten three preoperative shots instead of two, to make sure I did not wake up on the table again.

After the scar tissue had all been cut out, the graft from the back was deftly stitched into place around the lips, outlining the normal shape. The stitches were left dangling to attach a pressure dressing. When I heard Dr. Cramer issue instructions to start putting the dressing on, I felt my stomach relax and my breathing return to normal, and I knew the cutting and stitching had ended. I was totally awake now and was asked to sit up so that the full, bulky dressing—covering everything from the left eye to the chin, immobilizing the jaw so that the grafts would not distort—could be wrapped. The excised scar tissue, meanwhile, was not thrown out with the garbage. It was sent to the pathology laboratory, for complete study and examination.

For two days afterward I felt drowsy, so drowsy I refused all nursing care: baths, food, everything. My lips were so badly swollen they could not close enough to suck on a straw and my liquid intake was poor. I did manage to drink a little water from the glass, but most of it ran down the chin bandages and I was usually too doped up and disinterested to make the effort. At one point, I was told that if I did not take in more fluids within the next two hours, an I.V. was going to be started. But at half-past midnight on July 10, I drank a glass of chocolate milk. All was well.

The donor site on my back was weeping heavily, and a heat lamp was turned on it to try and dry it. The lamp was one of the few devices I encountered the whole time I was in the hospital that was not elaborate, expensive and overdesigned; it was nothing but an ordinary light bulb in a homemade wooden box. The head bandage was removed, revealing the blood- and fluid-stained dressings that, outlined in black by the sutures, surrounded the still-swollen lips. One cautious look in the mirror was enough to convince me that the cure had been worse than the condition. But in time, as wounds always do, it healed and steadily improved in appearance.

One day, quite unexpectedly, Dave Elwell paid me a visit in the hospital. He looked marvelous, with little to indicate that he was getting around on a wooden leg. In his dark blue suit, he looked every bit the executive, booming around the hospital and getting warm receptions from anyone who remembered him from the year before. He had flown to Rochester on business and learned that I was in Strong for surgery. He dropped the news that he had settled his suit against Mohawk for an astronomical $440,000, without the benefit (and fees) of legal counsel. It surprised me that he had been able to settle so quickly, especially without an attorney and while holding down his job. I was encouraged about my own case, but also had some doubts about whether I had done the wisest thing in rushing out to hire a lawyer right away.

After a week I was permitted to check out of Strong and stay with Grace at the Towne House while I waited for the hospital's prosthetic shop to make a chin-and-neck brace for me. It was to prevent any new contracting scars from pulling my skin out of shape again. I was supposed to wear the tight-fitting, plastic and fiberglas laminate, armorlike contraption twenty-four hours a day for the next six months. The shop told me it would take four days to make, but I pressured them to get it done in two so that we could return home to the children.

Then, when it was finished, it didn't fit right and I couldn't tolerate wearing it for any extended period—between two and twelve hours a day at first, then not at all, and Dr. Cramer was quite properly annoyed at me for rushing things. We returned home, myself looking worse and feeling less comfortable than when I had arrived nine days earlier.

Anyway, the brace didn't make much difference one way or another. The take was perfect. Dr. Cramer, meanwhile, was receiving an award from a medical group which was sending him on a tour of European plastic-surgery facilities for the summer, so my next surgery was not slated until the end of September. I was disappointed at this delay; psychologically, I couldn't do any substantive work until all the surgery was out of the way. So I whiled away the summer playing chess, painting, going to museums, picnicking with my family and gaining a new appreciation for life, my family and for my surroundings.

The seventh trip back to Rochester was on September 21, 1964. Grace and I drove a different route this time, with the overnight stop in Ithaca at a motel with an excellent restaurant. Nothing much had changed at the hospital in two months' absence. After his usual stone-faced perusal, Dr. Cramer scheduled a surgery for the left eye. Contracting scars there were pulling at the eyelid and preventing it from covering the cornea.

He and Dr. Zehl performed the operation. A three-by-five inch graft was shaved off the left thigh and horizontal incisions were made across the eyelids. The scars were cut out and the graft was stitched into the raw area. After a few days I was up and around. The dressings were changed and the grafts took completely. While waiting for the eye to heal, a large abcess developed on the left side of my neck from ingrown hair under the scar tissue, so Dr. Cramer, assisted by Nurse Surline, cut it open in the clinic, talking to me the whole time they were draining it and cutting away inflamed tissue. Then I had another eye examination nearby in Dr. Zehl's office. The right eye had improved to 20/15 with no refractive error. One eye, at least, was in excellent shape.

As I walked the hall during this visit, I met another patient, an old, charming and distinguished man, Charles Z. Case. He lived on a farm in Avon, New York, and had been in charge of transporting American armed forces in World War II. His parents had been on the fateful maiden voyage of the *Titanic;* his father went down with the ship but his mother survived. Case had attended Harrow in England; but he dropped out in the seventh grade and later went to work for Kodak over there. Eventually he became director of its English branch. One thing that always unsettled me about him was his monogrammed belt buckle (he wore trousers under his bathrobe on his daily walks up and down the hallway)—the initial wasn't his, and I never quite had the courage to question him about this little anomaly. He was an excellent chess player, the best I had faced in years, and we played every day. But he would not play in the evenings because his mind became so agitated he could not fall asleep. We read of his death in the *New York Times* just a few months later.

I was discharged on October 1. On our way home, Grace and I stopped overnight in Vestal, New York, and shared a chateaubriand at what was becoming one of our regular haunts. We followed our lavish dinner with a good double feature at a drive-in movie, and the next morning eagerly headed for home and the children. Five weeks later, we retraced our steps back to Strong. This was the big one coming up—the critical stage of rebuilding my new nose and the second-longest stay in the hospital.

In this stage they were going to cut a flap from my wrist and lay it open, leaving one end still attached. Then they would lift one end of the pedicle flap and lay it on the exposed wrist flap and stitch them together. From that moment on, for the next four months, my arm would be fixed by this band of flesh first to my chest, and later, in the next stage, to my forehead. I would be able to do nothing for myself, and would have to have private duty nurses seven days a week to perform for me the tasks I usually did on my own: washing, shaving, brushing my teeth, dialing and talking on the telephone, eating, writing, scratching, going to the bathroom, everything.

The night before, my left thigh, that miraculous pitcher of flesh, was shaved and scrubbed with pHisoHex to reduce the bacteria count. In the morning, I received extra doses of preop medication, an extensive scrubbing and lots of local needles around the edges of the pedicle flap that ran like a Sam Browne belt from my neck to my chest. Dr. Cramer lifted the flap, and this time the eyes above the masks danced in relief; the darkening was slight; the flap had a viable blood supply.

Conversation in the operating room was kept to a minimum so as not to wake me from my protective stupor; this was to be a three-hour procedure. The surgeons waited a few minutes to make sure the flap's color wasn't getting any darker, and then they harvested the left thigh for donor skin, placing that graft on the wound Dr. Cramer had just created in lifting the flap.

My good right arm had been shaved in my room the night before; now it was brought into view and draped. A C-shaped incision, resembling the flap of a purse, was made just above the wrist. Like the pedicle flap, the skin here was undermined, too, and folded outwards. The arm was laid on my chest, palm down, the wrist flap rolled open so that it pointed toward my chin with its raw side exposed. Then the pedicle flap was brought down from over the shoulder and laid on top of it so that the two opposing raw surfaces were making contact, and the margins were stitched together. Good color returned, indicating there was satisfactory circulation in both of them. The okay was given to apply the dressings and lock my arm in a perpetual civilian salute to the flag.

I was asked to sit up since I was fully awake but feeling no pain. Many hands supported me while a surgeon placed large pads under my arm, at my wrist and around my neck. He wrapped it all with gauze, and then plastered splints on the outside.

I rode out of the room on a Demerol high, which I would sometimes succumb to when emerging from sedation. The medication was so strong that I was kind of floating and I had no interest in food. I just wanted to be left alone and allowed to float. On several occasions I awakened back in my room and asked the nurse, "When are they going to take me down for surgery?" When the response was, "You've already been down and it's all over," my heart would leap and I would start to float in the happy world, sometimes giggling and not able to stop talking. The sensation was very pleasant. I could see how some longtime surgical patients get addicted. Fortunately for me, I was very much against the use of drugs, or otherwise it would have been a very tempting path to take.

Except for a little pain during the first couple of postoperative days, and the more intense pain of keeping my arm in a fixed position—it stiffened at the joints, the muscles atrophied and there was no way I could move it—my new situation was not unpleasant. Circulation was good at the fingertips, which meant that the splints and dressings were not too tight. I had some difficulty in sleeping at first, but I think it was mostly mental; I was worried about tearing the flap loose from its moorings. Eventually, I learned to move my arm slightly. The dressing began to loosen and I gained some motion at the elbow.

At one point, the flap shaded a little, an indication that the circulation was not as good as it had been right after surgery, but a week later when the splint was taken off it looked excellent. It had taken fully, and I was given a spongebath in bed, for which I was exceedingly grateful.

A new, lighter dressing was a little more comfortable, but the elbow and shoulders still hurt. Out of sheer desperation, I had a dressing and splint of my own design made. It was bulky, but firm, and, more important, it supported my elbow so that I could at last relax without putting a strain on the pedicle flap. For the entire first week I had actually been holding up my arm to keep from damaging the flap, and that had caused terrific pain to my shoulder. And, of course, there was no way I could exercise it to obtain relief.

The last stitches came out on November 22, and the next day the flap was worked on in the clinic. It was cut at the shoulder and raised until its original source of blood was cut off, making it dependent on the connection at the wrist flap for all its nourishment. The outer edge of the flap bled briskly later that night back in my room, but there was no pain. A resident stitched it up in my room without any anesthesia. Thanksgiving came on the twenty-sixth. Grace had brought the children up with her. Young children are not normally permitted to visit in a hospital, but Becky Keene, my constant champion, arranged for the boys to visit me. First, though, to amuse and befriend them she punched out each of their names on a label maker and pasted them on their jackets.

The boys were blasé about my condition and instantly ignored it. Grace had prepared them well. But they were entranced by my push-button speaker telephone and my bed. The phone was the standard one supplied by the phone company for conference calls. The bed was electrically operated, with buttons to raise and lower the mattress at the head, or legs or the entire bed as a unit. The boys all but ignored me as they climbed aboard and began to play submarine and spaceship games. It was a most pleasant distraction for them as well as me.

Later I was able to leave the hospital and join the family at the Towne House for Thanksgiving dinner. We had a guest with us, Mrs. Lane Johnson, a volunteer at Strong in her seventies who occasionally played chess with me. She had no family in Rochester. She was amused by the antics of our active little boys, and joined them on the floor in their games.

I had to be fed by my private-duty nurse, Marilyn Miller, but no one seemed to be fazed by it. Marilyn was leaving to get married. Her replacement, Annette Hancoski, also was with us. She had watched over me the night of the crash; we had not seen each other since. I spent the next two days with the family at the hotel and returned to the hospital only to sleep. Eating the hotel food was a real pleasure—they had a good chef and, because of our long association with them, we got great service.

But if the bland meals at the hospital were nothing to write home about, on many occasions, thanks to Becky Keene, I received much more delectable fare. Becky had close friends, Haron and Violet Saltoun, Iraqian Jews who had sold their home and business and come to America. Three of their five children had been afflicted with multiple sclerosis, and they believed it when they were told that they could be cured in America. The three unfortunate children had to be institutionalized when they got here, and the two parents made their life tolerable by making other people happy. Violet was a superb cook of Middle Eastern food, and, although she had never met me, the fact that I was a friend of Becky Keene's was enough for her. Every so often I'd receive a call from Becky: "Don't order dinner tonight, Violet is sending it in."

That evening, Violet's dark-haired daughter, Jackie, a charming girl, would drop off a trayful of exotic delights. It was always a full-course Middle Eastern feast: baklava and other pastries, all baked with the thinnest leaves, the sweetest honey and the best-tasting pistachio nuts; kebabs; lambs' tongues in rice; homemade candy and dry fruit. Each entrée was in its own, specially suited dish, which would be decorated in the style you find only in the finest restaurants. She had thin flat loaves of Arabic bread sent in by bus from Syracuse, and Haron always included a bottle of fine wine from his wine and liquor shop in Rochester.

There was always more than enough to feed my nurses and guests and patients and still have leftovers for days to come. On Christmas the Saltouns sent in so much food we were able to set up a large buffet in the solarium and feed all of the ambulatory patients and staff members on the entire floor. And if you ever thanked them or expressed your appreciation in any way, they only sent you more the next time. Besides their dinners for me, they held Sunday open houses for friends and strangers. It was over a year before we got to meet them personally, but we spoke frequently on the phone and they became just like members of my family.

The last delay of the pedicle flap was done on December 3. For three more weeks I languished, waiting for "the big one," while X-rays showed that no bone problems existed in the skull and sinuses. On December 21 the surgeons were scheduled to lift the flap from my chest and attach it to my forehead, to the skin they had grafted there, over a year before, after they had finished fenestrating the skull. I would have to remain in this grotesque position with my arm connected to my forehead by the flat band of skin until the flap had developed a new blood supply from the forehead, at which time it would be disconnected from the arm and formed, finally, into a new nose.

In preparation for it, cultures from my sinus were taken. Several cross-matches were made to my blood in case transfusions were required. A tranquilizer was ordered for me; several days beforehand, the forehead and the flap were already being washed with pHisoHex. On the night of December 20, Annette Hancoski signed the Operation Consent Order for me: "Patient has read above and approves. He is unable to use either hand to write."

15

Early on the morning of December 21, the action began. The shades were drawn, the lights extinguished, the telephone cut off, and I was transferred to the gurney and made comfortable on my pillow.

I preferred undergoing surgery the first thing in the morning because there was less time to stew about it. The worst part of almost any surgery is worrying about it beforehand. The rest is neither all that painful nor all that unpleasant, but no matter how many times you go through it, the worry beforehand is always there the next time.

Nembutol was given to me at 8:00; at 9:00 morphine and atropine, a poisonous alkeloid derived from belladonna; by 10:00 I was on the operating table, feeling no pain, the I.V. running. I was stripped and scrubbed over the eight different areas to be involved in the transfer of the flap—the forearm, neck, chest, shoulder, face, head, right hip and torso.

Sterile drapes were clipped into place. When it was determined that all sensation had ceased at the flap it was completely detached at its shoulder connection. It darkened, but the surgeons decided there was enough circulation to justify proceeding. A slice of skin was taken from the hip and used to cover the raw wound on the collarbone and chest left by the departed flap.

If the pedicle graft was placed directly over my open sinuses only the original sinus cavity surface would be lined with mucus membrane; the unlined surface of the flap would present a risk of infection. Dr. Cramer used a diamond-studded abrasion wheel at the end of a dental-type drill to remove the outer surface of skin all around the exposed sinuses and the bridge of the nose. Then carefully making incisions that bisected the mucus membrane lining the sinuses, cutting from the center to the edges, he was able to produce a viable layer of membrane to cover the cavity openings. This delicate maneuver accomplished two things—it not only covered the opening of the sinus cavities with a mucus membrane but it formed a base and lining for the pedicle flap as well.

The flap was set in place and stitched from the nose to the sinuses. But when it came to suturing it over the forehead's wide area of raw tissue and marrow-covered bone, there was insufficient good skin for the sutures to hold on to. Long stitches had to be taken from the back of the head (one of the few spots where the skin had been undamaged by the fire), run over the top, through the upper reaches of the flap and to the back of the head again like the strings of a banjo. As these long banjo stitches—called stents—were pulled taut they held the flap in place over the forehead.

When the last stitch was in place, the team members relaxed and took a look at their handiwork. I sported a thick band of skin that ran from the middle of my forehead to my right wrist, which was suspended right in front of my face. They pressed and rubbed the flap to see if the blood would leave and return properly. When it did, Dr. Cramer left it to the junior doctors to make a plaster cast over the right arm, hand, head and torso. It was supposed to prevent any motion, yet it had to permit access to my mouth and nasal opening, which were now overlapped by the forearm as though I were running interference in football.

It was 2:00 in the afternoon. Surgery had taken four hours. I was awake and sitting up in the operating room when the cast was put on, strong, certain hands holding my right arm fixed so it could not tug on the flap. When it was done, I lapsed back into the arms of Morpheus and was returned to my room. I did not leave that room again until the end of February.

I slept the rest of that day and night.

In the morning, an examination indicated that I could manage to turn my head slightly in my plaster carapace. My temperature was up and the cast had begun to irritate me in several places. Gauze pads were stuffed into those points to relieve the pressure while a heat lamp was beamed at the still oozing donor site, the right hip. For a few days it appeared that an ominous dark corner of the flap was going to spread, but by Christmas Eve the doctors concluded that it had not and that the remainder of the flap, notwithstanding a few discharges at the edges, appeared excellent. My temperature returned to normal.

The cast was continuing to cause me agony, though, and I finally convinced the resident to cut away the plaster at the pressure points. When he arrived in my room, he scared me out of my wits. He was packing a portable rotary saw blade. No matter how careful he was, I told him, he was going to slip. He reassured me. The saw, he explained, did not rotate, despite all appearances. It merely *reciprocated*, back and forth, over a narrow arc, wearing down the brittle plaster; if it touched any skin the supple flesh would merely wiggle back and forth in unison with the blade and not be damaged. Nevertheless, when the saw blade is in rapid motion, it is hard to tell; one must have faith in the doctor and not in one's own eyes. When my son Cory had to have a cast removed from a broken arm years later, the doctor did not take the time to explain how safe it really was, and Cory was frightened. All he did this time was cut into the cast over the left ear where it was causing persistent pain. His cutting covered the room with chalky dust.

Christmas came. Violet and Haron Saltoun supplied a sumptuous banquet. Many other friends in Rochester came to visit. The younger staff members—student nurses, doctors, and interns—went through the halls caroling, and adding an angelic touch to the day. And Christmas went.

The stitches holding the flap over the forehead were taken out on December 30. I spent New Year's Eve with Grace and another couple who had flown up for the occasion in my room, breaking open a bottle of champagne and a gift jar of Beluga caviar I had been hoarding.

A week later, the cast began to smell so foully that it made me physically sick. The nurses tried every technique they could in an attempt to mask the odor and clean under the cast, but the bandages themselves were too encrusted with pus. As more openings were cut into the cast, though, access was at least provided for them to scratch my many hard-to-reach itches. I would go into bizarre contortionist positions and they would be able to get at some of them with a long stick. I was living only for the day when this monstrosity would be off me and I could wash. That finally happened on January 12, 1965, some twenty-two days after I had been entombed. The sight of myself in the mirror with an elephantine flap from my forehead to my wrist was a little disconcerting at first, but the thrill of being scratched and bathed and oiled all over was more than enough to distract me.

For the next three days I supported my right arm with my bandaged left hand, afraid of putting any weight on it and tearing the flap, while Strong's orthopedic shop fashioned an "airline" splint I helped to design to take the cast's place. The splint was of polished steel and leather, shaped to the body and strapped around the waist and chest. The main steel support went up my right side under the arm and behind the head; there was no chin support. This allowed me to relax my arm without putting pressure on the flap, and still move my head around. At this point, the flap had grafted so well there was little danger of my tearing it off. I could move my arm around, and I soon learned not to worry about it; you can get used to anything. But even with my own splint I still had irritations at some new contact points.

Now the surgical procedures were going to be reversed—on January 18 a pedicle delay was performed at the wrist. By cutting off the blood supply for the flap at this end, the capillaries inside it would be forced to compensate by nourishing on blood from the forehead. I was returned to my room to await the day of final separation.

Very late one night, I was lying on my side, facing away from the door, watching the late show on my little TV set. Save for the blue-white glow of the tiny screen the room was dark, and the show I had on was spooky. I suddenly became aware of a presence behind me and turned around fast. I froze with terror. There, towering right above me, bathed in the eerie blue light of the TV set was a strange figure, nude to the waist, his right arm raised up as though he were about to strike. As my one good eye came into focus, I could see a glazed look in his staring eyes. He was mumbling something incoherently. I practically screamed. "What do you want? What are you doing here?" But the incoherencies just kept coming out of his quivering lips and he was still towering over me.

I was desperate. I pushed the button for the floor nurse. She was fortunately not long in coming and she ushered him out without a comment.

I was finally convinced that I had been faced not by a creature from outer space but by a patient recently returned from surgery, who was still under the disquieting effects of general anesthesia. He had on an airline splint not unlike mine, which is what was holding his arm up in the air, and he was completely disoriented. I was not bothered by him again.

Another delay of the flap was performed on January 27, and the blood supply continued to be good. It had now been five weeks since the flap had been fastened in front of my face. I would just have to bide my time until I was finally released from bondage.

One of my professional colleagues wanted to do something to keep me involved in the plastics field, so he arranged for me to review a technical book for a scientific journal. The book was sent to me, and after reading it by peering over my immobile arm, I dictated my review to Annette. She kindly typed up the manuscript and sent it off to the publisher. As a result of this effort, I was asked to join the journal's editorial advisory board. Meanwhile, Annette and the other young nurses took turns in caring for my daily needs, and I was beginning to enjoy their pleasant ministrations and constant attention so much that by the time Grace came up again the first week in February I was almost annoyed at her being there.

From the age of thirteen on, most people start to lose a little bit of their hearing each year. In most cases the loss is so gradual it is not even noticed. Significant deafness develops in only one man out of every thirty-nine.

Even before the crash, I was suffering from an ailment called otosclerosis, which translates as hardening of the ears. It is really a misnamed malady, since the bones do not harden with the onset of the disease; they become spongy. Predisposition to it may be inherited, but its exact cause is unknown; there is no cure. In it, calcium deposits around the bones of the inner ear immobilize the joints and interfere with the transmission of sound vibrations. My condition was originally diagnosed by a Philadelphia specialist after two other local specialists had failed to agree on a diagnosis; one of them had even recommended a series of a dozen treatments that would have proved totally useless.

Dr. John Frazer, Strong's ear, nose and throat specialist, studied the hearing tests conducted in Philadelphia and immediately confirmed the diagnosis of otosclerosis. He came to my room to discuss it. The progressive loss of hearing had developed in my remaining, good right ear, he explained; it was unrelated to the accident. The hearing in my burned-off left ear was normal.

He brought with him a medical chart to show in detail a corrective operation called a stapes mobilization which he wanted to do following my next plastic surgery, while I was still unconscious. In some cases, he warned me, a major nerve leading to the edge of the tongue that sensed the taste of salt was found just behind the eardrum and had to be severed to make room for a wire implant, and the operation itself was only about 90 percent effective. I considered those pretty good odds, and told him to go ahead.

Liberation from my shackle of transplanted flesh was scheduled for the morning of February 15. I couldn't wait. It had been fourteen weeks since I had been able to use my hands for anything. I'd had to be fed and bathed and taken to the toilet the whole time. Actually, at first I had been concerned about getting food up under my dangling wrist, but it turned out not to be a problem, except that being fed was a little drippy.

The preop medication was especially heavy and even more sedation was given intravenously in the operating room. After the usual scrubbing and draping, the surgery commenced. As soon as the pedicle flap was numb, it was disconnected from the wrist. My arm, stiff from the shoulder down due to disuse and atrophy, was lowered very slowly onto my chest. I was awake and aware of what was happening the whole time.

The flap itself was bleeding well, which was a sure sign circulation was good. The next step was making nostrils. The nostrils also had to be lined with mucus membrane. Dr. Cramer made an incision down the middle of the membranes, and undermined them. He brought the undermined layers out toward each other, and stitched them together forming a mucus-membrane tube in each nostril. They would become the lining of each of the two nostrils that would be formed out of the pedicle flap, which meanwhile was being held clear of the face. Some of the cartilage remaining in the right ala (which gives the nostrils its winglike configuration) was brought down to give the new nostrils a better shape. Now the flap, still hanging there, was stitched into place around the outline of that cartilage. Openings were formed by folding the flap under and stitching upward, onto the mucus membranes.

Something had to be done to give the nostrils shape and to let them breathe and drain while they were healing. Cotton was tried, but was unsatisfactory. Then pieces of a large-diameter plastic catheter were cut and slid up there. But the pressure on the newly released flap interfered with the circulation of the blood and they were quickly removed. Instead, gauze dipped in Vaseline was packed in each nostril, which confined breathing to my mouth.

As I have noted, long before this surgery, Dr. Cramer had suggested that I decide on the kind of nose I would like to have. It was a stimulating and intriguing decision to have to make, particularly since I had on more than one occasion considered plastic surgery on my original nose. By chance I came upon an advertisement in a magazine showing a large number of nose shapes, about twenty or so, and I cut it out. It was a perfect chart to start with, and yet it wasn't that easy a decision to make. I let my thoughts wander deliciously over the myriad possibilities of what I could look like, but I could not decide what kind of nose I wanted. But in the end it turned out I really didn't have any choice. Whatever came out was it. Even in the ordinary Rhinoplasty, the cosmetic "nose job," the patient usually cannot get the nose for which he or she hoped. In most cases, the outcome is an improvement, but chancy.

In my case, it was, too. At the end of surgery, I had a noselike feature right in the middle of my face. It was flat, tubular and red, but it had nostrils with a mucus membrane lining inside them that took in air and left no raw spots exposed. In time, even the normal, tiny nasal hairs grew inside the nostrils. The new nose appeared somewhat congested with poorly circulating blood but not severely so. This congestion has remained to some extent so that the nose is darker than the rest of the skin—but no more so than if I were a chronic drinker. There was even a little wing shape to the nostrils. The plan was to insert at a later date either some of my own cartilage or a molded silicone implant to give the nose its final, more normal shape. But the fear that the whole flap might be lost because the implant might cut off circulation or poke its way through to the surface caused the idea to be discarded. By then, anyway, I had adjusted to my proboscis and any potential improvements were no longer worth the risks, the pain and the expense.

No dressing was placed over the nose and only a light one around the wrist. For several days afterward, there was concern about damage to the capillaries in the flap transplant and I was forced to remain flat on my back to help circulation until the condition stabilized itself. I was not able to move my atrophied right arm at all and medication did not alleviate the pain in my shoulder. A week after surgery, I began five days of physical therapy and deep heat treatments that restored motion to my arm. I no longer needed private-duty nurses; I was able again at last to take care of myself and after that their visits were purely social.

The days remaining until I went home were taken up with removing the stitches and cleansing the surgical margins. Some areas around the nose were painful and bothersome. We devised some other plastic tubes, coated with Vaseline, that could be inserted into the nostrils to preserve their shape while they were healing and still allow me to breathe. These tubes let the mucus membranes grow and attach themselves to the skin with which it was forced into contact. I had to sleep with those tubes in my nose, and because they were greased with Vaseline they would slide out. I had to tape them in at night with adhesive tape, just catching an edge of the tubes with the tapes so as not to cut off the air passage. They were a little painful when they pressed on some sensitive area inside the nose, but they weren't too intolerable, and it became a challenge to devise a way to breathe and still keep them in place.

I always remembered the picture. It was a gimmick. It starts out in the beginning with Humphrey Bogart as a criminal hiding out from the police undergoing plastic surgery to change his identity. You only see him from the back until the bandages are being removed and there he is. No stitches. No scars. No swelling. Just Humphrey Bogart, a perfectly normal Humphrey Bogart.

Well, you don't look like that when you take off the bandages after plastic surgery. It never works the way it does in the movies when the bandages—all clean—are unwrapped two weeks later and the actor's entire face is changed and healed. At least, it never worked that way with me.

You're always disappointed with plastic surgery because you expect so much more. If they're going to perform a cosmetic repair like fixing your eyelid, you don't just walk in without an eyelid and come out with one on. You come out and you've got this big, tremendous, swollen, red-scarred, black-stitched, messy-looking thing called an eyelid, and you wish you were back the way you originally were and you think, "Why did I go through this just to look like this?" It takes weeks to months before it begins to assume even a slightly normal appearance. People don't realize that. The trauma of surgery always causes discoloration and swelling and I mean really *grotesque* swelling. I remember seeing the pictures of my three fingers after surgery—they looked like *knockwurst* about to burst. That's what you always look like after surgery, so it's always a letdown, and doctors don't tell patients it's going to look like that any more than they tell women they're going to have a depression after they give birth. I think the doctor should tell you it's going to look terrible for a while and you should be prepared for it.

It's not that I particularly wanted to look like Humphrey Bogart, but I at least hoped for the perfect-looking me underneath. Dr. Cramer had said to me, "Select your nose and we'll see if we can give you a nose like the one you select," but when it came down to the nitty-gritty it was impossible to even come close to any one of those noses.

My disappointment made me agitated, impatient and critical. I was anxious to get home. February 27 was finally set as the day of my discharge and I began making plans for my departure. I kept thinking about what I could bring home to my boys; it was difficult to shop from a hospital room. Then, remembering how they all loved to draw and paint, I designed a collapsible easel that all three of them could use at the same time. I picked a carpenter out of the Rochester Yellow Page directory and called him up. He came to the hospital, we talked over the design I had in mind and he returned with a very handsome gift for the boys.

Before I left, I underwent new hearing tests so Dr. Frazer could compare the results with the earlier ones in Philadelphia. They confirmed it: a stapes mobilization would be necessary. A hearing aid might have improved my hearing, but vanity, more than anything else prevented me, as it does many people, from resorting to one.

The last stitches were pulled out of my nostrils on the twenty-sixth and the following morning I was headed for home, the disassembled triple easel under my arm. I no longer sported the bandages that had covered the open sinuses and missing nose on all my previous trips home; my bare face was literally hanging out. I did, though, wear a hat to hide the grafted scalp and a black patch over the left eye because it was so unsightly. The eyepatch was the first thing that attracted small children; they always noticed that and little else of my disfigurement. Their first question invariably would be, "What happened to your eye?" I guess I did not as yet resemble the Man in the Hathaway Shirt.

When I returned to Strong in mid-March, I took the train alone once again. I spent the first night at the Towne House, mostly on the telephone calling all our friends in Rochester. The surgery was to be pretty straightforward—beef up the original grafts on the scalp which were too thin, bumpy and unhealed in a few spots. It was set for St. Patrick's Day, the day before my thirty-ninth birthday. First one, and then another graft of donor skin from my right flank and buttock were laid on the scalp after the diamond-studded wheel was used to abrade away the surface layer of skin.

Violet and Haron Saltoun sent in another banquet for my birthday, complete with a bottle of champagne. Annette Hancoski, my nurse, Mrs. Lane Johnson, the volunteer who had spent Thanksgiving with us, and one of my chess partners from Kodak, Bill Holleran plus his wife Jeanette joined me for the party. Then, while I was recuperating, I came across a classified ad in the paper. A retiring executive wanted to sell a telescope he had received as a retirement gift; he wasn't interested in astronomy. I got in touch with him and he came to the hospital, bringing the apparatus with him in several beautiful wooden chests. A deal was quickly consummated. When I returned home, the family was waiting for me when I got off the train in Grand Central with my gift and new hobby for them. We stopped off in New York, visited relatives and dined at an excellent Chinese restaurant in Greenwich Village, before making the drive back to Pennsylvania. I was in an excellent frame of mind.

The trip to Rochester on April 12 was my tenth for surgery. It was to be an otoplasty this time, to correct the cauliflower deformity of the right ear, the one with defective hearing, which had abcessed from the burns and healed with its upper half bent over. The original intention had been to pull the skin tight behind the ear to straighten the top of it, cutting off the excess and using it to cover the left eyelid in preparation for a later operation. But there wasn't sufficient skin left over, so that plan had to be abandoned. Instead, in a ninety-minute procedure, the doctors opened the back of the ear, cutting out some cartilage and straightening out the rest, and stitched the ear into its normal position.

This was again one of those times when I woke up in my hospital room and asked the nurse when I was going down to surgery. Once more I was told I had already been. What ecstatic joy! For the next three days I was given antibiotics as a precaution. I felt fine, though the drugs sometimes left a bad taste in my mouth. I played chess and received visitors and went home on April 18. It was one of my shortest stays.

I was going to have a month between operations. We used the time to take in the New York World's Fair. A good part of healing—more critical than the medical aspects, I think—is mental. If your mental picture is a good one, then everything progresses nicely. I was still in pretty bad shape physically. I'd been to the Franklin Institute in Philadelphia but this was the first time I was really going to be faced with crowds, very openly and visually in the bright sunlight and I tend to look worse in sunlight because the discoloration shows more. But I had to start the adjustment and I decided to start it immediately.

I had some apprehension about appearing in public not knowing what the reactions would be. But the World's Fair was an important test for me. There were large crowds there, first of all, and there were people there from all over the world—all kinds of people of every nationality, every race, every educational level. It was a cross-section and therefore it was good exposure for me to test the water and run the gamut of reactions.

I began to codify the different reactions I got from different people: I was impressed with the numbers of people who didn't react at all; most people didn't. They made normal eye contact, kept going and acted—convincingly—as if they hadn't noticed anything unusual.

There were other types as well. The elbow-nudgers would walk by, look at you and poke their partners so that they would not miss seeing what you looked like. Then there were those people who would stiffen their necks and not turn their heads, but follow you only with their eyes. There were those who would come back for a second look as though you were an animal in the zoo. I didn't mind so much their looking, but rather their looking at me as if I had no comprehension of what they were doing. This was beyond curiosity; it was rudeness.

But my emotional skin thickened rapidly; these things no longer bother me. In fact, now if people do *not* look at me I feel all but offended since I think of myself as being special rather than repulsive. And if someone does stare at me now with rude curiosity I think to myself, defensively, "I look this way because I was in a plane crash. What's your excuse?"

I did mind this overt behavior because I didn't want Grace and the children to be embarrassed by this seeming ridicule. But they were better about it than I was. Grace, especially, would never hesitate to call someone down for staring rudely.

Sometimes small children, and occasionally adults as well, ask Grace or the boys in my presence (as though I were incapable of comprehending), "What happened to him?" When they are told, they say "Oh!" and stare for ten seconds more and then go on to other pursuits, dropping the whole matter. Of course I get many direct queries and I think this is the healthiest approach. And I tell it like it is.

I was back in Rochester in mid-May. The railroad men recognized me now. I had never been one to make small talk with strangers in the past, but I began to do so now as people went out of their way to talk to me. My unusual appearance seemed to trigger a warm, friendly response, augmented, maybe, by the need for them to talk to mask any uncomfortable feelings they might have had.

This surgery was to replace the skin graft over the left eye so that it could eventually be worked into a viable lid. By the time I was taken into surgery I was completely asleep from the medication, but I remember waking up screaming each time I felt the needle penetrating the skin around my left eye. When I later apologized to Dr. Cramer for yelling so loudly, he said I had done nothing more than moan a little. In my mind I was screaming.

Blue dye was used to trace the area to be excised, and the skin inside it was carefully cut away. While this was going on, more anesthetics were being shot into the chest just below the right shoulder. I didn't feel those needles. A full-thickness graft of skin was cut out of the chest, trimmed to fit and stitched over the eye. The chest wound was stitched closed.

Once again, I experienced the exhilaration of discovering that surgery was over with when I thought it had not yet begun. I sometimes wonder if the surgery wasn't worth it for that feeling alone, a feeling like someone gets hitting himself on the head because it feels so good to stop. The ten-day stay at Strong was not unpleasant; my eye was only a little uncomfortable and there was only minor pain in my chest.

One day, Dr. Cramer came into my room and said, "Keep

this under your hat, but I've been offered two positions as head of plastic surgery—one in California and one in Philadelphia. Which should I take?"

Although it would have been out of character for him, I thought Dr. Cramer was teasing me because of the long trips I had been making to Rochester. But he wasn't joking. Of course, I suggested Philadelphia since it was only minutes from my home.

Since Dr. McCormack, the senior man in plastic surgery at Strong, was as young as Dr. Cramer, Cramer's advancement at the hospital was obviously limited. I thought nothing more about our conversation until a few months later he made the announcement that he had accepted the position at Temple University Health Science Center in Philadelphia. My long journeys would cease. I was happy for Dr. Cramer, since it was a well-deserved promotion for him. But I knew I would miss Rochester, and the many friends we had made during three years of treatment at Strong. I suspect we had more friends there than anyplace else in the world. But over the ensuing years many of them moved from Rochester to scattered outposts anyway, so that if Dr. Cramer and I hadn't deserted them, they would have deserted us. I consoled myself with the observation that nothing ever remains the same.

I left the hospital on May 25 with my right arm in a sling so as not to put a strain on the stitched-up chest. I would not have to return until the fall. Once again Grace and the boys met me at Grand Central Station and because we had had such a good time the last trip we again went for a Chinese dinner, this time in Chinatown.

I stopped wearing the sling after I got back home and a few days later all the stitches on the chest gave way. Coincidentally, so did the stitch in the eyelid. All this happened late one night. There was no bleeding, but I was understandably concerned. I called our family doctor, Dr. Broad. He told us to meet him at his office where he stitched me up again.

A very big event took place that June, one that improved my self-esteem and my outlook on life: I bought a hairpiece!

Even before the crash, I had been losing my hair. It had receded considerably, so that a good excuse for wearing a hairpiece was welcome. I shopped around at several studios recommended to me by friends until I was convinced which one was the best for me.

It was located upstairs on a building off Fifth Avenue in New York. I was ushered into a private room, seated in a barber's chair and given a sales pitch. The demonstrator showed me several sample hairpieces and then, with a flash of bravado, whipped off his own hair, eliciting shocked disbelief from his client and demonstrating the deceptive realism of the hairpiece, plus the ease in handling one. I think most studios employ bald men just so this act can be performed.

Assured that I wished to continue, indeed that I was *anxious* to continue, my demonstrator began to shape a piece of paper to the bald part of my scalp, cutting it and taping it until it resembled an irregularly shaped yalmulka. (Another studio I later patronized used plastic food wrap and Scotch tape to do the same.) The area to be covered was outlined with a grease pencil on the paper hat, which became the model for the "lace." Lace hairpieces have an open-mesh lace-fabric base into which your hairs are individually stitched. The fine holes in the pink fabric look like the pores of the scalp and therefore has a realistic look.

Color matching was the next step. A good-looking female assistant (they all seem to employ nice-looking girls, too) brought in bundles of human hair and skillfully blended them to match my own. A big to-do was made of this matching process, even though after several months of wear, the color of the hairpiece is bleached by the sun and cleaning to a discordant auburn regardless of what the natural color was. From then on, expensive hair dyeing becomes necessary, which turns the hair a monotonous, artificial, monochromatic hue and makes you look like a store-window mannequin. Or you can sneakily purchase touch-up hair sprays, pretending they are for your wife, and apply them every other day or so, hoping that the color isn't noticed by your friends as it runs off on your neck and gives you ring around the collar.

The lace doesn't last so well. It deteriorates, and sometimes your comb catches in it and tears it. It becomes a big maintenance problem.

Synthetic fiber hair holds its color and wears better; although it is always downplayed by the studio I suspect it is less profitable to them; I was paying close to $500 for each hairpiece, whereas I've seen the synthetics retail at three for $10. The temptation to buy one was great.

The expensive, custom-made hairpieces last at most for a couple of years. They are held on the head by either a clear adhesive applied like nail polish or with clear plastic tape with adhesive on both sides. They stick to plastic patches stitched to the underside of the lace at key points. One hairpiece maker bought his patches from the Tenenbaums prosthetics factory. Eventually, I developed an improved plastic which I sold to my hairpiece maker and to others, defraying the costs of future hairpieces.

There are other techniques for replacing lost hair—surgical transplants, implanted wires, hair weaving, and others—but either their own shortcomings or the delicate nature of my grafted scalp precluded my making use of them. Unlike the prosthetic nose, the hairpiece has no tendency to come off at an awkward moment. It can be solvent-cleaned at home or in the studio. It even feels like your own hair.

Putting on the completed hairpiece for the first time was a thrill. It takes weeks for it to be finished since each hair is inserted by hand and knotted in place. It is simply amazing how much the hairpiece can control your appearance. In spite of the fact that my face was a raw, disfigured conglomeration of unsightly features, to my eyes at least my new hair made me handsome. True enough, on the occasions when I viewed my profile in the three-sided mirror of a tailor's fitting room, this illusion was shattered, but then again I was shocked by that view even before my plane crashed. Every morning when I put on my hairpiece the transformation is startling, and I will sometimes greet myself in the bathroom mirror like a television commercial, "Hello, handsome!"

Shortly after getting the hairpiece I received word from my lawyers of the first settlement offer from the airline's insurance company. It was for $500,000.

16

A half a million dollars was a lot of money in those days. It still is, in spite of the beating our currency has taken from inflation. It was not easy arriving at a decision. But we reasoned that Dave Elwell had received almost as much without having to pay attorneys' fees; that my medical bills were high; that Workmens' Compensation had to be reimbursed, and that I had to pay back the salary I had been getting. Had I known just how good my lawyers actually were, a quick decision would have been easy, but they did not attempt to influence me one way or another. After anguishing over it for several days, Grace and I finally decided to reject the offer and to take our chances with a trial and a jury, as distasteful as that would be. We conveyed our decision to our attorneys and the impression we gleaned from them was that we had made the right one. As it turned out, we did.

A few weeks after the crash, as soon as he was sure I would survive, my brother-in-law had returned to New York City and consulted an attorney friend of ours, Ted Ellenoff. They had a long discussion of the legal aspects of the situation and Ted supplied Milton with a list of the five most prominent airline tort lawyers on the East Coast. With this list in hand, Milton spent the next few days going around the city interviewing and evaluating the firms. It was a job I think he relished since he was dealing from a position of strength; he had a hot case. Also, Milton, a senior executive with a soft-drink manufacturer, prides himself in being able to size people up quickly and separate the nonsense from the facts.

Eventually he found himself in the offices of Kreindler and Kreindler. Lee Kreindler was a down-to-earth type who quickly established a rapport with Milton. His firm's credentials were impeccable, and their fee turned out to be lower than all of the others Milton had interviewed—a flat 20 percent of the final settlement plus expenses. Some firms have been known to ask up to 50 percent. Besides that, 4 percent of their share would go to Ted Ellenoff for the referral and for services Ted would perform.

Everyone likes to think that their lawyer and doctor are the best there is. In our case, we had the record to prove it.

One of Lee Kreindler's first cases involved a plane crash in which a propeller was suspect. The young lawyer took three weeks off and went to work, without pay, for a propeller manufacturer in Long Island, rapidly becoming an expert. He went on not only to win the case and have it written into airline tort law, but to solve the actual cause of the crash.

The well-publicized case established the firm in the airline tort field and by 1963 about 80 percent of their cases were in aviation-crash law. They have taken a leading role in most of the major accidents over the last two decades—including the TWA mid-air collision over New York in 1961; the crash of a Northeast Airlines plane on Nantucket Island in 1958 that killed the chairman of the Atomic Energy Commission and twenty-four others and the Eastern Airlines jet that sucked a flock of birds into its engines and plunged into Boston Harbor in 1960. The firm has also been involved in several major foreign air crashes, including the first crash ever of a jet transport, outside Brussels in 1961, that took the lives of all twelve members of the U.S. figure-skating team. Again, he solved the cause of the crash, and the settlements he won were believed to be the first above the limits set by the Warsaw Convention of 1929, the original treaty governing international air crashes. Later, he led the American Bar Association team in seeking changes in that treaty. In three successful suits, the firm upset the principle of *lex loci delicti,* by which the state where the crash occurred had jurisdiction, and instead established that the state with the predominant interest in the case would hear it. He also won the case in 1962 where the government was held liable for the failure of air-traffic controllers to give accurate weather information. That had some application to our case.

At least six of the attorneys in his office handled one phase or another of my case. First, they probed my background. They obtained every document, birth certificate, diploma, honor and award belonging to my entire family. They selected, from among hundreds of family photographs, the ones that showed us in the most favorable light, indicative of the good life we had led. They assembled a three-volume portfolio which could just as aptly have been titled *This is Your Life.*

They interviewed Grace, and later me, taping many hours of conversation. All pertinent records were assembled, organized and catalogued. Note was made of any missing or questionable material. Lists of probing questions to ask were made. Copies were included of every single hospital record, plus periodic summaries by the chief physicians and surgeons. The medical photographer was kept busy making dozens of eight-by-ten-inch glossy close-up color prints, in triplicate, of each gory wound.

The FAA tower records were studied in detail. So were their training and operating procedures, and backgrounds of personnel. Special attention was paid to the tapes of their conversations with the aircraft and each other. The same thing was done to the airport's weather bureau and its personnel.

Copies of all Mohawk company records for the crew members and ground personnel—their training, background, experience, test results—were obtained. So were copies of all Mohawk's manuals for flight, training and operating procedure. My lawyers even got a court order requiring Mohawk to supply an identical Martin 404 so that they could take a moving picture from the cockpit as it took off from Monroe County Airport—to show the view the crew had of the field that day.

Early in the litigation process, Kreindler won a major point by getting the case moved to New York City rather than Rochester or Utica, the location of Mohawk headquarters. Awards are notoriously high in the city, usually smaller upstate.

The probing in my suit began. Kreindler & Kreindler took six thousand pages of depositions, filling twenty-six volumes, most of it taken by Attorney Milton G. Sincoff, whose questions —about aircraft, the weather, tower operations, medical factors —were knowledgeable and extremely sharp. The lawyers filled more volumes with maps, diagrams, radar charts, Weather Bureau reports, manuals, exhibits. Filing cabinet drawers were crammed with records.

One thing that my lawyers could not, by law, use in the proceedings, but could use as the basis for their embarrassing questions, was the report issued by the CAB investigation team on May 20, 1964.

The CAB placed the blame for the crash directly on the airline and cited evidence of "faulty judgment by the captain and failure by the crew to comply with company rules."

In its conclusions, the report noted that "the storm was known to the crew . . . and its intensity should have been immediately apparent to a professional pilot. The failure of the captain to properly appraise the weather conditions and his attempted takeoff into a severe thunderstorm raises serious doubts as to his judgment." It rehashed his record—the incidents, the reprimands, his failure to pass the company's proficiency flight check seven months before the crash—and faulted him for not completing the preflight checklist and for exchanging seats with Neff when the latter "had insufficient service" to be piloting the plane.

The report went on to lay out in detail how Dennis had not been given the latest available weather information, either by Mohawk's central dispatch office in Utica or by any of its customer-service agents at the airport where he stopped over that day, "contrary to the company's operations manual and the civil air regulations." It accused the controlling dispatcher at Utica of failing "to re-assess the worsening weather conditions and to convey this re-appraisal" to Dennis before he took off.

In addition to its blame-finding against Dennis and Mohawk, the CAB criticized another Federal agency. It noted that FAA personnel in the control tower that day were aware of the thunderstorm but did not bring it to Dennis's attention because they presumed he could see it, and singled them out for failure to do so. The FAA contended that Mohawk's system of dispensing weather information—keeping a file at Utica headquarters while at Rochester, for example, crews had to depend on United Airline's teletype updates—was in "substantial compliance" with the rules. The CAB thought otherwise. "Since the flight crews do not commence all flights at company headquarters," it stated, "this method of dispatching does not insure the travelling public that the Mohawk flight crews will receive all available and required weather information."

In its defense, the FAA maintained that the only jurisdiction its personnel in the tower had over a pilot was to refuse clearance due to heavy air traffic or low visibility, and that they were within their rights in clearing the plane since none of those conditions were prevailing at the time. They had no obligation, the FAA insisted, to warn the pilot of the weather, even though they *could* have done so. This was to become the key point of contention in the suit Copilot Neff's widow filed against the government.

With a report such as this, even though it was inadmissible directly as evidence, the airline's lawyers knew that their case was damaged beyond repair, that settlement on the best terms was the appropriate road. INA, the Insurance Company of North America, Mohawk's carrier, tried to settle the cases as quickly as possible. At least three or four were worked out in the first year after the crash. Others dragged on for five years —not uncommon in torts—and one case took over ten. The survivors, and the families of the dead, all took different tacks on the compensation for which they sued, according to the extent of their injuries and the advice they received. My lawyers made the decision to sue for $950,000 in compensatory damages and $500,000 in punitive damages. My personal involvement was miniscule. Except for rare taping sessions at my home between operations, a visit by Milt Sincoff to get my signature on documents when he was up in Rochester taking depositions and an occasional telephone call from Lee Kreindler, I was never involved. As a matter of fact, my one complaint to Kreindler was that he did not pay enough attention to me, a complaint I heard echoed by a friend I referred to the firm when he, too, was involved in a plane crash.

Over two years after the crash, I received a phone call from Kreindler. The airline's insurance carrier's attorneys had proposed a new settlement figure, but before they would make it firm and final they wanted to see me personally. I was agreeable to that, and a meeting was arranged at Kreindler's offices on Park Avenue.

Up to that point, all their attorneys had seen of me were photographs before the accident, and the series of devastating after-crash photographs Kreindler had assembled. Up to that point, they had seen more than I had.

Even my own lawyers found these photographs so hideous they refused to let me see them. One day I came in and insisted. Before he would turn them over to me Kreindler called Sincoff into his office and said, "Milt, Alan insists on seeing these pictures and I want you to bear witness that I am advising him not to." He didn't want the responsibility for what my reactions to them would be.

I did not look at them in his office. And I thought I couldn't look at them in the car because I might faint right on the road. So I knew I had to get them home and brace myself. That way, if I looked at them I would not pass out. Or if I did, it would be in the comfort of my easy chair.

I took the big manila envelope home and set it aside for several weeks. Finally I had the courage to take a peek.

I felt absolutely nothing.

Not even the slightest twinge pulsed through me. If I had been looking at those photographs and they had been of someone else I might have gone into a state of shock. But, somehow, seeing *myself* I wasn't affected by it. What I *did* do, though, was that after getting a chance to study the original damage and compare it to the current state of repairs, I wrote to Dr.

Cramer, thanking him once again and this time commending him on his miraculous skill. Until I looked at those photographs, I had not been made truly aware of how much damage there had been, and how little he had had to work with.

The large glossy color photos were taken with a sharp lens that captured all of the gory detail—then, the photos were enlarged: they provided a pictorial history of my condition from shortly after the accident through successive stages of healing and reconstruction. Every oozing sore, pus-filled wound, dry, blackened protruding bone, shiny exposed muscle and every hair and pore contributed to the contrast in textures. The pictures were taken from every angle with close-ups thrown in when needed. The "before" and "after" of every part of my body was included: my featureless, blackened face shortly after the accident; the dryness of the bone of the exposed skull; the skeleton of the hand exposed before amputation and rongeuring; the exposed shoulder muscles with a coating of grease making them look that much gorier. The after shots included the three swollen sausagelike restored fingers resembling a grotesque claw, the fenestrated skull and, worst of all, the pedicle flap stretched to its limit during surgery from its anchor at the forehead. It was not a pleasant dossier.

And so, when the time came, the lawyers for INA filed into Lee Kreindler's bright glass-and-steel offices, and they were visibly nervous, outwardly upset for putting me through what they knew must be an ordeal for me. As a matter of fact, it wasn't an ordeal at all. I was rather enjoying the experience. I knew I had them at a disadvantage. Only I knew that inwardly I was suffering not at all for looking the way I did. They didn't know that. At the same time, though, I did everything I could to put them at their ease.

There were four of them—kindly, pleasant gentlemen. I didn't try to present myself in any abnormal way to get greater sympathy from them. I dressed properly, and wore my prosthetic ear and hairpiece. But Grace was with me, and I suppose her outstanding charm and beauty made a sharp contrast to my disfigurement. They might have felt a twinge of guilt for saddling her with the likes of me for the rest of her life; she was, after all, a party to the suit. The meeting was short and amicable.

Shortly after that, on October 15, 1965, we agreed to the settlement. It was, at the time, a record—$675,000. Although it was tax free, I would not see all of it by any means. My attorneys' fees immediately skimmed $135,000 off the top. My hospital bills at Strong had to be settled. I had to reimburse Workmens' Compensation. And the Revlon Corporation had to be paid back for the two and a half years of salary I had been getting as an interest-free loan.

As with everything else, air-crash settlements have been the victims of inflation and continue to rise until awards to individual survivors or heirs have reached into the millions of dollars. Very often, however, an extraordinarily high jury award that makes the newspapers is often reduced considerably on appeal, or thrown out altogether. These reversals somehow don't make the newspapers. Neither do large out-of-court settlements, because they are not matters of public record. For instance, the widow of Copilot Neff sued the United States Government and won a judgment totaling $334,149.21. On appeal the verdict was reversed and the family received nothing.

Every passenger in our crash received some settlement or award. The smallest was $2,500; mine was the largest. My associate, Jerry Kurtz, who lost his life, had his case settled for only $300,000. Death cases are usually settled for less. I've heard it said, though the airlines obviously would deny it, that they prefer there be no survivors in a crash because that makes it less expensive for them. Chuck Wright, whose condition I think of as living death, settled for an amount in the area of $600,000. All told, the settlements totaled $4 million, exceeding INA's $3 million liability limit and forcing them to dip into the Lloyds of London pool for the extra million; Lloyd's was the reinsurer, covering excess claims.

In addition to settlements and awards, many passengers have flight insurance and most have life insurance. Some carry blanket, annual travel insurance policies. Others purchase them at the airport before boarding their flights. Those insurance policies are sold at the airport by vending machine or over the counter by pretty girls representing the firm or firms holding the concession there.

I had purchased one of those policies on the morning of July

2, 1963, at Westchester County Airport. It was an expense-account item paid for by my company. Under its provisions, I was able to collect $5,000—or $2500 each for the loss of two fingers. None of my other injuries were covered.

17

My summer vacation was over.

Dr. Cramer was to assume his position at Temple University some time after returning from his European tour. We were not scheduled to meet again until the second of October. During the four-month hiatus, while I waited for my financial settlement, I had an office built at home for the plastics consulting practice I planned to engage in when the surgery was finished.

I had published widely and well in my particular area of expertise. I had presented papers, moderated symposia, attended meetings of the appropriate societies and committees and generally gotten around. I had established some reputation in my field. With my newfound financial freedom, the next step to becoming a consultant was an easy one. After all, the definition of a consultant is anyone who has been out of work for more than six months.

The surgery planned for the October 2 visit was purposely kept simple. My only recollections of it are of the needles pricking the area around my nose. This was in preparation for raising the tip of the nose to a more normal position and allowing the upper lip, which had been pulled tight by the contracting skin above it, to relax. One small corner of the right nostril, which had been sore since the original nose-reconstruction operation eight months before, was repaired, and a contracting scar on the left cheek received a Z-plasty.

The work was minor repair work, but as luck would have it I caught a cold, probably from exposure in the air-conditioned operating room, and wound up having to stay in the hospital for ten days. I was footing the bills now, and I started to become conscious of the cost of a private room. And, of course, Becky Keene made sure that mine was the best—and therefore the most expensive—they had.

Two days after surgery, Dr. Cramer went to Philadelphia to hunt for a house. While he was gone I was checked infrequently by the resident staff, but I spent most of my time entertaining friends and socializing with the other patients on the floor. One of these patients was the very attractive twenty-five-year-old daughter of a Rochester physician, who was recuperating from surgery. Her name was Anne Parlow, and she wore the most exotic negligees, arousing the male staff to attend her on any pretext. She was also a chess player and we played regularly in my room, to the interruptions of her many would-be suitors. Although I had no private-duty nurses, most of the old ones came by and brought me up to date on the latest happenings in their lives. I received more than two dozen visitors in a ten-day stay, plus many more telephone calls and letters. But I had mixed feelings about being at Strong this time. Combined with the pleasure of seeing old friends again was the attrition of people I knew, made greater by the interval since my last visit.

The surgery I returned for in November was by no means minor. It was to give me a working left eyelid.

At this point, I still had a skin graft over my left eye. Little by little, through a series of operations, the opening had been enlarged by slits in the soft skin. Although you don't feel it, in a normal eyelid there is cartilage running along the edge to retain its shape. To prevent the skin from hanging loosely, it has to be stiff. What the surgeons were going to do was cut two long parallel slits between the epidermis on the surface and the mucus membrane on both eyelids, then cut out a strut of cartilage from a rib. They intended to slip that strut into the slits and close them up. Then I would not only have cartilage inside the eyelid but, by stretching bits of remaining eyelid muscles and attaching them to the lids, I could have a working eyelid again.

It sounds like a minor procedure to extract the cartilage, but an incision over five inches long had to be made and the first wedge of cartilage the doctor extracted was too short. A second wedge had to be taken. The struts were inserted as planned and I was sewn up.

When I revived I was surprised by the extent and the pain of the wound in my rib. I still felt nothing at all in the eye since it was grafted tissue, although in time some feeling would come back.

Dr. Cramer rushed off to a symposium in Cleveland the next day, leaving instructions that I return to Rochester in January, February and March for the next series of operations. He would not be making his move to Philadelphia till after that. Before he departed, he introduced me to his very first private patient, a young woman who had literally been scalped when her hair got caught in a farm thresher. Not only was her scalp torn off, but also an eyelid and an ear. As horrible as her injuries were, she looked marvelous. I did not realize she had a wig on; it had to be pointed out to me. She was certainly another walking monument to Dr. Cramer's skill.

I remained in the hospital four more days. On Tuesday, November 9, at about 5:00 P.M., we had just finished some jelly custard with dinner, when everything went black. I went out into the hall to take a look and all the lights were out there. I looked out the window. All the lights were out—everywhere I looked. I could view a wide area of the city from my fifth-floor room, and there was not a light to be seen anywhere except for automobile headlights. The Great Northeast Blackout had begun.

We were without electricity for eight hours. Flickering

matches, like fireflies, danced in the corners. The hospital's intensive-care patients and staff had to be moved into the surgical suite because it was one of the few places in Strong with an emergency generator.

I was the only one on the floor with a battery-operated radio, so we immediately started listening to the reports as they came in. As the staff members and the mobile patients jammed into my room, the whole thing became a joke and we all began to kid around. It was party time. One elderly woman in a wheelchair—I couldn't identify her in the dark—kept insisting again and again that it was a case of sabotage. She couldn't tell, in the pitch black, whether her audience had changed or not.

When I came back in December, the taxi driver who took me from the train station to the Towne House was one who had driven victims to the hospital on July 2, 1963. The floor nurses and aides were busy setting up a tree and hanging Christmas decorations. For the second year in a row I would hear them singing carols through the halls.

A web had formed between my nose and right eyebrow from a contracting graft. Removing it would be a simple procedure so I decided it would be a good time to have my stapes mobilization taken care of, and Dr. Frazer consented to do it.

The ear operation was a fascinating one. I had hoped it could be done immediately following the plastic surgery that was scheduled so I would only have to be anesthetized once. But hospital politics and scheduling were such—each department is allotted its share of time in the operating suite and nothing can be done, it seems, to change it—that it had to wait a day. As a consequence I had barely recovered from the anesthesia administered the day before when the same dosage was administered again and kept me unconscious for two more days. Looking through the eye-piece of a sophisticated microscope during the entire procedure, Dr. Frazer inserted a metal speculum tube into my outer ear to widen it as much as possible. Carefully cutting his way past the outer ear canal and down to the eardrum, he flipped the drum over and exposed the hammer bone in my inner ear. The eventuality he had warned me about in the beginning came to pass: the nerve that controls the taste buds was in fact blocking the inner ear canal. He had to cut it. Once he had penetrated into the inner ear, Dr. Frazer cut out the stapes, the wild bone growth and the mucus membrane. A piece of gel-foam and wire were lowered into the inner ear to make a new, artificial stapes.

My hearing should have been restored considerably even before surgery was over. It wasn't. Nor did I notice any improvement in my hearing when I woke up; in fact it seemed to have gotten worse. I went home and a large plug of coagulated blood worked its way out and it seemed as though there were some auditory improvement, but that was only illusory. The hearing is no better now than it was before the operation. The one thing I did notice right away was a slight numbness at the edge of my tongue; I could still sense the texture of foods, but with the nerve disconnected I now needed a little more salt than before in my food.

After my long recovery period from the double dose of anesthesia, Dr. Cramer decided to cut back on the dosage in future surgery until a threshold was reached that would still shield me from pain. I stayed four more days at Strong. My good eye became irritated, perhaps from the preop rub of pHisoHex, and I was taken to the eye clinic. I spent the rest of the time socializing and playing chess with the regulars and one of the nurses who had treated me in the days right after the crash and was at the moment another ear, nose and throat patient. Two days after I came home from the hospital, a local surgeon took out all but one of the stitches left from the minor nose-and-eyelid operation.

He couldn't see the last one under the coagulated blood. I finally located it and removed it myself with a pair of suture scissors I had "requisitioned" during one of my stays at Strong. Each time I left there I took with me large quantities of medicines, ointments, bandages and other supplies that had accumulated in my room and in time I had stowed enough medical gear to handle a major catastrophe.

A blizzard was raging and a snow emergency was in effect when I stepped off the train in Rochester in January 1966. I had to wait for a taxi and share it with other isolated travelers. It was very late before I made it to my warm, cozy room at the Towne House to begin calling our local friends.

The following morning when I checked into Strong a suitable room could not be found for me and we considered postponing surgery one day. While I waited to see if a room would become available, I paid a call on a researcher in pharmacology and anesthesiology at the medical school there, Dr. Harold H. Borgstedt. Dr. Borgstedt was coauthoring a book with me on epoxy resins; he was writing the chapter on toxicity, and we had yet to meet. When I entered his laboratory, he was performing experiments on a cat that was spreadeagled on a board with all sorts of devices and tubes protruding from its innards in order to evaluate the effects of a certain chemical on humans. I was a little shaken.

This was my thirty-sixth operation and it was again to be done on my nose. The I.V. anesthesia had been cut back quite a bit, per Dr. Cramer's most recent set of orders, and by the time surgery was over I could feel every stitch going in. Through my fogged mind I could hear Dr. Cramer telling me, almost angrily, to stop yelling.

The surgery was to add more shape to my nose, enlarge it and graft some skin on the upper lip. Recovery took awhile and because of the lip trauma I was forced onto a liquid diet. It was not only painful but the bandages were messy with blood. I couldn't move my lips, so when I drank anything it ran onto the bandage and together with the blood it smelled horrible. When the bandages finally did come off, the lip and nose looked raw and swollen and terrible, as the rebuilt areas of my face always did in the first days after surgery. I continually ignored the lesson that plastic surgery requires weeks, months, sometimes years of healing.

In the month before my next operation, my plastics consulting practice began to pick up. I also returned to teaching a course in plastics at the Philadelphia College of Textiles and Science, which I had been doing before the crash. If my appearance was disconcerting to any of my clients and students, I had no inkling of it. I behaved as if I were no different from the next guy, and the response was the same.

The first time that I taught again was as tough as the World's Fair had been. But, once I experienced it, I saw there was no problem. Again, my disfigurement was to my *advantage;* it held my students' interest.

I was unashamed to flaunt my appearance before them

after a while. I always started out in class with the sunglasses, but then took them off as they got used to me. Normally, my eye is more of a shock than the rest of me. When children see my eye, they never really notice the face. The question invariably is "What happened to your eye?" not "What happened to your face?"

I also teach at the Bucks County Technical School in a program for high-school students training to be plastics technicians. These are a tough group of kids. It was somewhat of a trial at first for me to walk the halls in that school. But then as the weeks went by I began to get friendly hellos from all the strange faces. Some began to learn what happened to me. I may be unusual, but then they saw I'm not as scary as I looked. Even the Frankenstein monster was a pathetic lovable creature and after you got to know him you began to sympathize with him. Sometimes I want to burst into the song from *Cabaret:* "If you could see [him] with my eyes, [he] isn't ugly at all."

I was back at Strong in March for surgery to improve the shape of the lower lip some more. A skin graft from the back of the neck—just above the hairline, so it would grow hair where a beard should be—was trimmed and laid in place, leaving no visible scar on the neck. Once the grafting was done, I was rolled onto my stomach. The burn scars had again contracted on the left side of my neck. A slice of skin from the back was used to relieve the condition. The operation was not an unqualified success. I had been telling Dr. Cramer that the tendons in the neck had been foreshortened, by the burn, but he refused to believe me. I know this is so because I can feel it even today when I pull my head to one side. Those tendons will bulge out at the neck in parallel rays, pulling the lower lip down in a distorted grimace.

The preoperative medication for this surgery was somewhat different: four needles instead of the usual two, given to me an hour before being called for surgery. One needle had morphine in it. Nevertheless, I still screamed through part of this surgery too. But once again it was over, and I returned to my room thinking I'd not yet been to surgery. I took the train home on St. Patrick's Day. The following day I turned forty. It was not my favorite birthday. I would have preferred to remain at thirty-nine indefinitely like Jack Benny.

Dr. Cramer had been making visits to Temple University prior to his move there. One week after my return home in March, I was able to visit him there to have the stitches removed.

My final trip to Rochester for surgery took place on May 8. The operation was to be a simple enlargement of the slit in the left eye, and I would only stay overnight. The morning after my arrival, I sat down to breakfast with the Towne House's banquet manager to outline our plan for a farewell party. We had actually been planning it since early March and had a tentative guest list all made up. We invited 130 people personally, plus several entire departments where I never got to learn individual names because I was unconscious when I came through. I knew a number of people by first or last name only, and with the help of Becky Keene, Florence Jacoby and Annette Hancoski, I was able to complete the list properly and get the invitations off.

I checked out of the hospital the morning after surgery and after many good-byes. To celebrate my liberation, Florence Jacoby and I went to Foxxy's Delicatessen for one last go at that great institution, New York kosher corned beef. It was pouring rain that day, with blustering winds, and the ceiling was low. At the Monroe County Airport, a Mohawk plane was forced to make an emergency landing when it couldn't raise its landing gear upon takeoff. The emergency fire engines and police were called out, just as they had been in July 1963.

That night I was supposed to pick Grace up at the airport. Mike Samloff, a doctor at Strong, and his wife Toni, a hospital volunteer, drove me there and we waited. An announcement came over the public-address system that the plane would be a half hour late; actually, it was circling in the gray soup overhead waiting for a break in the weather. The Samloffs and I went into the Café Avion to raise our sagging spirits. This was too similar to my experience. We were all very nervous and tried to reassure one another.

The plane finally made it down and pulled up to the ramp. Most of the passengers were businessmen, veteran air travelers. One by one they passed through the gate looking pale and wan, visibly unsettled by the trip. Then Grace appeared. Her colorful outfit was in complete contrast to their drab, rumpled business suits. She looked fresh, radiant and obviously not in the least upset. She was excited and had lots of anecdotes to relate. We drove back to the Towne House for a late dinner only to discover our New York accountant, in Rochester on business, sitting at the next table. He joined us. After dinner we collapsed into bed. We had several big days ahead of us.

In the morning Florence picked us up and took us to Annette's, where a very elaborate brunch awaited us. Then we went to Strong where Dr. Zehl tested the newly exposed left eye. I could make out the second line from the top—the two large letters—which meant my vision was 20/200, an improvement at least. A corneal transplant could improve the vision of the eye but Dr. Zehl's recommendation was not to have one done unless it became absolutely essential—namely, if my good eye should lose its vision for some reason.

When we were finished at the hospital, we rented a car and drove through the beautiful countryside to Newark, New York, to have dinner with Spencer Knight and his wife. It was a nostalgic and beautiful evening, and it closed the circle, for it was right here in Newark that the whole adventure had begun on that business trip to see Spence Knight on July 2, 1963.

The next day Grace took me on the grand tour of downtown Rochester. I had always been isolated in the one corner of it that encompassed the hospital and the motel, but she had gotten to know it fairly well. That afternoon we had an appointment in the lounge of the Towne House with Desmond Stone, the reporter, who wanted to interview us for a feature story he was writing on the party we had scheduled for the following evening; he and his wife were coming. We dined that night at the Samloffs.

The party was Sunday evening, May 15. We had brunch with Florence and her family and then returned to the motel to await the evening's festivities. We wanted it to turn out perfectly because we felt so grateful and thankful to everyone we had invited. It turned out even better than we had hoped.

Grace and I went to the reception room early to check up on last-minute details and to be on hand to welcome the first guests. But the maître d', Peggy Hogencamp, had seen to everything—a sign board announcing this was the place for our party; a table with a leatherbound guest book so we would have a memento of the party; an open bar running the entire length of the reception room; a long table crammed with hot and cold hors d'oeuvres. Peggy had always paid us special attention whenever we stayed there and we had become close. That night, she was so moved that tears filled her eyes.

We had arranged that the music during cocktails and dinner be provided by the same musician who had been playing at the Café Avion just before I boarded my flight the day I crashed, the short, stocky, fair-haired accordionist with the round face and the *gemutlichkeit* smile, Frantz Van Gennit. He strolled from group to group, playing favorites on request.

Guests began to arrive, and before long the room was jampacked with friends and wellwishers. The alcohol warmed everybody up and the food table had to be replenished more than once. Al Vragel, one of my chess-playing friends from Kodak, had volunteered to be official photographer, and flash bulbs popped as he posed us with groups of guests.

We gave Peggy the signal for dinner, and the entire back wall of the reception room folded, revealing the main dining room which had been set aside for the party. A buffet table groaned under a sumptuous array of delicacies—turkey, ham, shrimp, chicken and the *pièce de résistance,* a gargantuan baron of beef that had been cooked on a spit, and was being sliced to order by the head chef in his vertical *toque blanche.*

During dinner, Grace and I circulated among the tables, saying our farewells. Then, after dinner, I sat down at a small piano set up on the dance floor and, with Frantz accompanying me, played a medley of songs, picking out the bass with my bandaged left hand. It was my way of saying a very personal thank you and of dispelling any pity my appearance might evoke. It was also a moment, I could not help but notice, when many eyes welled up with tears.

Grace and I started the dancing.

The next morning we took the train for home.

18

I continued to appear in public at first to see what it would be like, and I found it wasn't so bad. After that I kept stretching my horizons all over the country and the world. Part of my interest in taking these trips, although I love to travel, was to see how different people reacted to me across the country and in foreign countries. I never hid myself.

In the summer of 1966 we boarded the S.S. *France*, and took ourselves and our station wagon on a three-month tour of Europe. My passport picture was taken while I still was wearing my plastic prosthetic nose. Now I had the real thing. I even wore sunglasses for that picture. But if any of this threw the customs officials, they didn't say anything about it.

The trip was a much-needed vacation. For me, it was a test to see how different people would react to the shock of seeing my face. When no one, anywhere we went, acted as though they had just come face to face with the ugliest American, I had the reinforced courage to keep traveling with little further thought as to how I looked.

Returning home also meant going back into the hospital and, after Strong, Temple University was a letdown, making me realize just how much I had really been enjoying my trips to Rochester.

Temple University Hospital consists of a complex of buildings, some horribly old, some concrete windowless fortresses built since my departure, interspersed with seedy commercial establishments and rundown row homes, all compressed into the black ghetto of Northeast Philadelphia. There is no green anywhere—no parks or lawns—and only a minimum of places to park, most of them metered along the heavily trafficked cobblestone streets that are slashed by trolley tracks. The main building is a modern brick skyscraper. No funds were expended to give it any sort of esthetic flair or exceptional comfort. When you enter the small, sterile lobby, you know they mean business, and business is what they get right down to. Whereas in Rochester I had been something of a personality, with all the benefits and privileges of one, here I was just another Blue Cross number with questionable financial credentials. And, since too many prior patients had departed with no known forwarding address, while a confused admissions secretary filled out a plethora of forms I was required to put down an advance deposit of several hundred dollars. Except for Dr. Cramer and one member of his staff at Strong who had moved with him, I knew no one. There was no coterie of friends to visit me or call, except of course my neighbors at home, forty-five minutes away. It was a whole new ball game.

The surgery, my thirty-ninth operation, was scheduled for September 19. I was assigned a private room on the tenth floor with a window view of Philadelphia and the student nurses' quarters. I could tell it was their quarters because they were sitting in their crisp starched uniforms in the stacked lounges, watching the passing scene below, or catching one last suntan on the roof clad in scanty bathing suits, too far away for any ogling by somebody with my limited eyesight. About eleven o'clock the night before the operation a nurse came in with a hypodermic needle. I was still scared of the sight of needles even though by now I knew they didn't hurt. I reared back and demanded to know, with maybe a little tremor in my voice, "What's that for?"

It was sedation for bedtime and she was fast reaching for me with the alcohol-dipped swab. I protested, explaining I had no difficulty falling asleep once I set my mind to it and that I liked late-night TV. It was a while before I'd convinced her that the eager intern had put down a routine order for me just in case I *might* need it, but she retreated, and I got to relax again in front of the boob tube.

Surgery was to further correct a droop at the tip of my grafted nose and shape it some more. During this operation the tissue at the tip was rolled under itself and, when resutured, resembled two fairly decent-looking nostrils. The outsides were thinned out a little more.

Once again, I was disappointed. Instead of a handsome, undrooping nose I left the hospital with a swollen tube of flesh with light-blue stitches that called even more attention to it. Fortunately, time heals most wounds (not all) and a more normal appearance returned. At this point, though, Dr. Cramer and I were still talking about the possibilities of a cartilage or silicone implant for my nose.

For two days, I watched the news reports of Surveyor II's soft landing on the moon and waited to go home. When I did check out, I had a refund due from my original deposit. I didn't receive it for several months. That taught me a small lesson. In the future, whenever I was being admitted to the hospital I told them it was for only a day or two (regardless of how long I planned to stay), so I didn't have to put out so much in advance.

Dr. Cramer took the stitches out a week later at his office in the plush, super-modern Skin and Cancer Clinic diagonally across from the main hospital building. I returned again on October 16, a bright, sunny Sunday afternoon, for what I thought was going to be one of the most simple and least traumatic surgeries, an eyebrow transplant.

Things did not start out well. A young lady came to take a blood sample and returned a little while later to take another one—the first one had been placed in the wrong tube. Then, the next day, when the second of two preop injections was given me in my room, I felt an itching sensation on my scrotum. It later developed into a rash all over my genitals. I had become allergic to one of the medications.

I already knew how hair was transplanted using small plugs, and that many people underwent the procedure as routinely as they would go to the dentist. It is possible to implant eyebrows that way, but they rarely look right. I had a further complication, too. The original graft covering the brow was so thin that there was not enough of a base to implant the plugs. So instead I underwent an amazingly complex procedure, in which an island of skin was transported from the back of the head.

It was one of my more interesting operations. In order to make the brow, the doctors had to take a patch of hair right at the edge of the hairline, cut it out, and leave it attached to a good vein or artery. Then they had to tunnel just above the ear and extend it all the way to a slit where the brow should be. With the hair removed by shaving, the hairline skin, attached to its blood supply, would be snaked through the tunnel and into place above the eye and stitched. It was quite a complex operation, painful, serious, difficult—and none too successful.

Dr. Cramer decided to do the left eyebrow first because it had the least promise of success. It was one of the worst areas of my head on which to work; it had all been burned, and the skin there was so thin it had already required several grafts. If the brow implant took on top of that, and I had a full eyebrow, then the right one would have been easier to do. I would have had two eyebrows then, but I preferred both or none; I didn't want to end up with only one brow if the left graft failed. And, unfortunately, the skin graft covering the left eyebrow proved to be too thin. When it was slit open, the surgeons found insufficient tissue below to attach the graft, and the skin was lying on bone that had been partly chipped away during the original grafting three years before. They had to move the brow graft above the normal position.

It was planned somehow to move the eyebrow to its proper location sometime in the future, but when it had healed only a few hairs had made the transfer successfully. Those few hairs do not stop growing as normal eyebrow hairs do, so I have to trim them periodically and decided to skip the second operation.

Instead, I took to wearing sunglasses in public, which make the question of eyebrows moot. Sunglasses—especially when the sun is not shining—are an affectation that lends an air of mystery and importance—at least to some people.

I came out of surgery, to my surprise, in terrible pain. I hadn't realized ahead of time what the extent of it was going to be. There was some concern on the doctors' part that the island would not take at all, and I was kept under close observation for several days to see if I would lose it. They also kept watch over the drainage from the incision in the thin skin behind my ear for fear of infection. The ulcerated sores that had developed on my genitals took almost two weeks to heal despite various salves and medicines. That can be an extremely unsettling experience when the cause is unknown. Finally, tests by Temple's chief dermatologist showed that I had become allergic to the sodium pentobarbitol in my preop injection and the drug was banned from my future use. I wear a Medic Alert medallion to warn would-be saviors of that fact.

I received a visit in my room from my old family doctor, Dr. Broad. To my regret he had decided to give up his general practice and specialize in anesthesiology. But he was preparing for his specialty at Temple, and he came by to tell me he had been present to observe both of my surgeries there so far as part of his training. I felt better knowing he had been there. I did not see Dr. Cramer; he was busy acting as host to a VIP doctor who had come all the way from Scotland to see him. I was, as usual, one of the proud exhibits.

On December 7 I was to have both my eyelids slit open in the outpatient clinic. Dr. Cramer's pleasant nurse had me lie down on the table and pointed the massive overhead lighting right at my eyes. She washed my face with pHisoHex and set about organizing the instruments the maestro would require—rubber gloves, mask, sutures, scissors, scalpel, sponges, needles, and more. Finally, enter the maestro: and, because he was in a shirt and tie I assumed this was going to be the proverbial piece of cake. He mumbled his greetings and began a minute study of my eyes as though they were the main course at dinner. I was quite calm about the whole thing, thanks to twenty milligrams of Librium I'd taken before we drove down.

The gloves went on with a squeak and then I felt needles

jabbing me all around my eyes. The pain from them was so excruciating I turned and twisted my entire torso in anguish, but I kept my head absolutely still. I moaned with each shot, hoping that I was telegraphing enough pain so that they would stop torturing me. Eventually, they did. There was no more pain after that. I could hear my skin being cut and the stitch needles going in, but I didn't feel a thing. While Dr. Cramer and the nurse were working, I heard her say "Ooops." I told her, "No oopses, please! You're working on my eyes." She had dropped the scissors. Then there was some confusion as to what size suture to use; she had put out the wrong one.

The right eyelid was still being held together by the operation performed on it in September 1963. The lids had softened enough so that when the small connection between them was cut, they were not supposed to contract. The cut was made, five very fine sutures were put in to close the edges and everything seemed fine—except that the lids were not quite straight after three years of irregular tension. The result is that when I sleep, part of the eye stays exposed, which may someday cause me some difficulty. The left eye, which looked like a lazy exclamation point lying on its side after its last surgery, was slit open to about five-sixths its proper width, which is the way it has remained. Unfortunately, the edge of the upper lid came undone somewhere along the line. The eye closes even less well than the right when I sleep so I occasionally use drops and ointment to protect it. A raw, red edge of subcutaneous tissue is constantly exposed which has not been able to heal by itself. It is the only unhealed area on my whole body. Someday, I suppose a small graft might be done on it if there is enough base for one.

My eyes experienced only slight irritation after this surgery. I was expecting much worse. One week later, Dr. Cramer removed the stitches, and now I no longer sported my eye patch—it sometimes touched the eyeball anyway and could be very uncomfortable—and relied on the sunglasses completely to protect my eyes and my vanity.

Around this time, I had been banging up my mangled left hand doing chores and shopwork around the house. There was some slight bone exposure and infection; hot soakings and antibiotic ointment helped. I use the hand constantly as though it were a normal limb, but it is very fragile and damages easily.

When it does, I don't feel it because the grafting has made the surface insensitive to feeling.

I took to wearing a modified black bowling glove on it. I call it my German intellectual glove, my Dr. Strangelove glove.

The black glove is normally a concealment of a missing hand; a mechanical claw would be a much more usable device. But there's something very elegant in wearing a black glove rather than a claw.

I only wear the glove in public and whenever there's company at home. I wear it only for cosmetic reasons and it's still part of that snob approach I have—a disfigured hand being an indication of a low class. I don't wear it when I am with the family or when I am alone. But when the children have their friends over they quickly run in ahead of their friends and say "Put your glove on." They don't like to have their friends walk in when I don't have it on. They're very protective that way.

Many times one of my hospital stays coincided with some of the catastrophic events of the 1960s—the assassinations of John Kennedy, Robert Kennedy and Martin Luther King, the 1967 Arab-Israeli War, the Great Blackout—but I never felt that the decade was passing me by. I didn't feel that way at all. In fact, I became a much more involved and active person after the accident than before.

I wasn't very active socially, politically or in the community prior to the accident, but afterward I wasn't tied down to regular work—as a matter of fact at that time I wasn't really doing anything—and I had long periods in which I could become more involved.

It's difficult to pinpoint an exact cause-and-effect relationship. Perhaps it was the fact that I was at home more now. Perhaps it was my physical appearance; or because of the erroneous rumors that had spread about our newfound wealth; even close friends believed that the settlement was well over a million dollars. At any rate, in the fall of 1966 one of our local politicians—a township supervisor and a Bucks County Commissioner for a number of years—was running for Congress against the Republican incumbent and he asked me to join a small brain trust group he was setting up.

There were five or six of us, mostly professors, and we advised him as to what political activities he should engage in and what programs he should support. I produced a series of radio commercials for him, which he put on the air. Unfortunately, Bucks County was primarily Republican territory and he lost.

This was a busy time for us. I was teaching one day a week at the college in Philadelphia; I was regularly attending the meetings of the Bucks County Chess Club; we were looking at private schools for the boys; my consulting practice was growing as was our social life.

I was also appointed to the township's arts and culture commission, which was organizing a concert band and arranging for the construction of a gazebo in our local park. Eventually I became chairman of the commission. Now I was in the public eye. My picture appeared in the newspapers fairly frequently and my appearance, distinctive if not exactly distinguished, actually became an asset.

I became chairman of the Delaware Valley Section of the Society of Plastics Engineers, and a member of its board of directors; and I became chairman of the Parent-Faculty Association of our boys' school and a member of its board of trustees. I had to get up in front of audiences frequently and talk to them as either an M.C. or a community leader.

For Christmas and New Year's Grace and I and another couple went on a Caribbean cruise aboard the *France* again, where the crew remembered me from the transatlantic voyages and treated me as an old regular. But the surgeries were to continue and after three months I checked back into Temple with a little trepidation. Surgery this time was intended to join the three fingers of the left hand to their knuckles with pins. It was the pins part that unnerved me. I had no conception of what that meant, but my imagination ran wild with thoughts of metal rods being implanted in my bones.

I was installed at first in a tiny room on the ninth floor—the only private room on the floor. All the others were shared by two to four patients. I was not too happy with the accommodations; I had become used to much better. So later in the day I was moved to a large corner room on the fifth floor. The trouble here was that the psychiatric wing was at the other end, and their corridor opened directly into ours with only a small desk, and a nurse occasionally sitting at it, as a protective barrier.

Having had weird experiences in the past even with normal patients, I walked down the hall to check out the situation for myself. Reassured, I went back to my room. That evening, I was visited by a resident anesthetist, a Chinese woman who had great difficulty communicating because of her thick accent and I became unsettled again, at the thought of my life in the balance and in her hands in case emergency instructions had to be rapidly understood. As it turned out Dr. Broad was going to be in charge, but I didn't know that then.

After she left I was watching TV and going through some *New York Times* chess games with a small set I always traveled with when, at 9:30, Dr. Cramer called. He was too tired to come in and see me himself, but he assured me he would be there the next morning, and sent in another doctor to look me over and have a chat.

I spent a very restless night, waking up many times—something I almost never do. In the morning I was told I would be going into surgery earlier than scheduled and given only one needle. This was a little disturbing, but I tried to put myself to sleep through sheer force of will. It didn't work; when I was wheeled down to surgery I was wide awake. I was left unattended in the large, chilly, brightly lit operating room which was a beehive of activity with people coming and going everywhere. Finally Dr. Broad came in and started to prepare my arm for anesthesia. Knowing he was there made me feel comfortable and I even opened my eyes and watched for a while. But then it took him five needles to hit the right vein. I can remember the green-clad spectre scrubbing my arm and armpit with a chilling solution and rough gauze before inserting the needle that would desensitize and immobilize my entire left arm—then, nothing.

When I awoke I was in my hospital room. Grace was there at my side, almost an apparition to me in my dazed condition. She had several chocolate bars—for which I often got an aggravated yen right after surgery. A nurse popped her head in to ask if I wanted any dinner. In my stupor, I told her no. By 8:00, after Grace had gone home to be with the boys, I was able to get down a dinner of chocolate bars and toast.

As I emerged from somnambulance my hand was extremely painful. It was one of the few times I had really been bothered by postoperative pain and I started taking Darvon every three hours. Dr. Cramer came in in his street clothes to check on me and to tell me what had been done.

The arm had been elevated in surgery to drain blood from the hand and a tourniquet applied. The three fingers on the left hand—middle, ring and pinky—were already one bone short. In addition, they had rotated 90 degrees away from a normal position and were not linked at the knuckles. What was left of the pinky, twisted and sans its fingernail, was not touched while an operation, called an arthrodesis, was performed on the other two digits to remove cartilage between two of their bones and fasten them so that they could grow together.

Incisions were made to expose both knucklebones. More bone fragments were picked away, shortening the fingers even more but allowing them to be rotated back to their normal position. A stretch of Kirschner, or K, wire was passed through the back of the hand, into the nearest fingerbones and out again, then pulled tight until the fingerbones had made contact with the knuckle and the position of the fingers looked proper.

I was released the next day, my hand hurting more from the straightening out than from the surgery, I think, and Grace and I headed out to the car to find a ticket on the windshield. She had parked at a defective meter, and when we stopped a policeman to explain the situation to him, all he had to say about it was "Tell it to the judge." At home, things didn't get any better: more ulcerous sores on the testicles, lasting four days, there were also scabs and ulcers on my right wrist, probably from the difficulties of getting the I.V. started. I was supposed to soak my hand in hot water every day and try to flex the wired fingers. One day, while I was doing this, the skin tore over one of the surgical sites and started hemorrhaging badly. I also found an infection behind one knuckle, oozing pus. I put through an emergency call to Dr. Cramer's home in a panic, and made an appointment to see him. But I could not get one for a few days, and by then the conditions had cleared up.

A few weeks after the hand surgery, I noticed a soreness under a heavy, overlapping, pocketlike burn scar on the chest. An abcess had developed, and I had to have it lanced at Dr. Cramer's outpatient clinic. As for the hand itself, the wires were not taken out for three months. Before they were, the wire on the ring finger had broken through the skin. At least that gave me some idea as to its size. I still thought of it as a pin, not a wire, so that seeing it made it not so bad somehow.

The wires came out as part of my forty-fourth, and next to last, operation, back at Temple, on June 6, 1967. Right at the start I was cold from the scrubbing solvents evaporating all over me in the cool of the operating room, and I began to shiver and my teeth to chatter. The hand was anesthetized and the one protruding pin was pulled out with a pair of pliers easily enough. But for the other pin a small incision had to be made, and as this one was yanked out I let out a scream, so suddenly and loudly that it made everyone in the room jump. I could hear someone make a comment about the bone being shattered, but at this point I was past caring.

The left thigh, the source of new skin for so much of my reconstruction, was to be called on once more now, for a graft above the left ear where the brow implant was still unhealed, pink and wet. Some good skin had to be sacrificed in order for the graft to take; the tissue itself was scraped with a knife to start bleeding, and the thigh donor skin was held down with transparent steri-strips that permitted the doctors to keep the ulcerous skin under observation in case infection set in.

Dr. Cramer was busy; Dr. McCormack was down from Strong, and getting the grand tour from him, which included a visit to see me. Dr. McCormack was bubbling as always. And I was recuperating, not in my dark, dreary room in the old building, but in the tenth floor of the newer pavilion with its clean, bright, modern look, and its two inspiring vistas—the city of Philadelphia below, and across the way the student nurses catching their suntans, as they had been doing when I first checked into Temple. Between watching them and the Six-Day War on TV, I was sufficiently distracted.

Before I was set to go home from the hospital, I got word that one of our good friends, an engineer with RCA, had been killed in an automobile accident while riding home from work. I was home in time for his funeral and to pay a condolence call, bandaged and all.

I went to his funeral feeling guilty. I had gone through worse than he had, but I had come out of it in good shape. This man had not. He was dead and had left a family. And I felt guilty

—guilty because I had lived and he had not. A string of deaths followed his—family, friends, acquaintances. With the news of each one, I not only felt the sense of personal loss, I felt the pangs of guilt again for having survived.

I wasn't going to have any more surgery for a year in order to allow the scars to soften and assume their final shapes. So in the summer of 1967 Grace and I packed our boys into the station wagon and drove cross-country, traveling at a pace that would not exactly have challenged the pioneers.

All along Dr. Cramer had been telling me, "You have to decide when enough is enough," and at the last surgery I said to him, "You're right, this is it. There's no sense going on. Unless you think there's something more we ought to do."

"Not unless you do," he said.

And I didn't.

The only thing really left that he could do would be the nose implant; there was very little other major surgery that would be worthwhile. I had reached the point of diminishing returns and I had integrated myself into a new life-style. I had learned to live with the deformity and the disfigurement, and I'd found as I became involved in various activities that, since I was functioning perfectly well—better than I ever had before —there was no sense going on with it.

I went in for surgery for the last time on May 26, 1968. Grace and Leigh dropped me off at Temple Hospital and left once I was comfortably settled in my room. The room, at least, was a refurbished one this time, private with a full bath, facing the front of the hospital with a view of the concrete, windowless laboratory building of the new medical school. At the opposite end of the hall, where before there had been the psychiatric wing, was now gynecology. At least I was going to be safe.

Two student nurses, as adorable as ever in their stiff pink and white uniforms, helped to settle me in and check me over. They were followed by a medical student who wrote up my history. He was shaken by my story—his grandmother had died of 50 percent burns and he also flew quite a bit since his father was an airline executive. After he left, I had the rest of the evening off. Institutional roast beef was served for dinner, and I was ravenously hungry. But I had forgotten to take my Nelson knife with me and, since I didn't want to bother anybody on the staff, I just tore into the meat with my bare hands.

Dr. Cramer came by to see me later that night. He told me that he had succeeded in arranging for me to appear with him on a local television station to discuss plastic surgery, until the station director got a look at the photographs of me. Instantly he said no.

I was awakened at 6:30 in the morning for a preoperative shot, and again an hour later for a second. As I was being wheeled to surgery, I suddenly realized it was my sister's birthday and wished her a happy birthday mentally. Surgery started at exactly 8:30. I didn't even need an anesthetist this time; it was all going to be done under local.

Scars on my face were going to be revised. After prepping me and draping everything but the face, the surgeons did a Z-plasty to a scar on my chin, changing it from a vertical to a horizontal one. A scar below the lip was Z-plastied in just the reverse fashion. Next, blue dye was used to trace a crease from my nose to the corner of my mouth. Two incisions were made, and wire sutures were inserted at the base of the nasal bone and used to pull up both sides of the lip to form a cupid's bow. Excess skin was trimmed off the nose, and the edges of the scars on the left side were sandpapered with an emery-cloth drum-bit attached to an electric motor.

Again I thought I could remember screaming in pain during surgery, but Dr. Cramer told me later I hadn't. In fact he said I had slept through most of it and when I started to come to toward the end he had refused to use any more anesthetic in order to avert any complications.

I was back in my room by 11:00, but I didn't wake up until late that afternoon. Grace was there as usual, cheerful and comforting. When I examined myself in the mirror, I discovered that in addition to the dressings all over my face there was a pad covering the left eye. I assumed, happily, that grafting had been done to it, and learned only later that the eye had been patched only to protect it from the scrub solutions.

I was famished but found that I had been restricted to liquids so that I would not disturb the new tissues around my mouth by chewing. But late that night, long after Grace had gone home, I had a craving for pizza. My night nurse, an elderly woman who remembered me from the year before when she had treated me, ordered one over the telephone. But it began raining hard and the shop refused to deliver. So I had to content myself with various juices from the hospital refrigerator. I spent the next few days doing consulting work from my hospital bed and watching television—the returns from the Oregon primary, the disappearance of the submarine *Scorpion* with all hands and the Philadelphia-produced *Mike Douglas Show,* which was showing a pilot's eye view of takeoffs and landings. I found that apropos. Four days later I was out of the hospital.

I was back twice within a week to have the sutures around my lip removed. It was only then that I found out that the other sutures—the wire ones—were going to be left inside my lip for good. The hope was that scar tissue would form and prevent them from cutting through the tissue or the nasal bone, or being rejected by the body. Not only did none of those complications develop, but I am not even aware of their presence and they don't inhibit my lip movement at all.

There was no fuss, no fanfare when I departed. This was going to be the end, except that Dr. Cramer did ask me to meet with one of the world's most prestigious plastic surgeons, Dr. John Marquis Converse, for what further recommendations he might have. Actually, I think Dr. Cramer may have had a subconscious desire to show off his own masterpiece to another master. The consultation was arranged for Dr. Converse's Park Avenue office rather than at the more traumatic Institute of Reconstructive Plastic Surgery at University Hospital, where he is the director and where most of his world renowned surgery is performed.

I was ushered into his impressive office, and he greeted me warmly. He was a man of great charm and elegance. Another doctor, whom I took to be his assistant, and an attractive secretary were also present throughout our meeting. Dr. Converse examined me, and then his assistant did the same. When they finished, Dr. Converse dictated a letter to his secretary while I listened, praising Dr. Cramer for his work but offering no suggestions for further surgery that we had not already considered. I was a little disappointed, but I expected him to say that. I extended my thanks and headed for Pennsylvania Station. All the way home, I marveled at what I had witnessed.

Now it was over. Forty-five or 46 operations, depending on how you were counting, 24 separate hospitalizations totaling 415 days over a period of five years, at a cost of more than $75,000. No records were set—there are people who have been burned worse than I, who have spent more time in the hospital and more money (especially with skyrocketing medical costs), been given more blood and plasma, been under the surgeon's knife for more hours. But I did become the subject of a number of scientific papers presented to the medical community at symposia and in their journals, not so much for the fact that my treatments were unique (though many of them were being tried for the first time) but that, considered together, they made such a fascinating case history. A few years later, Florence Jacoby became a staff member at Strong as Burn Nurse Clinician, with the responsibility for training other nurses in burn care. She wrote a technical paper called "Current Nursing Care of the Burned Patient" that won her an award for the outstanding paper in her field. A book, *Nursing Care of the Burned Patient*, followed, which won wide acclaim. I was able to attend the reception in her honor at Strong after the book was published and before she went on a worldwide lecture tour, disseminating the knowledge she had acquired.

The day after I came home from Temple for the last time, I was sitting in my office on the second floor of our home. It was raining as it had been all week. My back was to the large glass doors that faced the woods behind our property. Suddenly, a bolt of lightning smashed into one of the large old wild cherry trees that towered over the house, reducing the tree—literally —to splinters. I was thrown from my chair to the floor. Paintings fell from the walls. Slivers of the tree thirty feet long had been blown into a neighbors' yard. I wasn't hurt, but I began thinking that somebody up there was not letting go of me just yet. And contrary to the old adage, lightning did strike this tree again, not once more, but twice more. Our insurance company rated us as an obvious untoward risk, and canceled our homeowner's policy.

I returned to Rochester a number of times after my last discharge from Strong, for purely social reasons. One of those times was, by coincidence, the fifth anniversary of the crash. Becky Keene was retiring as public-relations director for the hospital and we were invited to the party in her honor to be held July 2, 1968.

While I was in Rochester I decided to go through the whole thing again. I wanted to be doing the same things at the same time on the same date. I drove out to the airport.

I went through all the motions I had gone through then, just to jog my memory, to get the atmosphere of the day's date. I stopped in at the Café Avion and spoke to the waitress who had been on duty that day, and who may have served me. Then I went to the Mohawk ticket counter and was taken back inside to the operations office. From there I made my way over to the weather bureau and the control tower on the other side of the field. When I explained who I was and why I was there, doors were opened for me and stories started pouring out of the mouths of my hosts. I was in the tower cab at 4:49, the exact moment of the crash. As if to set the stage for me, the sky darkened ominously at that very minute, but this time it did not rain and there was no thunder nor lightning. Then I returned to the Towne House, taking the route the ambulances had taken, passing Strong on the way.

I had experienced nothing. I was a stranger to this scene, an interested observer, a reporter doing a story. Nothing more. Perhaps what emotional involvement I might have had I've expurgated in the writing of this book.

The one thing I still hadn't done yet was to fly again.

It took me a while to overcome my fear of flying. And, though for quite some time Grace flew up to Rochester and thought nothing of it, sometime after her bumpy ride on that last visit, she became fearful too. It got to be worse for her than for me.

For a number of years, we arranged things so that we didn't have to fly. If we took vacations in the United States, we either drove or took a train. There were still many places to explore in our own country that we had not seen, so it was no problem, and we had some marvelous vacations. And for trips abroad we went by ship, a mode of travel I enjoyed immensely. The problem was that Grace gets seasick just seeing people off on a ferry; that avenue eventually closed itself off to us.

By now it was over five years since the crash had taken place. We were planning to spend the Christmas holidays in

Portugal and time did not permit us the luxury of sea travel. Thus, we found ourselves at Kennedy International Airport in New York.

Franklin Roosevelt's famous phrase, "The only thing we have to fear is fear itself," is so correct. I was apprehensive—about being apprehensive. I took Librium to calm me down. It relieved me of all fear, but it wasn't necessary. Takeoff was smooth, the flight was comfortable, and after that I was able to fly without any undue stress. I kept taking Librium before takeoff for a few more years only because I did not know how I might react. Eventually, I stopped taking even that, and I've come to enjoy flying again as much as most people who fly.

That was the last hurdle.

EPILOGUE

My ordeal was over. Or was it? I could now take stock of how I had fared, both physically and emotionally. If I had learned one thing, it was that it doesn't matter to me what I look like. It may matter to other people how I look, or how *they* look. But not to me.

I suppose it's nicer to be handsome than ugly, just as it's nicer to be rich than poor. But it is not such a terrible thing to be very ugly. It's not *me* that's ugly—it's just my face; I was damaged by an external force for which I was not responsible. I was upset when I first found out that my face had been destroyed, but that feeling was only momentary. I live with this new face, but remember I am looking out from behind it. It feels like my face and I *feel* no less good-looking than I did before.

I lost my face, but not my identity. I have never suffered an identity crisis. I know who I am, what I am, and where I'm going. And except for this autobiographical exercise, I very rarely indulge in introspection.

I have a stable emotional makeup; few things can really rock me and I can turn off unpleasant things quite easily. That's why I think I could have adjusted to any kind of crippling infirmity. If I had lost a leg the way Dave Elwell did, I think I would have made the most of it and functioned as well as he did. I think I could even have adjusted to the total paralysis suffered by Chuck Wright. I would especially regret the loss of sex function, but I know I could adjust to it.

The only important thing to me is being alive. I'm not talking about survival and the will to live; that's another matter. I'm talking about being aware; knowing what is happening. That's what is important. It makes no difference—arms, legs, ears, whatever. Only a functioning brain counts. Just put my head with a functioning brain on a platter. That's all I need.

And what about the matter of survival? In my mind the question never came up. I didn't know I had been put on the critical list and I don't think it would have made any difference if I had known. I never thought to myself, "I'm going to survive." I never made up my mind to fight for my life. I just survived, and there were no two ways about it. I never considered the possibility that I wouldn't.

I have funny feelings about death. I don't fear dying but I hate getting old because it brings me closer to death. It's the knowledge of imminent death that I find abhorrent. It's not the physical part of it, the pain of dying, but the thought of *not being*. I once read a story that haunted me for quite some time about a girl who was attacked by a grizzly bear in her sleeping bag as she camped with friends in Yellowstone National Park. As the bear was chewing and clawing her, she shrieked to her friends, "Oh my God, I'm *dead!*" At that moment she had abandoned all hope. She was not dying. She was dead.

Perhaps I can trace these feelings back to my father's suicide when I was sixteen. Apparently he was very depressed. In those days depression wasn't treated as readily as it is today and people rarely sought professional help. My father had reached middle age and was undoubtedly experiencing a midlife crisis.

He also was encountering some financial difficulties. Sometimes he was taken in by clients with "hot" deals and this time he had gotten involved with a man who claimed to be one of the top executives of the Rainy River Klondike Goldmine in Canada. I can remember several occasions on which this man was a guest at our house for dinner. My mother would rush to Sutter's French Confectioners on the Grand Concourse and Fordham Road to bring home a Boston cream pie which he claimed to love. The man traveled in the company of a young, attractive blonde "nurse" whom he always brought to dinner along with a cloth sack containing a large sample of ore with a thick vein of gold running through it. He also flashed some photostats of news articles about the "big strike." My father was taken in by all of this and made what was for him a sizable investment. That was just one of the ways he lost money. There were others.

One night I was out visiting a girlfriend in New York's Washington Heights and returned home very late to our apartment in the Bronx. It was snowing lightly even though it was the end of March. There were considerably fewer cars in those days and even fewer parked on our street, so that when I spotted my aunt's dark blue Packard parked directly in front of our door, I knew something must be seriously wrong. I was trembling when I entered the apartment. My uncle had received the call and broke the news to my mother as he was doing to me now. "Your father killed himself. They found him hanging on the back of his office door."

My father had written suicide notes to each of us on a yellow legal pad. Helen's and mine were a page and a half long; my mother's was considerably longer. I only read it that one time, then stored it away in a box with his worthless stock certificates and my other most treasured possessions.

His death was totally unnecessary. Neither his mental condition nor his financial one were so bad that simple remedies could not have been found for both. And for him to have known his grandchildren and for them to know him would have brought much joy.

What upsets me most of all is that he *knew*—he experienced that moment that separates life from death. He knew that he was going to cross that abyss—now.

The fight for survival is a normal reflex action. There are

many people with emotional imbalances who lose the will to survive, but for most people that will is involuntary. And so what I did, what I accomplished, was not unusual or different in any way from what any other normal person would have done. Every day, one hears stories of unbelievable tests of man's mettle; somehow people rise to the occasion every time.

So why should I be any different? When I hear of other people's trials and disasters, I shudder. I'm sure these other unfortunate people, if they learned of my story, would opt for their own brand of trouble. As my mother often said, "If everyone threw their troubles into the middle of a desert and you had to choose, you would walk in and pick out your own."

My experience has not been all that bad, anyway. I came out of it with all my faculties and I didn't develop emotional hangups. I have no more fear of flying now than I had before and even less fear of fire. I don't think I would hesitate to run into an inferno to save my children. I know now what the trauma is like, and if I survived it again it couldn't be any worse for me than it was at that time. Besides, the improvements made in burn treatments and plastic surgery in recent years have been monumental, almost doubling the knowledge and advances made since the beginning of recorded history. With the newer methods, healing would have been better and scarring less. The future holds even more promising possibilities including the regeneration of missing body parts.

The problems that the accident caused me are really minimal. I have several skin areas with little sensation because they are grafted, but even grafted skin develops new neural paths so that some sensation returns. I have no sensation on the back of my hand if it is touched very lightly, but I can sense pressure beneath because the nervous tissue has apparently regenerated. Every now and then I cut the back of my hand and bleed before I notice what I have done. I feel no pain, and this can pose a minor danger.

When I touch my forehead I seem to feel it somewhere else but not at the point of contact. The only problem it has ever caused is that on occasion I can't locate a minor itch to scratch.

I find that I catch cold considerably less frequently since the accident and I tend to feel that this is somehow due to my frontal sinuses not having a bony cover over them allowing any tendency for pressure buildup to abate. A crazy theory you say? Who can tell? Dr. Cramer felt that a bone or prosthetic implant to reseal the sinuses might jeopardize the skin graft on the forehead. My semiprotected sinuses are sensitive to extreme cold and become painful in subzero weather, but other than that and the disconcerting bulges they make when I blow my nose, they create no other difficulties.

In addition to the unsightliness of my bulging sinuses, my scalp under the hairpiece is quite unpleasant to look at. It is non-uniformly rough and pebbly with indented areas where bone had to be chiseled away. Grace and the children never seem to react to it in any visible way and the hairpiece conceals it from other eyes.

My left eye is the only real remaining problem. After the accident I couldn't read the top letter on the eye chart. Actually, I couldn't even see the chart; the burn scar covered the cornea and blocked the vision. But when the eyelid was reconstructed, the corneal scar began to rub away, becoming thinner and thinner, so that now, if I cover my right eye, I can make out a number of details, but the vision is very blurred and hazy, and not in alignment with the image seen by the right eye. So I just don't use my left eye at all. As a result, I have some difficulty with depth perception, particularly when parking the car close to the curb, playing tennis close to the net or threading a needle. Obviously one can survive quite well with only these handicaps.

I could have had a pair of authentic-looking prosthetic eyebrows made just the way my hairpiece was, or I could even pencil them in the way some women do. But wearing heavy-rimmed sunglasses or reading glasses is just as effective. Little by little I trimmed my vanity down so that now I only wear sunglasses to keep the sun out of my eyes. After all, the Mona Lisa doesn't have eyebrows, either.

The hearing in my right ear never did improve in spite of the surgery. It is odd that the prosthetic ear is the one with the good hearing. Every night I remove and clean the prosthetic and glue it back in place again the next morning with rubber cement. I could have had a real ear reconstructed, using an implant of either silicone or my own cartilage, but it would have required a number of complex operations and the results are often not worth the effort. Cases have been described to me of patients who underwent the operations only to be so disappointed in the result they sank into deep depression until the ear they had just had rebuilt was amputated and replaced with a plastic substitute. The plastic ear is uncannily real looking especially when new, before it's color begins to change. I rarely have problems with its becoming unstuck at embarrassing moments.

My nose could have turned out better; maybe we stopped the process too soon. Dr. Cramer had brought in a maxillary dentist whose specialty was carving surgical implants for facial features. But on further consideration—the restriction on circulation, or the chance of rejection, or the implant working its way through the skin due to the effects of gravity or friction, all of which might have jeopardized the entire project—it was decided to leave well enough alone. We took what we had and made the most of it. So I have this red tubular piece of flesh for a nose. But, you know, it doesn't matter!

The lips did not come out badly although the grafted skin above and below them have scars that contrast noticeably with the surrounding tissue. They have reasonably normal sensation but I have less muscular control over them than before. My teeth were never effected in any way. But I am always surprised when my dentist reminds me after an X-ray of the implanted wire loop below the nose. I never remember that it is there.

I lost a portion of my sense of taste, mainly to salt, when they performed the ear operation; and my voice has changed slightly because of the changes in the sinuses. I used to receive compliments for its resonance. I don't get many any more.

Dr. Cramer had advised me to avoid the sun as it was bad for the scar tissue, and I did, for many years. Now I no longer concern myself. I play long hours of tennis on the sunniest days and enjoy the beach whenever I can. The only trouble is my nose gets so much darker than the rest of my face that I remind myself of the Straw Man in *The Wizard of Oz.* At first I used to wear long white ducks when playing tennis to hide my scarred legs from people. Eventually I graduated to shorts and even took to going shirtless on the beach. Now I don't hesitate to strip in the locker room. That's progress!

I was never that fond of swimming so I didn't miss it. Although the hairpiece could tolerate the water, it isn't the best thing for it, but at least it would stay on, which is reassuring. So I've pretty much restricted myself to wading in the ocean.

I shave every morning, sometimes twice a day if I am going out again in the evening. Part of the skin on my face, particularly on the right side, is the original. Unfortunately the grafted skin on the left side and around the lips grows hair rather unevenly or not at all so that I can't grow a beard or a mustache to hide the scars and discoloration.

There are times when I wonder whether my disfigurement seems repulsive to Grace. It has not in any way affected our relationship. I wonder why it has not. I wonder how she *really* feels. I know my own feelings but I can't imagine anyone else's. Nor can I imagine how I would react in reversed circumstances. What would it be like for me to walk into the room knowing that Grace was in there burned and disfigured? Would I faint? Would I be repulsed by her? Maybe. But I would never let her know that from anything I said or did. Is that how she is protecting me? Perhaps. But when I look at myself in the mirror, I try to see the real me behind that strange mask. I hope she sees me that way too.

Long before the crash we had discussed what we would do if something happened to either of us. If I died I would have wanted her to remarry. But we never considered the possibilities of becoming disfigured, crippled or paralyzed, or of becoming a vegetable. You just don't think of these things. I know I would not abandon her if she had experienced one of these things. I guess the marriage vows sum it up: ". . . in sickness and in health."

People said to me in the hospital, "You're strong and you're going to get through this," and I did. They said the same to her, "You're strong, you'll handle this," and she did. It might seem that we were extraordinary, but it doesn't seem that way to either of us. I think nearly everybody would react the way we did. You rarely encounter people who run out on someone when they have gone through something like this, and when they do, you can be sure they would have run out whether they had gone through it or not. The disaster gave them the excuse they were looking for.

Grace stood by me; she was totally supportive; she helped

me in every way. My children have too. Tod and Cory can't really remember what I looked like before the crash except from pictures; Leigh was a little older, so that he has a more real memory. It's obvious that my appearance doesn't bother them. Leigh has even looked at the medical photographs and Cory and Tod have had fleeting glimpses. They have not gone through them picture by picture, not so much because they are of me but rather because of the gruesome nature of the pictures. They all saw a movie I had received of the crash taken shortly after impact and used by the airport emergency squad as a training film. It was sent to me, indirectly, by the fire chief. They all think it is "boring." And they love to go in an airplane. They say, "Gee, we haven't been in a plane for a long time." They know how I was burned but it doesn't bother them.

Very often when I discuss the accident with people who have the fortitude to bring the subject up, they are taken aback when I tell them that not only do I have no regrets about what happened, but that if I had the chance to go back in time to 4:49 on the afternoon of July 2, 1963, and have Mohawk Flight 112 lift off safely from the runway into all the unknowns that would ensue, or to have it end as it did, I would select the latter option without hesitation. I know what the results were down that path; there are no unknowns. It's the unknowns that we fear. I like what I've got. I may have been disfigured but my life has been enhanced.

My life is considerably more relaxed and pleasant now. I have few pressures, financial or otherwise. I have security and independence. I have good health, vigor and spirit, and the leisure time to do as I like. I was able to spend a great deal of time with my boys while they were growing up. My time is my own and I spend a great deal of it at home, usually in my office. I can spend my time on consulting, or teaching or community affairs or charity work as I desire. I can read what I want whenever I want.

Grace and I spend time together regularly, playing tennis, and dining and meandering about the back roads of the Bucks County countryside and beyond. We have a very active social life and many marvelous friends. I'm active in several challenging and worthwhile organizations. Tennis and chess are my passions which I indulge at every opportunity. Why would I want to change any of this?

The independence to spend so much time with my family is the greatest benefit of all. It has brought us very close together. I can attend all the boys' athletic events and cheer them on. Cory and Tod have developed into outstanding athletes. Leigh's plan for a career in medicine was influenced greatly by what happened to me. We take long vacations together and travel on almost every holiday—Christmas in Portugal, a summer in Ireland, another Christmas in England and Wales, a circuit of Scandinavia, another of Europe, a cruise to the Caribbean, drives to Canada or the West or wherever the whim and time take us. Now that the boys are older they tend to go off more on their own, or with friends, but we had our good years with them and it was more than enough compensation for the hurt and the pain.

So in terms of the plane crash I was fortunate. In terms of the stock market I was not so lucky. Even financial independence is fraught with dangers. I don't know if the fear of losing what you have is worse than not having had it at all. We took our settlement and with very expensive and substantial professional advice invested it in a conservative blue-chip portfolio just in time to catch the recession of the late sixties. True, the income continued to come in, but it was fixed during this inflationary spiral, while the sickening drop in the market and its unprecedented slow recovery were shattering. I even began to feel responsible for the drop, as though my entrance into the market had caused it. How did I ever miss out on New York City municipal bonds?

I can only speculate as to what life would have been like if I had not crashed. I would still be part of the daily rat race—the pressures, the difficulties of just surviving. I don't think my life would be as rewarding as it is now.

Not only have I made changes in my outlook on life, but so has Grace and even my mother. My mother would always caution me, "Save your money! Don't keep throwing it out on things; you never know when you are going to need it!" She drummed this into me all my life. After the accident her attitude, as well as Grace's and mine, changed radically. It became: live for the moment because who knows what tomorrow brings —a complete reversal.

The accident also relieved me of the pressures of a midlife crisis, the kind of thing that overwhelmed my father. When men reach middle age and start reviewing their lives, they often find that they haven't achieved their goals and time is beginning to run out. So I was lucky. Because this happened to me when it did, I didn't have to worry about success. For a long period my mind was on other things, my survival and my recovery, so I had no time for introspection. Financially I had made it, even if it was by the back door. And a new, exciting life was beginning for me.

I experienced a real renaissance. I felt as though I had died, like the phoenix, and was reborn again from my ashes with new vistas and new aspirations. I do things now that I never would have done before, never would have been able to do before.

Was it worth all the pain and suffering? We can remember that we experienced terrible pain and that we suffered, but somehow nature protects us from reexperiencing the actual pain sensation.

Anticipated pain is far worse than remembered pain. When we think back to excrutiating pain, our body systems do not undergo any physiological changes. But how we think about the hypodermic needle just *before* it is jabbed into our flesh determines whether our heart pounds in our chest, our hands perspire, our blood pressure shoots up, or we faint.

Prior to the plane crash I had never suffered any serious or continuous pain. Like everyone else, I had suffered little traumas throughout my life, but nothing on this scale. But the human body, and more importantly the human mind, is capable of tolerating just about anything. It learns to cope. And so I learned, raising my pain threshold as I confronted the increasing pain load because I was weaned off general anesthesia. And when the load became too much, the miracle of self-hypnosis intervened.

The purpose of pain is not to torment you; it is to protect you by warning you something is amiss in some part of your body. If you suddenly feel a pain in your toe, you look down and you may see that it is cut or a splinter is sticking out of it. The message loop is complete. There is no further reason to continue sensing the pain; it no longer serves a useful purpose. Therefore, you should be able to switch off the pain once you've got the message. I guess that's what I have learned to do.

Very often people complain to me about their aches and pains when they suddenly stop themselves and say, "What am I complaining about after all you have been through?" But in spite of what I "went through" I empathize and cringe with them in their own pain. I cringe more at the pains I haven't had than at the ones I did. I've experienced those and I have put them to rest.

There is always some interest in how I now relate externally to my experience. How do I feel when I read about another plane crash, for instance? There are a lot of them, almost one a day. I know, because I clip them for a file I keep. Sometimes I have a desire to contact the survivors to offer them encouragement and the benefit of my experience, but I don't do it unless specifically asked or if I learn that they are having a problem adjusting. I don't feel I should impose myself upon strangers and I also don't want to make a career out of my disfigurement. But I have been able to help on several occasions, and that has been extremely satisfying.

Being handicapped is without any question, a state of mind, not a condition of the body. I never once thought of myself as handicapped or limited. On the contrary, I usually feel physically superior to most people. Frankly, there are times when I use the fact that others consider me handicapped the same way a beautiful woman will use her looks to have her way. For example, because the sun used to burst into my scarred left eye when I faced into it playing tennis, making it difficult to see even with sunglasses on, my opponents were obliged to allow me to play with the sun at my back and they had the disadvantage. The problem is much less bothersome now, but I still accept my opponent's offers to continue the arrangement.

Handicapped is not synonymous with invalid. Grace and I once encountered a very attractive couple in a New York restaurant. She had been born without arms; he was blind. He fed both of them as she gave instructions. Neither of them showed any uneasiness. And so neither did the curious onlookers. It was an inspiring scene.

Much to the amusement and amazement of myself and my family, and in spite of my most unusual features, I have frequently been mistaken for other people. One such incident took place in a French restaurant on the shores of the Delaware in New Hope, Pennsylvania. We were sitting at a table overlooking the river when a charming middle-aged lady approached our table excitedly and gushed, "Aren't you Mr. ——— —from Los Angeles?"

I tried to convince her it was a case of mistaken identity, but it took some doing to get her back to her table in dismay and I suppose some embarrassment.

On another occasion we had just driven into London from the north and pulled up in front of the Connaught Hotel to ask for directions to our own hotel. The doorman bent down and peered through the car window at me. "You're kidding me, arn't cha?" he said. "You know the way as well as I do!"

"What do you mean?" I asked.

He beckoned over a second doorman and reported, "Here now! This bloke says he don't know the way to Brown's Hotel."

His colleague eyed me up and down, too. "Aren't you the chap who parks his car in front of here every morning?" he wanted to know.

When I finally convinced them there was no connection, they said, "This other chap was in a plane crash. What happened to you?" We were dumbfounded.

Not long ago, a retired gentleman, who sits on a bench sunning himself with his ever-present portable radio, winter and summer, at our local tennis club, asked me where my brother was. I told him that I didn't have a brother. He replied, "Well, that other fellow you sometimes play with looks just like you. I thought he was your brother."

That other fellow he referred to was an acquaintance. I don't know how it happened, but he had been badly burned about the face, especially around the mouth and chin; his nose looks like his untouched original. To me, there is absolutely no resemblance between us, but I recognize there is a look—the contraction of the scars especially around the lips—so that to strangers, at least, there is a similarity. I guess if you have seen one burn patient you've seen them all.

Another time, we had just the opposite experience. Grace and I drove to New York to have dinner with friends in their apartment near Lincoln Center. When we entered the elevator in the lobby it went down to the basement instead of up to the floor we wanted. The car stopped. The door slid noiselessly open and in walked a man, casually dressed, carrying a laundry basket of freshly washed clothes.

In a fraction of a second I recognized an old high-school classmate whom I had not seen nor had any contact with in over twenty-five years. Just as quickly as his face had registered with me, so did his name, and I blurted out, "Burt!"

Without a moment's hesitation, he responded just as excitedly, "Alan!"

We quickly filled in the gaps in each other's lives. He had no knowledge, prior to this meeting, of my accident, yet uncannily he was able to see past my face, which had to be totally strange to him, and span twenty-five years to bring back the memory of who I was. Is it possible that one uttered word after all that time was enough of a clue? Or is it something more? And if so, what?

A great many handicapped people write books. This may be a form of emotional catharsis. As Elie Wiesel has said, "Whoever lives through a trial of the spirit or who takes part in an event that weighs on man's destiny or frees him, is duty-bound to transmit what he has seen, felt and feared." He may well be right.

Today, I live more intensely than before. My accident and disfigurement have given me an edge. I regret nothing. I feel no bitterness. I blame no one. I am a victor of circumstances, not a victim.

I know what I have now: life. And life is everything.